QADDAFI

His Ideology in Theory and Practice

by Mohamed A. El-Khawas

ISBN 0-915597-24-1
ISBN 0-915597-23-3

AMANA BOOKS
58 Elliot Street
Brattleboro, Vermont 05301

Production by Maple Leaf Press
Brattleboro, Vermont

Designed by Deborah Maynard

Cover photo: UPI/Bettmann Newsphotos

ABOUT THE AUTHOR

Mohamed A. El-Khawas is a Professor of History and the Director of the Office of Faculty Development, College of Liberal and Fine Arts, at the University of the District of Columbia, Washington, D.C. He is the author of several books and articles on the Middle East and Africa, as well as co-author of *American Aid to Israel: Nature and Impact*, and Associate Editor of *The Search: Journal for Arab and Islamic Studies*.

CONTENTS

PART TWO
Foreign Policy: A Challenge and a Response

To my family

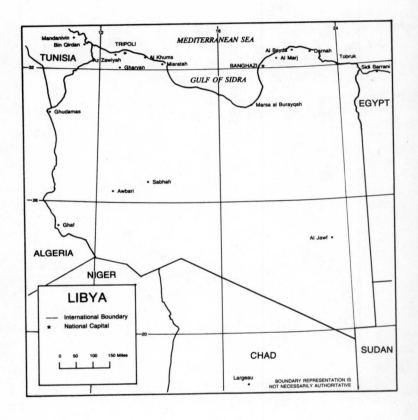

CHARTS, MAPS AND TABLES

Charts

Development in the Number of Male and Female
Students in the Public Elementary Education (1st Phase of
Obligatory Education)
Development in the Number of Female Students in
the Public Preparatory Education (2nd Phase of
Obligatory Education)
Development in the Number of Female Students in
Public Secondary Education

Maps

Tables

Participation in U.S. Presidential and
Congressional Elections, 1960-1982
Completed Housing Units Between 1969-1975
Completed Housing Units Between 1976-1978
Number of Female Students at Universities Between
1968/1969 and 1976/1977
Number of Female Students at Qar Younis University
Between 1968/1969 and 1976/1977

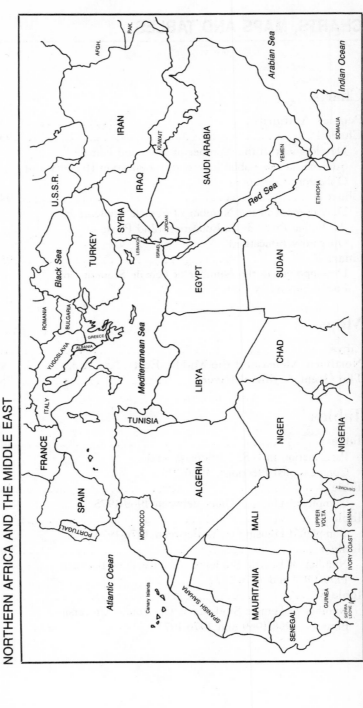

NORTHERN AFRICA AND THE MIDDLE EAST

PREFACE

This book is a product of many related efforts over a four-year period. It began with a series of lectures at Howard University (Washington, D.C.), Towson State University (MD), and Benedict College (Columbia, SC) in 1982 as well as papers delivered at the 1982 joint meeting of the African Heritage Studies Association and the National Conference of Black Political Scientists (New Orleans, LA) and at the African Studies Association (Boston, MA) in 1983. In the following years, as Muammar Al-Qaddafi became more controversial, my interest in the subject continued. This was reflected in several articles dealing with Qaddafi's domestic and foreign policies that appeared in the *The Search* (1981), *American Journal of Islamic Studies* (1984), *International Journal of World Studies* (1984), and *Africa Today* (1984). I'm grateful to the editors of these periodicals for permission to use them in this book; they all have been revised and updated to reflect changes that have taken place in Libya since their publication. These revisions have benefited from additional research which took me to Libya and Egypt as well as to several European and American cities. I've interviewed both sympathizers and foes of Qaddafi and have verified information from several sources prior to its inclusion. No identification is given of individuals or groups in order to maintain anonymity and to protect my sources. In addition, both Arabic and foreign published materials were used to present a well-balanced analysis of Qaddafi's ideology as it has been outlined in the Third Universal Theory and implemented in Libya.

Through these various approaches, I've tried to maintain objectivity in presenting an analysis of one of the most controversial leaders in the world today. Such an attempt at objectivity is likely to lead to criticism from both the right and left. Nevertheless, the book is written in a straightforward manner, seeking to show what Qaddafi has done in Libya since 1969 and to describe the problems he is now encountering.

I'm indebted to many friends and colleagues who have given me valuable assistance during the course of my research and writing. Special thanks go to many Libyans for their invaluable help, support, and encouragement to complete my task. Without their assistance, this book may never have taken form.

Mohamed A. El-Khawas
Washington, D.C.
April 7, 1986

INTRODUCTION

The Making of a Revolutionary Leader

O N SEPTEMBER 1, 1969, MUAMMAR AL-QADDAFI—
then a virtually unknown officer in his late twenties—rose to
leadership in Libya, an oil-rich country in North Africa with
about three million people. He engineered a successful coup and ousted
the weak, aging King Idris Al-Sanusi, who was out of the country.
No one then could have suspected to what extent he would effect
events—in the Middle East and elsewhere—in the decades to follow.

Over the years, Qaddafi has emerged as a charismatic, complicated
leader, full of contradictions—generous, proud, vindictive, and
egotistical. He is convinced that he can do no wrong and consequently
has no patience for different points of view. He is totally committed
to his people and his cause. For him, no tactic is inappropriate if it
advances his cause. His tenure in office has been filled with one crisis
after another—often self-generated because he resorts to maneuvers
rather than compromises to achieve his objectives.

To understand Qaddafi's actions and ideology, it is important to
examine his past, especially the circumstances and the environment
that have contributed to his political evolution. The major national
and regional events in the late fifties and sixties helped raise his political
consciousness and led to his decision to stage the coup.

Childhood: Lean Years

Qaddafi was born in a tent in An-Naja in 1942 in the midst of World
War II, when North Africa became a battleground in the power struggle between Axis and Allies. His parents, Bedouin descendants of the
Kathathfa tribe, were poor. His father was a farmer, who supported
his family by a meager harvest and a small herd of goats and camels.[1]
When Qaddafi was old enough, he helped his father work the land
and look after the herds.

His political education began at an early date as he spent evenings
listening to his father's accounts of the Italian occupation and the Lib-

yan national resistance throughout the years of colonial domination and control. He was told about his family's involvement in the struggle against the colonizers – a struggle that resulted in the killing of his grandfather and the wounding of his father in the post-World War I years.[2] These stories ignited in him a strong sense of nationalism and a dislike for colonialism.

From the outset, Qaddafi was different from other children. He was not interested in playing games with his cousins; instead, he preferred to occupy his time by listening to his father's stories about Libyan folk heroes and historical events. Although he was serious and intelligent, he was forced to delay his formal education because of his family's poverty. There was no local elementary school for him to attend, and his family could not afford to send him away. When he was seven or eight, his father hired a teacher to tutor him at home so that he could continue to help in the fields. His early education was confined to reading the Qur'an and learning numbers. Two years later, his father reluctantly sent him to Sert school, eighteen miles away from home, because he wanted a better future for his son, who had shown a quickness and eagerness to learn. Since they had no relatives or friends at Sert and could not afford to rent a room, Qaddafi slept in the mosque and visited his family on weekends, breaks, and holidays. Since he did not have any money to pay for transportation, he walked and hitchhiked rides on camels and donkeys along the eighteen-mile trek.[3]

Older than the other students, he was able to finish elementary education in four years at Sert. His social experience at school left its imprint on Qaddafi. It made him dislike social inequality and stigmatization, but it also provided him with opportunities to develop a strong personality and to show leadership qualities. He was one of few Bedouin boys at Sert school. Because of their Bedouin background and their poverty, they were outcasts in school. Although Qaddafi was not bothered by such treatment, his fellow Bedouins were discouraged. Qaddafi counselled them, instilling in them a sense of pride in their Bedouin heritage. He encouraged them to work hard to prove that they were as capable as anyone of learning and excelling in education.[4]

Qaddafi grew up during a difficult period in Libyan history. Although Italian colonialism came to an end in the closing days of World War II, Britain and France were left in control of Libya. The post-war period witnessed an upsurge in Libyan nationalism, accompanied by calls for independence and national unity. Following independence in 1951, however, foreign influence continued to prevail in Libya. Having few developed natural resources, Libya had to live on foreign subsidies and was forced to lease military bases to Britain and the U.S. Qaddafi was critical of the presence of foreign military bases on Libyan soil. In his view, these bases were not intended to serve Libya's national interest, but only to promote colonial interests in the Arab world.[5] He also criticized King Idris for Libya's economic dependence on the West and for placing Libya in the Western orbit and on the fringe of the Arab world.

Throughout the fifties, Qaddafi manifested open hostility toward foreigners, whom he considered colonialists. A good illustration is provided by an incident in which Qaddafi refused to stand up when the inspector of English, Mr. Johnson, visited his classroom. In a show of defiance, he crossed his legs, tore up a paper in his hand and held up a key chain bearing Gamal Abdel Nasser's picture. Such an attitude resulted in a sharp exchange between Qaddafi and Johnson and in his being sent to the principal's office. Although the inspector insisted on dismissing him from school, the principal, Esnousi Najjar, an Egyptian, decided against any disciplinary action. Instead, he gave him a word of advice: "Don't do such things any more. Do as Nasser did."[6] Qaddafi would remember these words.

Political Activism: From Teens to Adulthood

Qaddafi's politicization was accelerated by the turbulent events in the Arab world. His teenage years witnessed the outbreak of Arab revolution that challenged corrupt governments, as well as an upsurge in Arab nationalism, a convulsion against European colonialism. Qaddafi closely watched these events and reacted in his own way to express his support or condemnation. For example, in 1954 when the Algerian Revolution, an effort to end French colonial rule, broke out, Qaddafi gave speeches at schools and mosques supporting the national liberation struggle in Algeria. He also collected contributions and donations for the Algerians from his neighbors and friends in An-Naja.[7] A couple of years later, he protested and expressed concern over the fate of the five Algerian revolutionary leaders, including Ahmed Ben Bella, who were hijacked to France while flying between Tunis and Casablanca.[8]

Events in Egypt caught Qaddafi's attention and made him notice the charismatic leadership of Nasser, who by then had emerged as the spokesman and leader of Arab nationalism. Qaddafi saw the Egyptian revolution that erupted under Nasser's leadership as ushering in a new era in the Middle East. Not only had Nasser's revolution put an end to monarchy and corrupt party politics in Egypt but it had also initiated a strong nationalist policy that gained him the animosity of the leading Western powers and the admiration of progressive and radical forces in the Middle East. When Nasser nationalized the Suez Canal Company in 1956, Britain, France, and Israel jointly attacked Egypt in an effort to overthrow Nasser and to put a lid on the rising tide of Arab nationalism, which threatened Western influence and Western presence in the strategic Middle Eastern region.

Young Qaddafi was moved by these events in neighboring Egypt, which proved to be able to stand up against the tripartite attack. Qaddafi admired and respected Nasser, who emerged from these 1956 events stronger than ever and who became the force behind Arab nationalism that challenged the European presence in the Arab world. As Qaddafi later said, the tripartite attack on Egypt "made me love and admire Gamal Abdel Nasser more and more."[9] Qaddafi was taken by Nasser's charisma, anti-colonial stance and his bold initiatives that bewildered the West. As one observer said, Nasser's policies "had left an indelible mark on the mind of [Qaddafi]. . . The leadership of Nasser and the determination of the Egyptian people had fired the imagination of [Qaddafi] and prodded him to question the very purpose and existence of the Libyan Government . . . [Qaddafi] wondered what the state meant to the poor and generally backward villagers and [Bedouins]; their lots had definitely not been improved. Yet they were the people who needed [most] to be helped."[10]

In his early years, then, Qaddafi was influenced by Nasser, a dominant figure in the international scene during the fifties and sixties. Nasser's socialism, Pan-Arabism and anti-colonialism aroused the masses far beyond Egypt and provided the Arab intelligentsia with potent ammunition for their political agitation. Young Qaddafi was greatly inspired by Nasser's dynamic Pan-Arabism and socialism. In 1958, for example, Qaddafi celebrated the union between Egypt and Syria by giving "a big party . . . at Sebha School."[11] Three years later, he organized a demonstration at Fezzan protesting Syria's break with the United Arab Republic (UAR). His action resulted in his expulsion from secondary school. He was the only one out of the sixteen expelled students who was denied the right to study in Fezzan. He had to move to Misrata to finish his secondary school education.[12] Thus, his political activities and agitation caused troubles for him and his family.

At that time, he was in touch with active political groups, namely the Baathists, who stood for Arab socialism, and the Al-Ikhwan Al-Muslimin (Muslim Brotherhood), who advocated the return to classic Islam. Although Qaddafi was religious, he saw merits in the socialist ideology. However, he decided not to join either group because he rejected factionalism.[13] Another reason was that he had already made up his mind to enter the Military Academy upon graduation from secondary school. Membership in any of these political groups would have undermined his chances of obtaining admission to the Military Academy.

During these years, Qaddafi became engrossed in reading every book and article on Nasser he could find[14] because he had secretly decided to follow Nasser's footsteps in order to change things in his native country. Like Nasser, his goal was not to launch a coup d'état to change the government but to start a revolution that could bring about fundamental changes in the socio-economic and political structures in Libya.[15] This led him to decide on a career in the military. He even advised his close, politically-minded friends to pursue a similar career. He even went as far as taking the application of Muftah Ali, a Bedouin, and registering him in the Military Academy.[16] He did so because he planned "to form a nucleus of Free Unionist Officers whose long-term purpose was to make a coup possible by gaining sufficient support for it within the army."[17]

Qaddafi entered the Military Academy in Benghazi in 1963 and graduated two years later. It was during these years that he became convinced of his country's need for weapons as well as for "economic . . . progress based on sound principles to build up a society of justice and satisfaction."[18] In 1966, he was sent to Britain's Sandhurst Military College for a study tour of four and a half months. It was there that he realized the backwardness of his country and changed his views on Britain. He admired Britain's material progress, especially in the agricultural sector. He showed no interest in its culture, however. He was "proud of [his] values, ideas, heritage and social character."[19] He did not hide his feelings. For example, he hung a picture of his family's tent in his room in Britain and wore the Libyan national dress, *Al-jird*, in downtown London. When his study tour ended, he did not visit other European countries, except Italy for two days, on his way home.

Upon his return from Britain, he entered the university to study history, while continuing his career in the military. In 1967, he was moved by the defeat of the Arab armies at the hands of Israel. These events convinced him and his friends of "the soundness of the goal we had been working for, and it urged us to continue our struggle."[20]

A Revolutionary Leader

Qaddafi has had a stormy and controversial career. He is the prod-uct of the turbulent Middle East and the troubled times of the fifties and sixties. In his youth, he became a revolutionary because of fun-damental disagreements with his government's policies. He especially criticized the government's failure to use Libya's oil wealth for develop-ment, its inability to prevent the British from using their base in Libya to attack Egypt in 1956, and its failure to support the anti-colonial struggle in Algeria. In his view, these policies kept Libya on the periphery of the Arab world and in the Western orbit. In response, Qaddafi and a few of his fellow students formed a secret group at Sebha in the late 1950s, a group that met regularly to formulate "the organiza-tional procedures which would enable them to pool their individual resources towards one final aim – revolution."[21] Qaddafi also printed and distributed an underground newspaper.[22]

Over the years, his group mushroomed into a full-fledged underground movement whose goals were to overthrow the monarchy, to end political corruption, to redirect Libya's foreign policy, and to confront the economic and social problems of the country. They wanted to end Libya's dependence on the West and to bring it back into the Arab fold. Although all of these were pressing issues, they had to wait for the opportune time to move against King Idris.

In 1969, Qaddafi, together with other Free Unionist Officers in the army, ousted the king in a bloodless coup and established Libya as a republic. The coup gave him the opportunity to shape the country according to his ideas. Since then, Qaddafi and Libya have been in-exorably bound together; he is the architect of the new Libya and is personally responsible for all of its recent political, economic, and social developments.

From the outset, Qaddafi planned to turn his coup into a revolution,[23] transforming Libya from a traditional, conservative state into a modern, progressive one. This called for a major structural transformation of society—changes in roles and functions, in attitudes and behavior. In his initial steps to pave the way for major structural change, Qaddafi found it necessary to put his Revolutionary Command Council (RCC) in charge of the government and to rule by decrees. With the suspension of the constitution and the outlawing of political parties in 1969, Qaddafi moved to fill the vacuum, making himself the undisputed leader and architect of his country's course.

Qaddafi's disillusionment with Libya's established structures led him to consider setting up a new form of government. It also was necessary to educate the masses, to raise their level of political awareness and to train them for active participation in the affairs of the country. His search for a new, more viable political system led him to reject both Western democracy and communism on the ground that they were not suited to the Arab people and culture. To a great extent, this stance was a psychological reaction to the long years of colonial domination of the Arab world, including Libya. It also was a manifestation of his militant nationalism, in which resentment and fear of the West were intermingled.

Initially, his admiration of Nasser led him to borrow Nasser's model of the Arab Socialist Union (ASU), a single, mass political party designed to maximize political participation of the working people at all levels. His experiment with the ASU ran into serious problems, however, largely because the traditional power brokers remained well entrenched in their local communities.[24] As a result, the masses were still denied any real opportunities to play a significant role in the political process. Qaddafi thus decided to abandon Nasser's model in favor of an ideology more suitable to his country's needs. This turned out to be his own Third Universal Theory, which had been in the making for some time.

His theory is a blueprint for major structural change in the political, economic, and social realms and is designed to address the chronic problems of exploitation, class dominance, and unequal opportunities that existed in Libya under the monarchy. Its objective is to set up a democratic, socialist state where power and wealth are placed in the hands of the people as a whole.

Qaddafi planned to guide the masses and prepare them to take over the instruments of government. To do so, he organized People's Committees and popular congresses throughout the country as structures to involve the people directly in the political process. He sought to do away with all forms of exploitation by implementing his own brand of socialism where the nation's wealth would be redistributed among the people. In addition, he revived Islam as a means to combat social ills and injustice.

Qaddafi took several years to put his theory into practice in Libya. When the new political structure was fully operative, he dissolved the RCC which had ruled the country since 1969. Although Qaddafi resigned his official government post to devote more time to the revolution, he has continued to function as the head of state, largely because his position as the leader of the Al-Fateh Revolution has given him tremendous power, resulting in his continuing dominance of the political scene. He is undoubtedly the man responsible for making top-level decisions. In addition, the majority of the people are uninvolved in his new form of democracy despite its theoretical premise that all of the people must participate in the political structure.

To deal with the passivity of his countrymen, Qaddafi has encouraged the formation of Revolutionary Committees throughout the country. They act as the guardians of the revolution by spurring the masses to carry out their revolutionary duties and to stay on the revolutionary path.[25] Over the years, they have gained power and strength as People's Committees and popular congresses have failed to live up to Qaddafi's revolutionary expectations. Consequently, Qaddafi has become increasingly dependent on the Revolutionary Committees to push his ideas forward and to uphold his system of government. He also has shown intolerance for other points of view, an attitude that has led to the rise of opposition at home and the formation of several anti-Qaddafi groups abroad.[26] Qaddafi has directed the Revolutionary Committees to act against his critics and opponents, whom he considers "the enemies of the Revolution." These committees have used often heavy-handed tactics against the opposition: they have periodically carried out crackdowns on opponents at home and are thought to have dispatched "hit squads" to murder Libyan exiles who have criticized Qaddafi in Europe or in the United States. Despite these measures, Qaddafi has not completely silenced his opposition. His position is in no immediate danger, however, because he has systematically weeded out his opposition inside the country and has had some success in doing so abroad.

Attacks on Libyan expatriates have made Qaddafi one of the most controversial leaders in the world today. He seems not to abide by

the principles of international law or by the conventional rules of
diplomacy in conducting his country's foreign policy. His use of aggressive tactics to achieve his policy objectives has led to sharp criticism
by several major powers, including the U.S. Yet this criticism has not
caused him to change course. It is remarkable how little Qaddafi has
changed.

As for his foreign policy, Qaddafi was determined to reverse Libya's
passive role in international politics and to get it actively involved in
the Arab world. His nationalism dictates that Libya should gain absolute independence from the West. Thus, shortly after coming to
power, he closed American and British military bases in his country
and nationalized several Western-owned financial institutions and
businesses.[27] By these actions, he sought to free Libya from its
dependence on the West and to reaffirm its independence. He wanted
Libya to deal with any major power, regardless of its ideology, that
would serve Libyan and Arab interests.

His policy of non-alignment was intended to keep Libya out of cold-
war conflicts. However, events have led to a deterioration in relations
with the U.S. Qaddafi considers the U.S. "hostile to the Arabs"[28]
because of its unlimited support for Israel, support that guarantees
Israeli military superiority over any combination of Arab states. At
the same time, the U.S. has refused to sell arms to Libya and other
progressive Arab states.

Qaddafi, a tough-minded revolutionary, has shown open and
unrelenting hatred of the U.S., which he charges has exploited the
Arab world by planting the seeds of division and by dragging the Arab
countries into the cold war. Further, he views U.S. actions to keep
its Rapid Deployment Force in the Red Sea and Persian Gulf and
to have the Sixth Fleet in the Mediterranean Sea as threats to Libya
and part of an American destabilization campaign to oust him. To
counter these American threats, Qaddafi has formed an alliance with
the revolutionary, leftist governments of South Yemen and
Ethiopia.[29] In addition, he has repeatedly called upon neighboring
governments to deny the U.S. the use of their naval facilities and airfields and to close foreign military bases on their soil. He has also
moved closer to the Soviet Union, which has been willing to sell him
arms to strengthen his military capabilities.

Qaddafi sees himself as the savior of the Arab world. As Nasser's
self-proclaimed heir, he believes that he is destined to finish the task
of building Pan-Arabism and the liberation of Palestine, yet he has

failed to promote Arab unity through diplomacy. His sense of mission has caused him to be tactless and impatient with other Arab leaders who have not responded positively to his pleas to form a union with Libya. Further, he has provided funds and training to dissident groups in neighboring countries, groups which have been striving to overthrow their governments. Such assistance has resulted in a souring of relations with Egypt, Tunisia, and the Sudan during Al-Nimeiri's regime.

Qaddafi's attitude toward Arab states is also determined by their stance on Palestine. Qaddafi does not recognize Israel and is committed to the use of force to end the Zionist occupation of Palestine.[30] As a result, he has rejected any attempt to negotiate–directly or indirectly–with Israel. He strongly opposed Anwar El-Sadat's peace initiatives, including his historic visit to Jerusalem and the U.S.-engineered Camp David Accords. Instead, he has provided financial and material assistance to the Palestine Liberation Organization (PLO) and Syria, both of which have been engaged in active fighting against Israel.[31]

His uncompromising stance on Palestine is part of his broader support for the right of dependent peoples to self-determination and independence. Qaddafi has placed Libya in the forefront of the struggle for national liberation, making it the center of international resistance to colonialism. He has provided military training and financial assistance to several liberation movements conducting armed struggles against colonial rule and has assisted groups in many countries to overthrow their pro-Western regimes and to bring revolutionary changes. Such assistance has drawn sharp criticism from several nations, including the U.S., which have accused Qaddafi of supporting international terrorism and pursuing a policy of subversion and intervention.[32] To show their displeasure with his policy, some governments initiated punitive measures against Libya, such as closing Libya's People's Bureaus (embassies), expelling Libyan diplomats, severing diplomatic relations, or imposing economic boycotts.

Despite these measures, Qaddafi has continued to support revolutionary groups in neighboring states to achieve his foreign policy objectives. This is part of his well-financed, world-wide campaign to support revolutionary movements that are seeking to bring about political change by the use of force. Qaddafi considers his financing and training of foreign insurgencies to be part of his campaign to combat colonialism and imperialism which, in his view, have hindered Arab unity and development.

His appearance on the Middle East scene was timely because the front-line Arab states were in need of external assistance in the aftermath of the 1967 war. Other Arab nations such as Iraq, Algeria, and Morocco were preoccupied with internal problems or border disputes. Consequently, not only was revolutionary zeal on the downtrend, but also the Arabs had suffered a humiliating defeat at the hands of Israel in 1967. The Arab world desperately needed a psychological boost. Qaddafi's appearance thus helped to lift the Arabs from the doldrums and to raise their low self-esteem. Furthermore, his tough bargaining with oil companies in the early 1970s generated huge revenues that enabled Libya to give financial assistance to the front-line states to acquire more and better weaponry as well as to aid the Palestinian resistance in fighting Israel. Because of Libya's oil revenues, this financial assistance did not hinder development efforts in Libya until the U.S. oil embargo against Libya in 1982.

Qaddafi and his fellow officers have been said to be "the new hope of the Arab world." They have been termed "the post-setback generation"[33] who are not only fired by Nasser's ideology but are also dedicated to finishing what Nasser started, no matter how difficult it will be or how long it will take for their efforts to bear fruit. It is within this general framework that Qaddafi has developed his ideology and policies. He sees himself as Nasser's heir, largely because of his belief that Nasser's successor in Egypt—Sadat—betrayed Nasserism. His objectives are to unify the Arab world, to restore Arab dignity, and to liberate Arab land from foreign domination.

In his view, revolution and unity are "two faces [of] one issue where the past, present and future intersect."[34] Like Nasser, he is committed to Arab unity and socialism. In his words, "so long as the revolution continues, it will not stop seeking Arab unity."[35] He acknowledges that his Pan-Arab drive might at first lead to a collision with other Arab governments which are preoccupied with their national problems and which have turned their back on Arab unity. It is his conviction that Arab unity is a necessity if the Arabs are to reclaim their proper place in history. As he says, "There is no way for any Arab other than unity."[36]

Qaddafi's cultural revolution was staged to revitalize the Islamic-Arab heritage as a means of freeing the Arab individual and nation. He hopes to galvanize the Arab masses and to encourage them to take power away from the governments which have too long directed policies and interpreted national interests. His objective is to crush these forms of government and to replace them with new ones dominated by the people and modeled after his Third Universal Theory.

In view of the controversy surrounding Qaddafi, it is pertinent to understand the ideas and methods of the man who influences the destinies of Libya and the Arab world. This study examines Libya's domestic and foreign policies which have been directed by Qaddafi and influenced by his ideology. It is therefore different from other studies that have tended to focus on one or the other aspect of Qaddafi's actions. It is specifically designed as a brief but complete summary of Qaddafi's ideas and policies; as such, it should prove useful to student and layman alike.

The book is divided into two sections. The first section outlines the principal elements of Qaddafi's thought as it appeared in the *Green Book*, which contains an authoritative exposition of his theories. It highlights his views on other existing theories and thus provides a basis for understanding why he developed his own theory and how it differs from others. A sound grasp of his system of ideas is indispensable to understanding recent developments in Libya. In addition, it offers a description of the new Libya which has been constructed in ways that follow Qaddafi's theory. It also exposes the multiplicity of problems and issues that he has encountered in putting his theory into practice. Qaddafi has not merely suggested an abstract theory to set up a utopian society; he has systematically implemented his ideas in Libya, thus arousing interest among friends and criticism among foes. This discussion helps test the claim that his theory provides practical, humanitarian solutions to problems that have proven to be intractable in both the East and the West.

The second section analyzes the substance and direction of Qaddafi's foreign policy as well as the U.S. response to his challenge. His ideas and actions have aroused much fear over the direction of the Al-Fateh Revolution, particularly since his revolutionary goals appear to be having repercussions on neighboring countries. Significantly, Qaddafi has made no secret of his desire to export his ideology and to establish a Pan-Arab or Pan-Islamic state under his dominance. His style and actions have made him a controversial leader and have put Libya on a collision course with the U.S. and other nations.

PART ONE

QADDAFISM

Theory and Practice

QADDAFI'S IDEOLOGY:

The Third Universal Theory

Q ADDAFI HAS SEVERELY CRITICIZED THE PO-
litical theories and economic models prevailing in the world
today. He argues that neither communism nor traditional
democracy has dealt effectively with the many problems plaguing contemporary societies. Their lack of success is caused primarily by their
failure to put power and wealth in the hands of the people as a whole.
Instead, through representation or deputation, they have deprived the
masses of authority and have concentrated power in the hands of a
privileged class or group. Furthermore, Qaddafi argues that both
capitalism and communism have kept the masses away from any meaningful opportunities to share the national wealth. In his view, capitalism
has failed because "it elevated man without considering collectivity,"
while communism "emphasized the collectivity and forgot man."[37]
His theory aims to correct the shortcomings of both systems. Its application therefore is not limited to Libya. It can be applied anywhere
because it deals with today's human problems and provides solutions
that neither Western democracy nor communism has offered. It places
man and natural law at the center of the system on the grounds that
"man is the basis of everything; . . . law is made for man," not vice-
versa. Natural law "does not change but it acquires new dimensions
with the evolution of human knowledge."[38]

The purpose of this chapter is to examine Qaddafi's Third Universal Theory, particularly his views on existing theories and models that
provide an important basis for understanding why he prepared his own
theory. This examination will shed light on the solutions he proposes
to the problems that seem to be insurmountable in both the East and
the West.

Communism and Democracy: Targets of Criticism

Qaddafi rejects both communism and Western democracy as political
systems because the people as a whole do not directly rule themselves.
Communism, in advocating the rule of the proletariat, places the instru-

15

ment of government in the hands of a single party, which dominates the entire society. Such a system is authoritarian because it concentrates political and economic power in the hands of one party whose membership is limited to a small number. The result is a proletarian dictatorship, which keeps the majority of the people from participating in the political process and denies them their fundamental rights to political and economic freedom. Neither does it enhance national unity, for many segments of society are alienated and on the periphery of their society. It is thus misleading to think that the proletariat rules in a communist state; instead, a small elite monopolizes power in the name of the working class, who still remain exploited for ideological ends. It is the rule of an oligarchy who seek to further their ideology without any genuine popular participation, even though their ideology advocates the welfare of the people.

Qaddafi also objects to the methods and instruments used in Western-style democracy to control authority and to make legislative and administrative decisions, all of which have failed to bring the people into direct participation in the political process. He cites the use of the plebiscite as a method allegedly used to consult the masses on complex national issues. Yet the plebiscite is usually initiated by the ruling party or the military regime which then manipulates authority and monopolizes the state's propaganda machinery to pressure the masses and ensure the plebiscite's passage. For the most part, the people are left uninformed and unaware of the complexity of the issues embodied in the plebiscite. Furthermore, the opposition is left with no alternative other than to cast a negative vote, if it dares to do so. In many countries, a plebiscite is often conducted in an atmosphere of intimidation and oppression, where voters are forced to go to the polls or face threats of a fine or imprisonment. In such an atmosphere, people are afraid to stay at home on voting day and feel compelled to say yes to avoid retaliation by authority.

The undemocratic nature of the plebiscite is evident in the tendency of military regimes and dictators to use it as a convenient means of increasing their dictatorial power. It helps to legitimize their ever-increasing authority at the cost of depriving the masses of any meaningful participation in the political process.

In the final analysis, the plebiscite is not an effective instrument to ensure the presence of democracy or to safeguard against tyranny. For Qaddafi, it is a blow against democracy because people are forced to choose between "yes," or "no." Such a limited choice does not give the people an opportunity to express their feelings and opinions on an issue. They are indeed gagged in the name of modern democracy and are allowed to utter only one word, "yes" or "no." To him, "this is the most cruel and oppressive dictatorial system."[39]

Qaddafi also argues that parliamentary democracy is far from being democratic because the people are not directly in control of the instruments of government. It is a form of indirect democracy based on the concept of representation of separate constituencies. Representatives are often professional or seasoned politicians whose main concern is to be reelected. They act on behalf of their constituencies and strive to promote and defend parochial interests which are often in competition with one another as each tries to obtain the largest share of national appropriations and projects. This situation encourages divisiveness, regionalism and factionalism and therefore does not help to cement national unity. Inevitably, too, national interests must take the back seat when constituent interests are involved.

Qaddafi contends that Western democracy does not ensure the establishment of a government of all the people. At best, it is a government representing the majority and, at worst, when many people do not vote, it is a government of the minority. In either case, a sizable portion of the population is left without representation. In 1976, for example, Jimmy Carter was elected President of the United States with less than twenty-eight percent of the American people voting for him.[40] Many people apparently feel that their votes will make little difference in the outcome of an election. Others do not find a perfect candidate and refuse to choose the lesser of two evils. Consequently, they do not bother to participate in national elections. Voter apathy is quite common in the U.S. as more and more citizens decide to stay away from the polls on election day. As Table 1 shows, there has been a continuous decline in the number of Americans voting in presidential elections since 1960. In 1980, the turn-out was the lowest of any presidential election over the past two decades. Nearly half the Americans of voting age stayed home on election day.

The picture looks even dimmer when congressional elections are examined. Although the turn-out for congressional elections has always been low, generally far below that for the presidential elections, it is interesting to note that mid-term elections have always had the lowest turn-out of any elections. In both the 1974 and 1978 congressional elections, nearly two out of three American voters stayed away from the polls. The alienation of voters has thus resulted in a sharp decline in the level of political participation and the decline seems irreversible. This problem is not unique for the U.S. Other countries have experienced similar problems and have attempted to remedy the situation by imposing fines or by taxing non-voters.[41]

Qaddafi argues that, in Western democracy, people play a minor role in the political process, their participation limited primarily to casting their votes to elect representatives. The electoral system is corrupt because "votes can be bought and falsified."[42] Furthermore, the majority of the people cannot afford the high cost of running for

TABLE 1

Participation in Presidential and Congressional Elections, 1960-1982

Year	President (%)	U.S. Representatives (%)
1960	62.8	58.5
1962	--	45.4
1964	61.9	57.8
1966	--	45.4
1968	60.9	55.1
1970	--	43.5
1972	55.2	50.7
1974	--	35.9
1976	53.5	48.9
1978	--	34.9
1980	52.6	47.4
1982	--	38.1

Source: U.S. Bureau of Census, *Statistical Abstract of the United States: 1984* (104th Edition). Washington, D.C.: Government Printing Office, 1983, p. 262.

elected office. Only the rich can run and get elected and, consequently, control and dominate the positions of governmental power. Authority is thus concentrated in the hands of a few representatives who, despite their claim that they act on behalf of the masses, actually usurp the people's authority and sovereignty. This is particularly true in parliamentary democracies, where the legislative and executive branches of the government are controlled by the party that wins the election even if only by 51 percent of the votes. This is government of the party and not of the people. Such a regime cannot be representative of the whole people if 49 percent of the voters are dissatisfied with that party.[43]

Two or multi-party systems also do not represent the people as a whole. Rather, the political parties that compete for the instruments of government are specialized groupings of people who share interests, outlooks, culture, location or ideology. They compete for the chance to take power and to have their party dominate the rest of society. If anything, their competition heightens the struggle for power and ultimately makes impossible "any achievements of the people" or "any socially beneficial plans."[44] Since the winning party typically controls both the executive and the legislative branches of the government, it is difficult for the system of checks and balances to function properly. In reality, the ruling party governs on behalf of the people, but without any meaningful representation of the people.

The losing party forms the opposition, but it lacks sufficient means to act as a popular check on the ruling party. The losing or minority parties are generally too weak and ineffective to mount meaningful opposition or to prevent corruption and waste. Nor do they have the power and resources to pressure the government to serve all the people rather than special interest groups. Such parties tend to be either co-opted by the ruling party, banned entirely, or harassed by having their leaders rounded up or forced to flee the country. Often, the opposition parties are allowed to exist as long as they are willing to play the game according to the rules set up by the ruling party. Any deviation from these rules would result in the suppression of their political activities. Under these circumstances, opposition parties are unable to serve any useful function in the political process, although their mere presence helps the government pretend that democracy exists and that all people are playing a role in running the government. Thus, opposition parties serve to deceive the masses who in fact are robbed of any real power.

In addition, Qaddafi contends that party politics is not in the interest of national unity. Because it encourages regionalism and special interests, it divides rather than unites the various segments of society. He argues that party struggle for power is "politically, socially and economically destructive to the society."[45]

Qaddafi therefore rejects the concepts underlying single, dual and multi-party systems. He concludes that "the party game is a deceitful farce based on a sham form of democracy which has a selfish content based on manoeuvres, tricks and political games."[46] He doubts that a ruling party can serve the interests of the people as a whole since it represents only a part of the people and is established to further those interests. He says, "No party or parties embrace all the people and therefore the party or . . . coalition represents a minority compared to the masses outside its membership."[47] In his view, the party system is a "modern tribal and sectarian system,"[48] in which power struggles among political parties can tear the society apart since the ultimate goal for each party is to stand solely in power and to exclude all others. In his view, no single party, sect or tribe should be allowed to crush others for its own benefit or interest.[49]

Qaddafi insists that, in a genuine democracy, the authority of the state must rest in the hands of the people, not of the party. He categorically rejects parliamentary democracy since it is based on the principle of majority rule, the concept of representation and the delegation of authority. He says,

> The mere existence of a parliament means the absence of the people, but true democracy exists only through the participation of the people, not through the actions of their representatives. Parliaments have been a legal barrier between peoples and the exercise of authority.[50]

He adds that

> direct democracy . . . has been replaced by various theories of government such as representative assemblies, parties, coalitions and plebiscites. All [have] led to the isolation of the people from political activity and to the plundering of the sovereignty of the people and the assumption of their authority by the successive and conflicting instruments of governing beginning with the individual, on through the class, the sect, the tribe, the parliament and the party.[51]

Qaddafi's Direct Democracy: A Solution

As a solution to the shortcomings of today's democracy, Qaddafi suggests that power should be removed from the hands of parties, classes, or individuals and be placed in the hands of the people. He advocates the creation of a popular democracy in which the people as a whole are not only the source of power but also the instrument of governing themselves, without intermediaries, representation or deputation.[52] It would be a genuine democracy derived from the will of the people and designed to bring about direct mass participation in the political process for the benefit of society as a whole. Under the system he proposes, there would be no room for party politicking or for opportunistic politicians to control and dominate the political system, promoting their interests while sacrificing the interests of all others. All the people would become decision-makers and would have control over the state's affairs, with no one representing them or speaking in their name. Qaddafi hopes to maximize popular participation in the state apparatus where policies are formulated and carried out. In such a system, every citizen would have an equal opportunity to participate in political activity. Such mass participation, he believes, would heighten political consciousness, enhance national unity by creating a strong sense of communal belonging, and create a responsible citizen who is closely identified with the nation's goals and who has a strong sense of his rights and obligations toward the society. In such an atmosphere, the problems of governing would be solved since legislative and administrative decisions would be made and their implementation supervised by the people themselves. Authority rests in the people.

To implement his direct democracy, Qaddafi suggests a horizontal reorganization of the society, from the grass roots upward, where the people's participation in the political process would be guaranteed at all levels and in all matters. He advocates forming popular congresses and people's committees on local, regional, and national levels.

Basic Popular Congresses (BPC) would be organized locally, according to place of residence, so that the entire adult population would be members of a congress. In his view, regular meetings should be held, with people expected to attend to discuss, debate, and vote on all matters. Each BPC would choose a People's Committee, to act as its executive tool and be in charge of implementing its decisions. In fact, People's Committees would administer the organs of local government, thus replacing bureaucrats and technocrats in local administration. They would be staffed by qualified personnel in order to carry out the BPC's decisions in various administrative and technical fields. They would also be accountable to the BPC, which would review their work and make changes if needed.[53]

Each BPC would also select a secretariat, responsible for making preparations for holding its session and preparing its agenda. The secretary would preside over its meetings, recording its decisions. All local secretariats in a given municipality would form the next level of participation, that is, Municipality Popular Congresses (MPC), with each MPC choosing a secretariat, to act continuously for the MPC at the regional level.

The General People's Congress (GPC) would be organized at the national level, representing all social groups within the country. Its membership would include the secretariats from the Basic Popular Congresses and the People's Committees as well as from unions, syndicates, and professional associations.[54] It would be the highest political authority and the instrument of government in the country. The structure he envisions is different in nature from a parliament or congress, however, because it would function only as a coordinating body receiving input from other levels; it would debate their resolutions and formulate policies and actions based on their recommendations. The GPC would also select the national secretariat, confirmed annually; its function being similar to that of a cabinet or council of ministers since it would be in charge of the day-to-day operation of the state apparatus. The main difference is that neither the secretary-general nor the secretariat would formulate policy; their operational function would be limited to the execution of decisions already made by the General People's Congress.

Qaddafi believes that once these levels of political participation are completed and once the popular congresses and people's committees are established and carrying out their intended functions, the state will wither away. The people will then become the authority by directly controlling the instruments of government and by being in charge of decision-making in all political, economic, and social spheres. He argues that there can be no true democracy without popular congresses and people's committees everywhere.[55] In fact, Qaddafi advocates the establishment of people's committees in all businesses and educational institutions. These committees would be chosen by and from

People's Authority

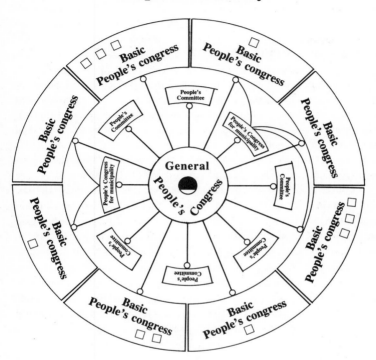

Terminology:

General Secretariat of the General People's Congress
General People's Committee

○   Congress Secretariat

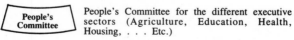

People's Committee for the different executive sectors (Agriculture, Education, Health, Housing, . . . Etc.)

Syndicate or association or union

the people working in these places. They would administer all fields of work and production. Under such a system, each social group would be governing itself.

Economic Socialism

Qaddafi believes that the source of contemporary economic problems lies in the exploitation of man by man which has been allowed to exist in one form or another under both capitalism and communism. Monopoly power, for example, has been manipulated by the individual under capitalism and by the state under communism, leaving the majority of the populace in no position to satisfy their material needs. Consequently, man is no longer in control of the means to ensure his economic well-being; instead, he has become increasingly dependent on others for survival. Such dependence has set in motion a chain reaction. Qaddafi explains, "Man's freedom is lacking if someone else controls what he needs. For need may result in man's enslavement of man. Need causes exploitation. Need is an intrinsic problem and conflict grows out of the domination of man's need."[56]

In his view, there can be no political freedom as long as wealth is concentrated in the hands of a privileged group or of the state. Although Qaddafi recognizes that classes cannot be eliminated simply by granting equal civic and political rights, he insists that economic exploitation of man by man must be wiped out through a just and wide redistribution of wealth among the people.[57] There is no political or social freedom unless it is also accompanied by economic freedom where citizens are free to satisfy their basic needs without relying on someone else. Economic dependency is a form of enslavement and therefore must be eliminated if an egalitarian society is to be formed. In Qaddafi's view, then, a new economic order is necessary.

Public and Private Ownership

Qaddafi rejects capitalism, communism and Third World socialism because they have all failed to solve the pressing economic problems of modern society and have not adequately met the challenge of development. In his view, these different *isms* simply transfer property from the extreme right to the extreme left or to various intermediate positions. He argues that they are all unjust because they have deprived the majority of the people of wealth. Capitalism places

ownership in the hands of a few individuals who exploit the masses
for their own class interest. Communism, on the other hand, sets up
another form of monopoly which prevents the people from owning
or controlling the means of production. Since the communist state
is motivated by profit-making and a strong desire to safeguard its interests, it has turned out to "perform the same functions" as a capitalist
state with "no difference between them." The net result is "a Marxist
state which is the other face of the capitalist world."[58] As for
socialism, although it divides ownership between public and private
sectors, it allows the emergence of a small group of wealthy people
just as capitalism does, leaving workers to receive only part of the
profits.[59]

Qaddafi seeks to establish a new brand of socialism that does away
with the "vertical ownership" of capitalism and with the state monopoly
of communism. He favors the creation of "horizontal ownership" where
ownership is jointly shared by a broad base of people. Its primary goal
is to distribute wealth widely and justly among the people. Wealth
therefore would not be monopolized by the state, as it is under communism, or by a few individuals, as it is under capitalism. Instead,
all productive sectors of the economy would be controlled and directed
by the people through joint ownership.[60]

In his view, joint public ownership provides a sound base for
economic development because people would be in charge of the
economy and, consequently, would be motivated to accelerate production to increase their income. He therefore opposes the establishment of large corporations, whether they are owned by individuals
or by the state. Instead, he argues that these conglomerate companies
should be converted into joint-stock companies and that the public
should be given equal rights to buy and own shares in these enterprises.

Qaddafi's socialism does not do away with private ownership. He
indeed encourages the development of the private sector as long as
it is non-exploitative in nature. He stresses self-reliance by urging individuals to undertake any production or service to satisfy their needs
but without exploiting others. Private ownership therefore would not
be expropriated from one group and given to another, nor would it
be taken over by the state as long as there is no exploitation. However,
he insists that all holdings that are beyond the satisfaction of individual
needs should become the property of the people through joint
ownership.[61]

Qaddafi seeks to satisfy the material needs of man "through the liberation of these needs from outside domination and control."[62] He therefore suggests three types of economic activities:

- Individual Production: Each man works to meet his own needs. . . Each man becomes the private owner of his source of income, without assistance from anybody.
- Socialist Production: This is the activity of partners in collectively-owned undertakings. Thus, all the productive factors work together. The production therefore belongs equally to the three factors of production [workers, raw material and machinery]. Likewise, these factors of production work together to define the sharing out of the production.
- Public Services: This means services rendered by a number of individuals to other individuals in society. These are usually vital services such as health care, education, administration, etc. The whole of society works together to meet the needs of each individual so that they can continue to provide a service to others.[63]

His objective is to place wealth in the hands of the masses and to make it possible for each individual to meet his basic needs without reliance on someone else or encroachment on the rights of others. In his socialist society, exploitation of man by man would be eliminated, and accumulation of wealth beyond personal needs would be outlawed.

Workers As Partners

Qaddafi's socialism seeks to end the exploitative relationship between workers and employers. In his view, labor problems have not been solved under communism or capitalism. Marxism offered simply a makeshift repair, resulting in no real difference between workers employed by a state under communism and those employed by individuals under capitalism. Both groups of workers "suffer from the same hard conditions and exploitation."[64] They all ask for improvement of their situation, an increase in their wages, and fewer working hours.

Qaddafi acknowledges that the reform of labor laws has "made the problem less severe than it was in past centuries"[65] by granting many rights to workers. Labor problems have continued, however. Qaddafi says,

Important historical developments have taken place which

contribute to solving the problem of work and wages, i.e.,
the relationship between the workers and the
employers. . . The developments include fixed working-
hours, wages for additional work, different types of leave,
minimum wages, profit sharing, and participation in administration. In addition, arbitrary dismissal has been
outlawed and social security has been guaranteed along
with the right to strike and whatever other provisions are
found in almost all modern labor laws. Of no less
significance are the changes in the field of ownership such
as the emergence of systems limiting income or outlawing private ownership and transferring it to the
state. . . Despite all these not inconsiderable
developments . . . the problem still basically exists.[66]

Although workers have made some gains in obtaining higher wages,
better benefits, and in some cases, a percentage of the profits, these
gains are more charity than a recognition of their rights in what they
produce. Qaddafi contends that labor problems will not go away as
long as workers are looked upon as wage-earners, not partners. The
exploitation of workers lies in the disproportion between their wages
and their labor and efforts in production. Thus, reform of wages has
not found a lasting solution to the problem of workers. In his view,
"wage-workers are a type of slave, however improved their wages may
be,"[67] whether they are employed by an individual or by a state. The
continuation of labor problems is largely due to the failure of both
capitalism and Marxism to deal with the problem of workers' right
to what they produce.

Qaddafi argues that workers should be considered as producers
because they constitute an essential part in the production process.
Since workers, machinery, and raw material are all essential to the
production process, they all must be given equal rights in what they
produce.[68] It is suggested that

[the production] would be shared three ways between the
various equal factors. The first third of the production
should go to the workers, and thus the second third for
raw materials, but since raw materials are part of the
nation's wealth and therefore belong to the people, this
second third should be enjoyed by the people, once it is
paid back into the general budget of society. The remaining third is the share of the production unit and, finally,

also belongs to the people, since the people own all the
factories and companies, having bought them with their
own budget in order to provide a job to all the productive
forces of the nation.[69]

Qaddafi believes that the wage system is incapable of treating
workers as partners because it has been originated and manipulated
by the owners, with workers merely reacting to its problems and trying to reform them. His ultimate goal is to abolish the wage system
under which workers do not receive a fair share from what they produce and must rely on someone else to satisfy their material needs.[70]
Nor does it give them an incentive to work hard since they will receive
their wages whether production goes up or down.

Qaddafi instead suggests the establishment of a new partnership in
which producers would be considered partners, not wage-workers, in
the production process. Under his system, producers would not receive
wages but instead would get a share in production that is equal to
their effort, capacity and efficiency. This new arrangement should
motivate them to work harder to increase production since their income would fluctuate depending on their contribution to the production effort. Their gains or losses would thus be commensurate with
their labor. Such a system would not only eliminate labor exploitation by employers but would also put an end to labor unrest. Producers would see themselves as an integral part of the production cycle
and would control their destiny by working for themselves.

Qaddafi argues that workers' emancipation can be achieved by "the
overthrow of the employers and the abolition of those laws which con-
secrate exploitation."[71] This is the only way to free workers to meet
their needs. He therefore advocates that workers should take over
factories and companies, becoming part of the management and
organization of production units. "Workers' control" means that they
would be "full-fledged masters of their own company." They would
choose people's committees out of their own ranks to be in charge
of the socialist corporation "whether [the tasks] are company concerns,
production matters or workers' problems."[72] People's Committees
would replace the capitalist or state bureaucratic management. These
committees would promote the welfare of the working people rather
than the welfare of an individual or state. It would be in the workers'
interest to step up production, improve the quality of their product,
increase its value and produce goods to meet consumer needs. To
ensure sound economic policies, production unit congresses would

be established to make collective decisions which would be carried out by People's Committees in each unit of production.

Qaddafi believes that this new partnership would eliminate the exploitation that characterized the relationship between employees and employers under both capitalism and communism. He contends that his socialist solution not only guarantees economic freedom of the working masses but also eliminates class struggle on all fronts—political, social and economic.[73] Thus, the workers' revolution will lead to freedom and equality "once exploitation and injustice have been rooted out for good."[74]

It is generally acknowledged that it is not an easy task to ask the workers to take over factories and start managing production units. In Libya, for instance, it took a whole year to explain the concept of "partners, not wage-earners."[75] It was only then that the workers marched on factories and took over the management. Such a system requires the politicization of workers who have been accustomed to the traditional relationship between employers and employees. Political education is needed to ensure that workers understand their new responsibilities and shoulder their duties under the new partnership in the production process. They must guard against sabotage by those elements who oppose the socialist system. Workers also have to double their efforts to "show exceptional prudence in the management of its productive units, try to maintain productivity, and ensure that work is well organized and constant." This is essential for the success of the workers' revolution since former employers "would do all they could to sabotage the revolution and recommence their oppression and tyranny of the workers."[76]

It is not enough to put the national wealth in the hands of the people, for reactionary forces are waiting for the proper time to destroy workers' gains. In Chile, for example, the Allende government nationalized foreign companies and placed national wealth back in the hands of the people. However, the government was overthrown as a result of a conspiracy between Chilean reactionaries and world capitalists who objected to Allende's socialism. His downfall was accompanied by workers' loss of whatever gains they had obtained during his tenure in office. According to Libyan interpretation, this was possible because of the lack of political awareness among Chilean workers, who were manipulated by capitalists and conservatives to demonstrate against Allende's socialist program.[77] Thus, the absence of revolutionary awareness among the underprivileged classes in Chile was partly

responsible for the failure of Allende's revolution. This is also true
in the case of Egypt. Egyptian workers "proved to be incapable of
preserving the achievements of Nasser['s] revolution,"[78] when the
counter-revolutionary forces became active again after the untimely
death of Nasser. To avoid these mistakes, workers must be politically
educated; they must understand the socialist revolution; they must
participate in the national dialogue and take part in the decision-making
process.

Land and Its Usage

Qaddafi rejects private ownership of land because farm workers,
who toil the land, are forced to sell their labor for low wages and to
rely on the landlords for their livelihood. Another reason is that such
practices lead to competition among individuals to increase their land
holdings, while depriving others of the right to use land to make a
decent living.

Qaddafi also objects to state ownership of land because individual
initiatives are suppressed in favor of collectivism. Under such a system,
the state is in control of the means of production and, as such, farmers
are in no position to fulfill their material needs without reliance on
the state.

In his socialism, Qaddafi makes a distinction between ownership
and use of the land. He insists that land is not private property; it
cannot be owned or monopolized by the state or by individuals. Since
land is the collective property of all the people, any citizen has the
right to work the land to meet his basic needs by himself and for
himself. The land therefore belongs to those who toil it. Farmers
should be allowed to use as much land as they can toil by their own
family without relying on hired labor.

Thus, his concept of land is based on communal, not individual,
ownership. Under such a system, individuals and their heirs will be
allowed to use the land for farming or pasturing only as long as productive work is done through their own efforts and without depending on others. They can also lose that right if they have outside help
to work the land. This fits well with Qaddafi's objection to the wage
system, which he views as a form of enslavement.

The same land concept applies to housing. A citizen is entitled to
build a house for his own family use, but not for the purpose of renting it. In Qaddafi's views, housing is a basic need and therefore should
not be rented out or owned whether by the state or by individuals.

He rejects the concept of rental housing because of the inherently exploitative relationship between tenants and landlords, who can forcibly evict tenants for almost any reason. Rents also can become excessive because the landlords are in the housing business for profits. Because of this exploitative element, Qaddafi insists that every occupant should have the right to own the dwelling house in which he lives.

All in all, Qaddafi's socialism strives to wipe out economic exploitation in all its forms and manifestations. It advocates that the only legitimate economic activity is for man to satisfy his basic needs— food, shelter, clothing, and means of transportation—by himself and for himself. This will eliminate the possibility of exploiting others' labor for self-enrichment whether in the agricultural or industrial sectors. Self-maintenance would be guaranteed but accumulation of wealth in excess of one's needs would not be allowed. These concepts are reflected in Qaddafi's insistence that the wage system be abolished and that man either work for himself to meet his basic needs, work for a socialist corporation in which he is a partner (not a wage-earner) or perform a public service to the society, which will then provide him with basic needs.

Social Reconstruction

Qaddafi's examination of contemporary societies led him to conclude that they are "essentially composed of predetermined models built [on] exploitation, oppression and injustice and constructed by the [societies] of exploitation."[79] This intolerable condition has come about as a result of inequality, lack of freedom, and a straying from religion, all of which have led to the hegemony of one class over another and the rise of different forms of discrimination based on sex, color, or creed.

To solve these problems, Qaddafi suggests "a radical change in society and culture so that life will be founded on healthy bases."[80] His objective is to incite the masses everywhere to "destroy the predetermined models, which are the products of exploitation" and to set up a new society that is based on respect for life "as nature demands."[81] He seeks to introduce a new social structure based on equality, freedom and a return to religion in order to eliminate social injustice. This is not a utopian society but one based on rehabilitating human values that have been suppressed or disregarded when industrialization was accompanied by dehumanization. He proposes a social order that takes into account the material and spiritual needs of man and their influence on the process of forming a nation and on relations between the individual and social institutions.

The Family, the Tribe and the Nation

Qaddafi argues that a society has several social structures centrally important to its vitality; they are the family, the tribe, and the nation, all of which are non-political in nature. These social bonds are essential to the individual as a source of differing advantages, privileges, values and ideas. These are strongest at the family level and progressively weaker at each higher level. Qaddafi fears that these values, along with their material benefits and social advantages, are threatened by extinction whenever any of these social institutions are lost.[82]

The family is the most important social structure, the one in which man has close direct and personal relationships. It plays a significant role in his evolution and development. For this reason, Qaddafi insists that any attempt to disperse or to weaken the family is "inhuman and unnatural" because an "individual without a family has no value or social life."[83] In contrast, if individuals are permitted to grow naturally within the family, both the family and the society will flourish.

As for the tribe, Qaddafi believes that it is "a natural 'umbrella' for social security."[84] Like the family, the tribe provides man with benefits, advantages and ideas; it also influences his behavioral pattern. Although many countries have attempted to weaken, if not destroy, tribes in the name of progress and modernization, Qaddafi believes that the tribe has a special role to play in the socialization process. From childhood to adulthood, persons gradually and systematically absorb tribal customs and traditions which influence their values, mores, ideals and behavior. Qaddafi suggests that this practical life experience in tribal acculturation can benefit society if it is transformed into a social education. To him, such education is not only practical and valuable but also much "better and more human than any [formal] school education."[85]

Qaddafi contends that the nation, an important unit, is often born out of a common origin and grows with a shared destiny through affiliation. The nation is the individual's political and social "umbrella," the bond of which is nationalism. It is a wider social structure than the family or the tribe, both of which are limited in their membership. Although he argues that "national fanaticism is essential" for national survival, he warns that it can get out of hand and become "a threat to humanity."[86] He feels that it is vital for societies "to maintain the cohesiveness of the family, the tribe [and] the nation . . . in order to benefit from advantages, privileges, values and ideals yielded by [their] solidarity, cohesiveness, unity, intimacy and love."[87]

Qaddafi makes a distinction between a nation and a state because, in his view, the state is an artificial economic, political, and sometimes military system "with which mankind has no relationship and has nothing to do."[88] It is created either by nationalism or by religious, economic, and military factors. The national state is composed of a single national group; it is viable because the political structure is consistent with the social structure. Such a state is likely to survive unless it falls victim to external aggression (i.e., colonialism and imperialism) or to internal strife (i.e., clashes with other social institutions such as tribes, clans, or families). Even under these circumstances, states will re-emerge as a national struggle breaks out to put an end to foreign domination or to express a resurgence of national unity. Another kind of state is born out of religious, economic, and/or military factors; it usually encompasses several national groupings. Its structure is artificial and liable to break up as each group gains independence under the banner of nationalism. This outcome is inevitable whenever the political structure is not consistent with the social structure.[89]

Qaddafi stresses nationalism as the basis upon which nations are founded and survive because, without it, nations are threatened with extinction. He argues that each group's social structure binds its people together and produces common needs that, in his view, must be fulfilled collectively, not individually. Group members are bound by a single nationalism and share needs, rights, demands or objectives. Qaddafi considers national liberation fronts as social movements instigated in support of nationalism, since they strive to achieve liberation from the domination of another group.[90]

In Qaddafi's view, nationalism is the social bond that can "[work] automatically to impel the nation towards survival."[91] Thus, when the bond of nationalism is broken, nations are threatened by civil strife, violence, and destruction. The same is true when individuals begin to disregard nationalism; their lives are damaged and so is the life of the nation. In his analysis, the social factor is essential for national unity. Although it can be challenged by religion, which may divide or unite national groupings, such rivalry would end, however, when the social factor dominates.[92]

According to Qaddafi, historical records reveal that there is a conflict between the social factor (nationalism) and religion whenever different nationalities are grouped together in one nation. He argues that although religion might be victorious at the beginning, nationalism will eventually triumph. This was evident in the recent history of the subcontinent of India. In the post-World War II period, the sub-continent was divided into two states along religious lines, so that the Hindus went to India and the Muslims to Pakistan. Religion, however, was unable to contain the rise of Bengali nationalism in East Pakistan. The Bengalis finally broke away from Pakistan and founded their own state, Bangladesh.[93] These events give credence to his argument that where there is a conflict between nationalism and religion, nationalism will triumph.

Religion and Society

Qaddafi puts complete trust and confidence in people and believes that social relationships are best guided by an unwritten ethical code that cannot be enforced by law. However, such ethical relationships can be influential only when they emanate from individuals. This explains the emphasis he places on religion, which provides the general outline for the relationship between God and man, between man and man, and between man and society. When religion effectively guides people in their daily activity, he argues, exploitation will be eliminated, and the world we live in will be much better.

Qaddafi advocates a return to religion, which, in his view, is "a fundamental factor in the life of man and is reflected [in] so many social considerations."[94] He stresses that "we do not require that religion should be Islam. . . Christians shall be real Christians by going back to the original Christianity, the Bible."[95] He says, "We do not intend to make followers of other religions our enemies. We also are not fanatic for this religion or that. We believe that religion is the foundation of man's life. We believe that every man should have a religion"[96] because without it man "knows no source of ethical obligations."[97] In addition, religion helps solve social problems. It leads to emotional stability, which, in turn, will lead to "social stability where there is no anxiety, no schi[z]ophrenia, social non-adherence, flight from reality by adopting hippie customs or becoming drug addicts or committing suicide."[98]

Although Qaddafi does not advocate that Islam be imposed on

others, he believes that there is a need to study the Qur'an, the holy book of Islam, because "the [Qur'an] is addressed to all humanity and is not the property of the Arabs."[99] In addition, "our Prophet [Muhammad] is for all nations."[100] Another reason is that "the Bible has been distorted. . . It has become a book composed by men. Only the [Qur'an] has not been distorted by anybody. . . It is a modern book compared with other heavenly books."[101] He says, "The Christian shall remain a Christian and will study the [Qur'an] or the original Gospel before it was distorted. The Jew shall remain a Jew, and shall study the [Qur'an] or the Gospel or the Bible, as the [Qur'an] is not our property alone."[102]

His recommendation to study the Qur'an stems from his firm belief that "all the guidance a man needs in running a state is to be found exclusively in the Qur'an."[103] In June 1970, he told the correspondent of *Le Monde*, "Read the [Qur'an] or re-read it. You'll find the answers to all your questions. Arab unity, socialism, inheritance rights, the place of women in society, the inevitable fall of the Roman Empire, the destruction of our planet following the [invention] of the atom bomb. It's all there for anyone willing to read it."[104]

Qaddafi sees religion as offering a natural law that can both satisfy individual spiritual needs and combat social illness such as discrimination and class differences. Without religion, morality would be eroded and social order would break down, creating chaotic conditions that law alone cannot handle.[105] This situation would cause divisiveness, instability and lawlessness, all of which would destroy national unity and hinder progress.

For Qaddafi, religion encourages morality and combats inequality, injustice, and corruption. It strengthens the fabric of society and improves social relations. It is seen as a key means of establishing a classless society based on egalitarianism and socialism. He says, "We need to go back to our origins."[106] In his view, it is only by applying the scripture that an ideal society can be established.

Women and Society

In his egalitarian society, there is no room for any form of discrimination because religious values and principles would be enforced. He considers sex discrimination to be "a flagrant act of oppression without justification."[107] Although there are biological differences between man and woman (i.e., menstruation, pregnancy, miscarriage, etc.), there is a role for each to play, matching their differences. He is concerned, for instance, that "to dispense with the natural role of woman in maternity—i.e., nurseries replacing mothers—is a start in dispensing with the human society and transforming it into a biological society with an artificial way of life."[108] Motherhood is the female's function, not the male's, because a child has a natural tendency toward her. Any attempt to take a child away from his or her mother is "coercion, oppression and dictatorship."[109] It is unjust and cruel to ask a pregnant woman or a breast-feeding mother to perform hard work. It is unnatural to transform women into men because all "must perform, not abandon, the role for which they are created."[110]

His starting point for these views is a belief that women are exploited and oppressed in most present-day societies, whether advanced or developing. He complains that "all societies nowadays look upon [women] as no more than an article of merchandise. The East regards her as a commodity for buying and selling, while the West does not recognize her femininity."[111] He therefore recommends a world-wide revolution to put an end to all materialistic conditions that hinder women from performing their natural role in life and that force them "to carry out men's duties in order to be equal in rights."[112]

In his view, the question of whether or not women should work is "a ridiculous materialistic presentation."[113] Society must provide work for all men and women who need work, "but on condition that each individual should work in the field that suits him [or her], and not be forced to carry out unsuitable work."[114] All human beings are created equal and free. Freedom, however, means that every person gets the type of education which qualifies him or her for doing appropriate work. In his view, although there is no difference in rights between man and woman, "there is no absolute equality between them as regards their duties."[115]

Minorities

Qaddafi also pays special attention to the problems of minorities which are caused by artificial barriers created by the majority who seek control of power and wealth. He argues that minorities have social rights that should not be encroached upon by the majority because such action is "an act of injustice." He insists that "the social characteristic is personal and is not to be given or taken away."[116] He warns against viewing minorities as political and economic minorities because such a view is "dictatorship and injustice."[117]

Qaddafi claims that minorities cannot "exist simply because of religion or beliefs." He argues that "every race has a majority religion and . . . a majority nationality." He therefore concludes that "it is a mistake that a person adopts a religion other than the majority religion of his race."[118] He insists that minorities are based on race, not religion or culture. In his view, there are only two significant types of minorities. The first involves minorities that no longer have nations or homelands of their own. They are the remnants of people whose nations disappeared in the course of history. Examples are the Gurkhas and the Gypsies. These minorities, having lost their homelands, have settled in new nations and have become part of them politically and economically. Despite this degree of assimilation, they have retained their own traditions, habits, religion, and often languages. Those minorities should be free to practice their own social and cultural habits.[119]

The second type is the minority that lives in another nation despite the fact that an identifiable homeland and race continue to exist. Examples are the Armenians and the Kurds. In his view, these minorities "should be free to return to their homeland"[120] because their problems will continue as long as they are denied the right to have their own nations. The only solution therefore would be to create a politically independent Armenia and Kurdistan. Otherwise, keeping them under subjugation by force is a "barbaric venture."[121]

Qaddafi makes a distinction between such minorities and the Jews who, in his view, "are not a minority."[122] In Israel today, there are two groups: the Oriental Jews, who constitute 55 percent of the Jewish population, and the European (Ashkenazi) Jews, who account for 45 percent. He argues that because European Jews have homelands and nationalities in Europe, they therefore have no right to settle in Palestine or to forcibly evict the Arab population. To Qaddafi, European Jews "have no right to leave their [European] nations to form a racist imperialist society in Palestine."[123] The Zionist claim to Palestine as a homeland is "a false claim,"[124] which has precipitated the long conflict in the Middle East, has threatened peace and security in the region, and might cause a third world war. He argues that only the Oriental Jews have the right to remain in the Middle East. Thus, European Jews should return to Europe, namely the countries of their origin. It is within this framework that he calls upon the Libyan Jews, who are now living in Europe, to return to Libya because they have the right to live in their native country just like other Libyans. He says, "I would welcome and will provide for the return of the Libyan Jews in Europe, if they wish to live in a new and free Jamahiriya. They will have equal rights and duties. They will be able to sit side by side with other Libyans in the Congresses, and decide with others the fate of their nation. Yet they will be able to practice their own religion freely, at home or in the synagogues. In the Jamahiriya society, all the people . . . have equal rights to power and wealth."[125]

Since the problems of minorities have continued to exist in both capitalist and communist societies, he believes that the only solution rests in his Third Universal Theory which places power, wealth and arms in the hands of all the people. Minorities will automatically become an integral part of the larger community when they participate directly in the political process and receive equal political and economic rights. In doing so, they will become conscientious and responsible members of society because they will no longer be treated differently from the majority or be placed on the periphery of the community. Once the political and economic problems of the minorities are solved, Qaddafi believes that nationalism, the most potent source of social unity, can become stronger.

Blacks

In his search for a new social order, Qaddafi could not ignore the problems of black peoples who have suffered tremendously from racism, which manifested itself both in European colonization of Africa and in servitude in North America. In his view, both colonialism and slavery were manifestations of European hatred of the black race. They were both the product of the Anglo-Saxon doctrine of white supremacy. The net result of centuries of enslavement has been a bitter feeling and a search for satisfaction derived from the need to rehabilitate a whole race. This condition has given birth to "a psychological motivation in the movement of the black race to vengeance and domination."[126]

Qaddafi sees no justification for one race to despise another or for a person "to boast at the expense of another"[127] whether because of color or national origin. Thus, discrimination or segregation is morally wrong because human beings are created equal. There should be no distinction based on color, sex, or creed.

He recognizes that "the black race is now in a very backward social situation" stemming from centuries of slavery and colonialism. He also points out, however, that

> such backwardness helps to bring about numerical
> superiority of the blacks because their low standard of liv-
> ing has protected them from getting to know the means
> and ways of birth control and family planning. Also their
> backward social traditions are a reason why there is no
> limit to marriage, leading to their unlimited growth, while
> the population of other races has decreased because of
> birth control, restrictions on marriage and continuous oc-
> cupation in work, unlike the blacks who are sluggish in
> a climate which is always hot.[128]

He argues that the only way for the black people to reverse these
conditions is to fight "to regain their dignity and respect." He feels
that time is on their side and that the black race will eventually "take
over power in various parts of the world."[129] He bases his prediction
on the inevitability of social historical cycles. Since the yellow and
white races have had their days of expansion and domination, it could
be expected that the black race will have its turn.[130] In his view, their
ascendence to power would be the first step toward regaining their
respect and placing themselves on equal footing with other races.[131]
Blacks, whether they are in North America or Africa, have many in-
centives to struggle for their proper place in the world community.
American blacks, for instance, are fighting for social, economic and
political emancipation; they are struggling to eradicate the injustices
of centuries of oppression and deprivation. He says, "The rise of the
black Americans is not due to the political or economic situation in
America, but rather due to the hereditary drive and the . . . hidden
anger against oppression. Socially, economically and politically, the
blacks want to be free from the daily oppressive and unjust and arbitrary control of the Anglo-American majority."[132] He predicts that
the burning desire for equality, freedom, and justice will drive blacks
toward revolution aimed at eradicating the "barbaric U.S. culture which
fosters [discrimination] . . . to maintain a system of domestic colonialism and [external] imperialism."[133]

Education

Qaddafi also seeks to liberalize the educational systems of the world
today because, in his view, they are inappropriate, inadequate and
irrelevant. For the most part, students are placed in a strait-jacket by
rigid requirements and methodized curricula and they are also forced

to learn in a highly regimented atmosphere. To him, this type of education deprives individuals of their natural right to choose the subjects they desire.

Qaddafi sees compulsory education as another example of deprivation of individual freedom because it is "a compulsory obliteration of a human being's talents as well as a forcible direction of a human being's choices." It is therefore "an act of dictatorship damaging to freedom because it deprives man of free choice, creativity and brilliance."[134] The net result is a stifling of the masses.

Because of such apparent deficiencies in educational institutions, Qaddafi advocates abolishing all educational methods prevailing in the world today. He calls for a world-wide cultural revolution "to emancipate man's mind from curricula[r] fanaticism and from the process of deliberate adaptation of man's taste, his ability to form concepts and his mentality."[135] This does not mean, however, that education should come to a halt or that people should turn their backs on education or that schools should be closed down. On the contrary, he values education as a means to train individuals in various fields of knowledge. But the training should be tailored to meet individual needs, not imposed by the state or influenced in specific directions by authority.

Qaddafi urges societies to make all types of education available so that individuals can choose from whatever subjects they wish to study. Failure to have sufficient institutions causes hardship on the people by restricting their freedom of choice and by forcing them to learn subjects they might not be interested in or even care about. He also criticizes societies that place restrictions on teaching certain subjects, whether in the form of a ban, a monopoly, or a distortion of knowledge in the educational process. In his view, these societies are "reactionary . .. . biased towards ignorance and hostile to freedom."[136] Education should be open and free because "knowledge is a natural right of every human being [of] which nobody has the right to deprive him under any pretext." He believes that "ignorance will come to an end when everything is presented as it actually is and when knowledge about everything is available to each person in the manner that suits him."[137]

Conclusion

In order to justify the need for his Third Universal Theory, Qaddafi has expressed serious reservations about and much valid criticism of the political theories and economic models prevailing in the world today. He argues that neither traditional democracy nor communism has successfully dealt with the many problems of contemporary societies. Their lack of success is caused primarily by their failure to place the instruments of government and wealth in the hands of the people. Although communism claims that power and authority are controlled by the working class, they are in fact dominated by a single party in which a cadre of elite members rules in the name of the working class. It is a government of the party leadership rather than of working people.

Western democracy, on the other hand, places power and authority in the hands of a few elected representatives who usurp the people's power and who rule on behalf of the people. In his view, parliamentary democracy is a form of "misrepresentation" because it is a government of the party and not of the people, since the masses are not directly involved in running the government and have no control over state affairs. Party politics has resulted in power struggles that are waged so that one party or coalition of parties can dominate the government in order to further a class or group interest at the cost of the rest of society. The party's struggle for power breeds a divisiveness that hinders rather than advances national unity and progress. For this reason, Qaddafi thinks that parties and party politics serve no useful purpose.

As a remedy for the shortcomings of both Western-style democracy and communism, Qaddafi's Third Universal Theory advocates the establishment of a "direct democracy" in which the people as a whole are directly involved in the political process and become the instruments of government, thus replacing representatives, deputies or intermediaries. Popular congresses and people's committees should be formed at the local, regional and national levels in order to ensure direct mass political participation at all levels and in all matters.

Under his direct democracy, the people's direct involvement in political activity is assured at the local level in the Basic Popular Congresses. Every citizen over eighteen years of age has an opportunity to represent himself on all matters before the BPCs. The success of his democracy hinges on the degree of political education and sophistication of the average citizen who will have to see the need for and the value of playing an active role in political discussion and the decision-making apparatus.

On the other hand, some form of representation is a necessity at the regional and national levels because it is physically impossible to gather an entire adult population in one location on a continuous basis to make legislative and administrative decisions and to formulate policies. In Qaddafi's scheme, each BPC selects a secretariat to send to the Municipality Popular Congresses (MPC) and the General People's Congress (CPC). It is a mistake to view these national groupings in the traditional roles of representatives, however, because there is no delegation of authority. They are not free to present their own personal views but are restricted to presenting decisions and resolutions already made at the previous levels and to transmitting the wishes of the people as expressed by the popular congresses. The General People's Congress (GPC) broadly represents all social groups within the country. Its membership is not limited to the leadership of the Basic Popular Congresses and People's Committees but includes representatives from unions, syndicates and professional associations. Thus, no group is left unrepresented at the highest level of authority in the country.

Qaddafi has replaced a cabinet with a secretariat chosen by the General People's Congress and subject to annual reconfirmation. The members of the secretariat, including the secretary-general, do not play the traditional ministerial roles because they are not authorized to make policies on behalf of the people or to speak in their names. They only execute decisions made by the General People's Congress.

Qaddafi's model attempts to avoid the pitfalls of Western democracy while it seeks to maximize popular participation in the decision-making apparatus of government. The success of his political system greatly depends, however, on the readiness and willingness of the average citizen to participate actively in the political process and in a way that ensures smooth operation of the government machinery, which is no longer controlled and managed by skillful and trained bureaucrats.

Western scholars have criticized Qaddafi's democracy as being unsuitable to heavily populated countries where, in their view, representation is essential and inescapable for the survival of an orderly democratic form of government. This is a valid criticism because Qaddafi's political model is still in the stage of experimentation in Libya. His theory requires a total overhaul of contemporary political systems and advocates radical changes which many societies might be reluctant to introduce for fear of causing political instability and chaotic conditions. Many leaders will undoubtedly prefer to maintain Western-style democracy since they are familiar with the rules of the game and any changes will mean new players and new rules which might not promote their group interests or ensure their power.

In the economic sphere, Qaddafi believes that neither capitalism nor communism has succeeded in solving economic problems and promoting development. Both models have deprived the majority of the people of wealth by concentrating wealth in the hands of a few individuals or by setting up a state monopoly. Public ownership is a dominant feature in his socialism. He also encourages the development of the private sector as long as it is non-exploitative in nature. He urges every individual to work for himself, but insists that what is beyond individual needs should be owned jointly by the public for the benefit of the whole. He advocates the establishment of a new partnership between workers and employers in order to eliminate that exploitation of labor that is found in both Western and Eastern societies. Because workers are an integral part of the production process, they should be given a fair share in what they produce. He therefore suggests abolishing the wage system in favor of giving workers an equal share in production commensurate with their contribution to the production efforts. This will not only eliminate labor exploitation but also will help increase production and efficiency because workers will gain or lose financially as production goes up or down.

Although this new partnership might eliminate a source of labor-management conflict, there is no guarantee that it can result in an immediate increase in production. In fact, it is likely that production will go down at the beginning, if Libya has the same experience as several other countries in the aftermath of nationalization. The success of his model will depend on whether workers are ready to take advantage of the new opportunity provided by socialism. Yet until Qaddafi's socialism has been fully carried out in Libya and has proven to be successful in tackling its problems of economic development, there is doubt that it could find its way into another society. What must be recognized, too, is that financial constraints would make his brand of socialism impractical for many Third World countries. Unlike Libya with its oil riches, many governments are struggling and can hardly make basic material necessities available for their people; in such a circumstance, it is doubtful that people can expect to work for themselves and to own the means to fulfill their basic needs.

Despite these problems, there are merits in Qaddafi's socialism since it seeks to eliminate the unjust distribution of national wealth which typically has been concentrated in the hands of a few individuals or monopolized by the state. His main objective is to redistribute wealth among the majority of the people and to ensure that basic human necessities are not only met but also controlled by individuals. He seeks to put an end to all forms of economic exploitation and enslavement of man by man, conditions which have characterized both capitalist and communist societies.

Qaddafi's social program is more controversial than his economic program; his ideas have been influenced by his national culture and consequently might not appeal to societies with different cultural backgrounds. He advocates a return to religion to strengthen the fabric of society. In his view, human behavior should be guided by an ethical code that cannot be enforced by law alone. Religion enforces morality and therefore motivates individuals to behave in a manner conducive to promoting cohesiveness and stability. Religion can also solidify national unity when it is compatible with nationalism.

A return to religion might be attractive to societies where a single religion dominates, as in Libya. Since Islam is Libya's main religion, it is understandable that Qaddafi would try to revive the basic tenets of Islam in order to eliminate social injustices and to create a classless society where all forms of discrimination would be wiped out. The return to Islam will also result in a cultural and political awakening based on Pan-Arabism that stresses a common heritage and destiny. But his emphasis on religion might not be the solution for other nations where several religions coexist or where religion is separated from the state and is left as a personal matter.

Qaddafi's views on women will undoubtedly be challenged by feminist movements in the West which have been striving for greater equality between women and men. They cannot accept his traditional views that would place restrictions on women doing certain jobs because of biological differences between men and women. Nor would they accept his argument on women's natural function as mothers, a pretext that has long been used to keep women at home and away from the job market. They feel that modern facilities such as nurseries and kindergartens are well equipped to provide excellent care for children and to free women to join the working force. They also insist that whatever jobs men can do women can do also.

Qaddafi's solution for the problems of minorities might not be widely accepted either, particularly in societies where the majorities prefer the status quo to ensure their continued domination of power and wealth. In his view, the problems of minorities will continue to hurt societies unless his Third Universal Theory is implemented. The only solution, he argues, is to place power, wealth, and arms in the hands of the people, as a way to grant political and economic rights on an equal footing for all. As is obvious, Qaddafi believes that it is necessary to implement his theory in its totality in order to cure social ills and to ensure the creation of an egalitarian, socialist, democratic society.

Qaddafi's attempt to draw a general theory, with its political, economic, and social components, is a gigantic task that can make him an easy target of criticism for those who are committed to other political philosophies. His Third Universal Theory, as outlined in the *Green Book,* is still very sketchy and needs further development and refinement. This must be done if it is to be widely regarded as a viable theory for other societies to adopt.

The systematic implementation of his theory in Libya is a practical step in the right direction in order to give the theory a degree of legitimacy and to demonstrate its workability. Such application will move the theory from the state of utopia into reality. It will also allow Qaddafi to make the readjustments necessary to put his theory into practice.

Nevertheless, it is a bold attempt to restructure Libyan society along new lines that have never been tried before. It is nationalistic in nature because it has rejected alien ideologies and instead seeks to support a national culture among Libyans and Arabs by stressing a return to their origins. It is based on trust in the masses and in their ability to be in charge of their instruments of government and national wealth. Its aim is to eliminate political and economic privileges of any group, class, or party in order to redistribute power and wealth justly and widely among the people. It seeks to establish a society based on egalitarianism and socialism. It is timely to examine whether such a system can succeed in Libya or anywhere else. Its success or failure in Libya will suggest whether it can also be borrowed by other societies.

LIBYA IN TRANSITION:

A Revolutionary Political System in the Making

O N SEPTEMBER 1, 1969, QADDAFI STAGED A SUC-
cessful coup, which ousted the constitutional monarchy of
King Idris, and put himself in charge of the country. His coup
was the fuse that ignited the Al-Fateh Revolution, which swept across
the land, "crackling and burning, and [clean-sweeping] its path, paving
the way for the new in place of the old."[138]

From the outset, Qaddafi planned to revolutionize the state structure and revamp society in order to bring the neglected majority into
the political process and to give them a just share in the national wealth.
As the founder and leader of the Revolution, he has been in a strong
strategic position to influence the substance and direction of every
change in the country. Between 1969 and 1977, for example, he
directed the efforts of the Revolutionary Command Council (RCC)
to create a new Libya and to alter the course of its history. Even after
he resigned his official post in the government in 1979, Qaddafi has
continued as the initiator of all major national policies and actions.

The purpose of this chapter is to examine Qaddafi's efforts to restructure the political life of Libya in accordance with his Third Universal
Theory. This assessment will, in particular, seek to shed light on the
ways in which his controversial theory has been implemented in his
country.

The Early Years

In his initial steps to harness the aspirations of the people to the
task of developing a viable political entity, Qaddafi found it necessary
to let the RCC, under his chairmanship, be the supreme authority
in Libya. Until the late 1970s, the RCC functioned as the state's chief
legislative and executive body and was assisted by a Council of
Ministers, which carried out the RCC policies and supervised the day-
to-day administration of the government. From the beginning, Qaddafi emerged as the initiator and orchestrator of all RCC actions and
activities.

Qaddafi's realism led him to recognize that democratization could not be achieved overnight in Libya and that the people would first have to be taught how to fulfill the role that he envisioned for them in policy formulation and in assuming the functions of government. Because the Libyans had been deprived of power for so long under colonialism and the monarchy, they could not be expected to assume their new leadership role right away. Therefore, he frequently invited the masses to discuss issues with him in public sessions, often long and televised. These sessions were used as a forum for politicization where opinions could be aired prior to his making final decisions.[139] He also directed the RCC to lay the foundations for wide-scale political participation and, in 1971, established the Arab Socialist Union (ASU), not as a political party but as a mass organization that was to encompass all people, in the cities, villages, and desert alike. It was intended to provide the masses with "an opportunity to participate politically in planning and supervising future policies."[140] The ASU thus became Libya's primary forum for political participation. In its operation, it sought to enhance national unity and to remove the destructive influences of party politics which, in the past, had only engendered regional, factional, and tribal rivalries. In Qaddafi's view, such party squabbles had betrayed the nation's cause as well as the Arab Revolution, and he saw no need to experiment with alien political systems or ideologies that contradict Libya's Arab-Islamic heritage.[141] He contended that most ideologies, whether to the extreme right or left, have caused fragmentation and have widened the gap between government and the masses. He thus insisted that no political system would be sound unless it was based on the people's participation and their direct involvement in running the country.

It is for this reason that the ASU was a mass, national organization, created specifically to "bring about collaboration among the popular working classes . . . and unite [them] with the revolution against one-class dictatorship."[142] Although the working classes formed 50 percent of the ASU leadership, the experiment failed to mobilize and politicize the masses. This was primarily because traditionalism proved to be much stronger than originally predicted. The ASU was unable to dislodge the close ties between the people and the traditional leadership or to "destroy public trust [in] and loyalty to traditional institutions and leaders."[143] Another factor in its failure was the complex organizational structure of the ASU which confused the populace and discouraged them from active participation in the political process.

Frustrated by the failure of the ASU, Qaddafi launched his Popular Revolution on April 15, 1973. In a major speech at Zwara, he announced a five-point program to revolutionize the administrative structures of the government by turning the masses against the inefficient, corrupt bureaucracy and by abolishing the outdated laws which had hindered the march of the revolution. He declared that

- all existing laws are to be repealed and replaced by revolutionary procedures;
- the country shall be purged of those who are politically unhealthy;
- civil liberties shall be accorded to the proletariat but not to those who disdain the masses of common people. Consequently, arms will be distributed to many sectors of the people who do not belong to either the armed forces or the militia;
- all those who belong to the caste of parasitic bureaucrats will be removed by the people, who . . . will be the instrument for the destruction of the bureaucracy; and
- the Cultural Revolution against all that is reactionary, misleading and ruinous to young people's minds is proclaimed.[144]

At this conjuncture, Qaddafi's aim was to remove the bureaucrats from their positions of authority and to weaken the bourgeois' hold on society; in his view, these groups "formed a barrier between the revolution and the masses."[145] This was a necessary step to prepare the people for the new role he envisioned for them in the new political structure based on the Third Universal Theory. As one observer said, the Zwara speech was intended "to take the people of Libya a first step forward towards the institution of a novel order of governing based on the complete decentralization of power." It set in motion a series of changes and put into practice Qaddafi's theory which sought "to give power to the people so that they would be able to govern themselves by themselves."[146]

Direct Democracy

Under Qaddafi's "direct democracy," the people as a whole are not only directly involved in the political process but also become the instruments of government, thus replacing representatives, deputies or intermediaries.[147] He proposes a reorganization of society from the grass roots upward. People's committees and popular congresses are to be formed at the local, regional and national levels to ensure direct mass political participation at all levels and in all matters.[148]

People's Committees

In 1973, Qaddafi moved a giant step forward to implement his belief that a true popular revolution must be ruled by the people. He called upon the masses to form People's Committees in every village, city, college, institute and factory.[149] He urged them to seize power and administer all places of work and production, including local governments.[150]

People were slow to respond to Qaddafi's call for People's Committees. In fact, students at the Faculty of Law at Qar Younis University in Benghazi were the first to set up a committee, which took charge of the administration and management of their college. Workers were slower in forming committees. Qaddafi had to speak out to encourage labor groups to take authority and power into their own hands by establishing People's Committees in their factories and companies.[151]

These committees are to be elected openly by the people in each unit or area and not by governors, directors or any other authority. Their leadership is to be collective; decisions would be made by unanimity and responsibility would be shared jointly. Because of these committees, the people as a whole would become the source of power in Libya. They would elect these committees and hold them accountable for translating their wishes into realities.

Since October 1973, People's Committees have become the official authority in the governorates and municipalities. The chairman of each committee has taken over the functions previously held by a governor or mayor. Directors in each governorate are elected directly by the people and are no longer appointed by the central government. This change has shifted responsibility to the masses, who now must keep a watch on these directors and hold them responsible for their performance.[152]

Similarly, People's Committees have taken over the management of institutions, public corporations and companies, including their boards of directors, which are now headed by the chairman of the People's Committee for each unit. University councils have been taken over by People's Committees, which include students, faculty and staff; each committee chairman has assumed the functions of the president of the university, and the chairman of the faculty council has become the dean of faculty. Other public institutions such as hospitals and government printing presses have elected their People's Committees to administer and manage their operations.

At the beginning, members of the People's Committees did not receive salaries. Serving on these committees was seen as a privilege, one that carried heavy weight, however, because their performance was closely watched by the people. This proved to be administratively inefficient, however. Salaries are now given to the chairman of the People's Committee, to the Committee secretariat, and to their assistants so that they can devote their full-time attention to carrying out their administrative duties. The membership term on the People's Committee is limited to three years, however, and a committee member can be removed at any time by a two-thirds vote. Resignation must be accepted and approved by the committee.

Currently, there are People's Committees everywhere in Libya. They have become an important political instrument under popular leadership that has made a strong effort to democratize the administration and to promote the goals of the Al-Fateh Revolution. Shortly after the People's Committees, the Basic People's Congresses (BPC) were established "as a higher authority and a means of supervision of the whole people over its parts as embodied in the popular committees."[153]

Basic People's Congresses

To help get the people involved in the political process at the grass roots level, Basic People's Congresses (BPC) were formed locally, according to place of residence, so that all people would be members of a congress. These congresses select their People's Committees. They also choose their secretariats which, in turn, constitute the Municipality People's Congresses (MPC).

Qaddafi made a point to attend the first BPC that was held at Tawergha in 1976. He went out of his way to explain the principles underlying his direct people's democracy and instructed the masses on what to do every step of the way. First, he stressed that BPC membership was not limited to men or political activists but open to all the people, including women, who constitute fifty percent of the population. He warned that the exclusion of women would not only keep the society divided but would also make a mockery out of the Third Universal Theory. Under no circumstances should decisions be made by only half of the people; they must be made by all the people in the BPC's jurisdiction. Realizing that social traditions might prevent women's participation, Qaddafi suggested that they could meet in separate chambers to express their views on issues before the BPC if traditions did not allow women and men to assemble in a single hall.[154] He emphasized that it is important for both men and women to participate in the decision-making process on all matters that affect their lives.

Second, Qaddafi did not want professional politicians and political activists moving from one BPC to another manipulating the political process and infringing on residents' rights to deliberate on issues before them. He therefore pointed out that only residents of the BPC area would be allowed to participate in its work. This means that "anyone who did not belong to the Municipality should not be admitted to the assembly."[155] Instead, they should attend congresses in their own areas. To give some order to the process, Qaddafi proposed that BPCs issue identification cards for their members, checking cards as people are admitted to meetings, to ensure that attendance is limited to people living in that municipality.

Third, Qaddafi proposed that a national agenda be drawn up, normally consisting of seven items, in order to ensure that similar issues were debated throughout the country. This means that each BPC was expected to abide strictly by the agenda. This was done in order "to prevent the Basic People's [Congresses] from degenerating into formless assemblies without purpose or discipline."[156] After discussion, the BPC would offer recommendations and resolutions, which would become policies binding on the people of the area.

Fourth, Qaddafi told the people assembled in the BPC at Tawergha that they were in charge of "every aspect of the life of the people, ranging from municipal services and economic development to foreign policy and the defense of the country."[157] He stresssed the seriousness of the task ahead because their recommendations and resolutions are "final and inviolable." He said, "No individual, body or institution would be entitled to alter or interfere in any way with these recommendations and resolutions, either by omission, addition, amendment or alteration." He made it clear that their decisions would be "the effective and final policy of their areas of jurisdiction." This is in line with his theory that "the people and the people alone have the prerogative and indeed the authority to [make] decisions."[158] This means that there is no veto over the people's power.

It was not an easy task for the people to shoulder the new responsibilities of running the government. From the founding of the Republic
in 1969, they had been accustomed to let the RCC, headed by Qaddafi, conduct the business of government in a dictatorial fashion. Qaddafi, having dismantled the traditional form of government, was now
asking the Libyans to control and direct the instruments of government in a way that had never before been done in the country.

Qaddafi was concerned about people's apathy, which could threaten
the implementation of his Third Universal Theory in Libya or
anywhere else. There was a need to motivate the people to take their
new responsibilities seriously to ensure the success of his experiment.
He therefore attacked passivity among the Libyans, especially as
evidenced by a small turn-out in the BPCs. Some people stayed away
because they were not familiar with his theory or were skeptical about
the outcome. Others attended the BPC sessions but failed to take
an active role in deliberation, probably because they were not sure
that they were indeed in charge of local and national policies and that
their decisions were binding on the state. To overcome this apathy,
Qaddafi reiterated that "their decisions will be binding not only on
the institutions of the state but [also] on him personally."[159] He also
criticized citizens who chose not to attend the BPC sessions, stating
that there is no place for those "who default on their political responsibilities."[160] In his view, failure to participate in the BPC is a betrayal
for both the individual and the nation. He made it clear that BPC
decisions are binding whether a person attended or not and whether
he liked or opposed the decisions. This was intended to motivate
people to attend BPCs and to take part in the political process, which
should be based on people's participation at all levels of the decision-
making apparatus. Qaddafi wanted to ensure that the BPC would function at the local level since it represents the backbone of the political
structure of his direct popular democracy.

General People's Congress

At the national level, Qaddafi established the General People's Congress (GPC), which includes representatives from all social groups
within the country. It is the highest political authority and instrument
of government in Libya. It is empowered "to study, discuss and approve the policies of the state, its general planning, budget, peace and
war treaties and to check and to guide the executive and popular
authorities."[161] The GPC's broad powers mean that no other body—

such as a parliament or other formal institution–is needed.

The General People's Congress has a broad base of representation. Its membership currently includes the leadership of the Basic People's Congresses, the People's Committees, the unions, the syndicates and the professional association.[162] These diversified groups act as a check and balance on each other, offering a way to ensure that no group, class or individual will absorb power and dominate the political system.

In November 1976, Qaddaffi found himself in conflict with the General People's Congress over "The Draft Declaration on the Establishment of the People's Power." The draft called for the abolishment of the Revolutionary Command Council (RCC), which, under Qaddafi's chairmanship, had ruled Libya, controlling both executive and legislative functions of the government. In addition, the declaration advocated "the dismantling of the government," including the presidency, the cabinet and all political and administrative structures that are commonly found in conventional forms of government. Instead, it suggested "the immediate transfer of power" to the General People's Congress.[163]

Qaddafi was eager to take the final step to complete the structure of his direct people's democracy. The GPC, on the other hand, was not ready to act on the draft, which would have immediately overhauled the entire political system that had existed in Libya since 1969. When it became evident that the GPC would put off the decision for a year, Qaddafi "threatened to relinquish power unilaterally."[164]

However, Qaddafi was persuaded to change his mind on the argument that the draft should be taken through the process he set up in accordance with his Third Universal Theory. The draft must first be submitted to the Basic People's Congresses, which would act on it and formulate their recommendations. Then it would be forwarded to the General People's Congress to finalize the decision. As a compromise, it was agreed to call "special extraordinary sessions" for the Basic People's Congresses to consider the draft between January and February 1977. The General People's Congress would then be convened to act on their recommendations.

The draft raised some serious issues: How much power would the GPC secretary-general have? Should Qaddafi be exempted by granting him extraordinary powers to keep the Revolution on its march? What role would the Revolution's leaders play in the new structure? What was the future of the RCC? These issues caused a heated ex-

change between Qaddafi and the GPC. At the end, however, Qaddafi got his way as the GPC bowed to his wishes, in deference to
his role as the architect of the experiment in direct people's democracy.

The GPC was against the proposal limiting the authority of the
secretary-general since everyone expected Qaddafi to be elected to
the post. It was inconceivable that the Congress would curtail Qaddafi's authority in the new structure. In their view, such action was
"tantamount to giving up the Revolution."[165] It preferred to make an
exception for Qaddafi by granting him extraordinary powers in order
to push the Al-Fateh Revolution forward.[166]

Qaddafi, on the other hand, argued against giving expanded powers
to the secretary-general of the GPC. He was determined to prevent
any individual from accumulating too much power. He was unwilling
to make an exception for himself out of fear that it might set a precedent, undermining the essence of his theory. In his view, there is a
definite relationship between the amount of power held by an individual
at the top of the hierarchical system and the amount of power exer-
cised by the people, for "the people's power is curtailed in direct pro-
portion to the amount of authority held by a single individual."[167]
When he persisted in his opposition, the GPC decided to endorse
his proposal and to limit the authority of the secretary-general.

Qaddafi and the GPC also disagreed on the role of the abolishment
of the RCC, whose membership was compromised of the Free
Unionist Officers who had led the coup in 1969 and who had
dominated the political scene since that time. It was suggested, instead, that the RCC continue to carry out the same functions as it
had since 1969, regardless of the changes introduced in the political
system.

Qaddafi could not agree to the continuation of the RCC, since it
would undercut his experiment in putting the instruments of government in the hands of the people. Its existence would rob the masses
of an opportunity to rule themselves.

As the stalemate continued, it was obvious that the GPC did not
want to dismantle the RCC unless its members were chosen to serve
on the GPC general secretariat, which would provide the political
leadership for both the congress and the nation. This meant that Qaddafi would become the Secretary-General of the GPC, while the other
four members of the RCC–Major Abd El-Salem Jaloud, Lt. Colonel
Abu BakrUnis, Colonel Mustapha El-Kharroubi and Major Khweildi
El-Hemeidi–would be elected to the General Secretariat.[168] This

compromise broke the deadlock, and the RCC officers came to occupy the highest offices in the nation. Thus, no change was made
in the national leadership since the same persons continued to
dominate the political process regardless of the changes in the political
structure. The real changes would have to wait until the membership
of the general secretariat was changed in future elections.

In addition to the general secretariat, it was decided to create a
General People's Committee to parallel the popular committees at the
local level and to direct the work at the national level. That decision
resulted in another round of disagreement between Qaddafi and the
GPC. The General People's Congress wanted the four RCC officers
to serve on both the General People's Committee and the general
secretariat of the GPC in order to keep the Al-Fateh Revolution on
the right path.

Qaddafi was vehemently against the proposal, arguing that "just as
one individual is not allowed to hold two positions at the level of the
BPC, so it is inadmissible for an individual, no matter how illustrious,
to hold simultaneously two positions at the top."[169] In his view, no
one should be permitted to serve on both the General People's Committee and the general secretariat. He was not willing to make an exception in this critical period of formation for it might set a precedent
that would undermine his theory of direct popular democracy. Qaddafi, along with the RCC officers, refused the proposition to combine
the two posts at the national level, saying "the combination of the
General Secretariat and the General Popular Committee was out of
the question."[170] He therefore asked the GPC to nominate a chairman for the General People's Committee. When the Congress failed
to do so, Qaddafi nominated Abd El-Ati El-Obeidi and, when the
voting was inconclusive, he named him as chairman.[171]

It seems likely that Qaddafi went beyond his power when he named
the chairman of the General People's Committee. He did so, however,
because he wanted to set up a structure at the national level that would
ensure the proper functions of the political process. It would have been
a setback if he had gone along with the GPC recommendation of allowing individuals to combine more than one post at the national level.
Thus, he was forced to overrule the GPC for the sake of preserving
his theory of people's power, upon which the experiment in Libya
was built.

The adoption of the Declaration on the Establishment of the
People's Power in March 1977 ushered the beginning of the era of the

masses (Jamahiriya) in Libya. Qaddafi then announced the birth of the Socialist People's Libyan Arab Jamahiriya. The General People's Congress now possesses both legislative and executive powers for the whole country. It formulates decisions, reviews policies submitted by the Basic People's Congresses, and supervises their implementation.

The General People's Congress openly elects a president to preside over sessions, to sign its laws, and to accept the credentials of ambassadors.[172] It also elects a General Secretariat to carry out its resolutions and recommendations, to make preparations for holding its sessions and to draw up its agenda. The Secretariat includes a Secretary General and a number of Secretaries, each of whom supervises one section of activities in the state. They are accountable to the Congress, which can dismiss them or accept their resignations.[173]

Thus, the functions of the previous council of ministers have been taken over by the General Secretariat of the Congress. However, its function is different. Neither the Secretary General nor the Secretaries make decisions to determine the general policy of the state. Their main duty is to implement decisions made by the General People's Congress. Further, they are responsible for carrying out the wishes of the Congress, which can terminate their services at any time if it is dissatisfied with their performance.

Revolutionary Committees

When the General People's Congress (GPC) convened in 1979, Qaddafi relinquished his post as its Secretary General and other official positions and titles except as the Leader of the Revolution. He did so because he wanted to devote all of his time to revolutionary activities. He also wished to separate the Revolution from the people's authority and civil administration. This separation has given him a monopoly over the Revolution, and has put him in a strategic position to influence the country's policies and priorities.

As part of his emphasis on the Revolution, Qaddafi called on Libyan revolutionaries in 1977 to form their own committees throughout the country. In response, Revolutionary Committees were organized in every office, business, and educational institution, and also in the Armed Forces.[174] These committees quickly became highly organized, with a structure parallel to the People's Committees. Both local and national units were established in an effort to coordinate activities and to gain efficiency in carrying out their tasks.

Membership in Revolutionary Committees is not based on election but is open to anyone who firmly believes in Qaddafi's ideology and his socialist society. Members have been said to be "handpicked zealots"[175] who serve as Qaddafi's "ideological shock troops,"[176] totalling about 3,000-4,000 people.[177] They have tremendous power because they are directly under Qaddafi's command and are only accountable to him. They operate completely outside the administrative framework of the popular congresses.

Revolutionary Committees are committed to pushing the Revolution forward and defending Qaddafi's newly installed political, economic, and social systems in Libya. They engage in revolutionary activities at the grass-roots level by providing guidance for the masses on how to carry out their duties, following the *Green Book*. They seek to raise the level of political awareness among the populace so that the people can execute their power by directing the instruments of government. Their duties have been outlined as follows:

- Inciting the masses to exercise authority.
- Firmly establishing the people's authority.
- Practicing revolutionary supervision.
- Agitating the popular congresses.
- Leading the popular committees and the secretariats of the congresses to the right way.
- Protecting, defending, and propagating the revolution.[178]

Consequently, their function is to continually encourage the popular congresses to intensify their ideological work, to help the masses make progressive decisions, and to get such decisions implemented by the People's Committees.[179] To do so, Qaddafi has asked the Revolutionary Committees to keep a close watch on People's Committees and to be sure that decisions made by the popular congresses are fully implemented. Any sabotage or deviation by a member or by the whole committee should be reported to the popular congresses in order to punish those who are responsible for not carrying out the wishes of the people.[180]

As opposition to Qaddafi's leadership and ideology has increased, Qaddafi has ordered the Revolutionary Committees to collect names and to prepare a list of the enemies of the Revolution. The list is submitted to the headquarters of the Revolutionary Committees for investigation and for appropriate action. In the Armed Forces, an immediate action is expected against any attempt to mount a coup.[181]

Thus, Revolutionary Committees are now in charge of combatting reactionaries, counterrevolutionaries, and foreign ideologies which might seek to undermine or destroy the accomplishments of the Al-Fateh Revolution. They have used agitation as a means to incite the masses against those who are "antagonistic to the people's power and the new socialist transformation." Yet, Qaddafi insists that agitation must be prudent: "No one is allowed to take an individual or unlimited initiative except in extreme situations where defense of the Revolution and the people's authority is called for." He also warned against "blind popular domination" because it can destroy the interest of the masses. He told the Revolutionary Committees to equip themselves with administrative know-how and political consciousness in order to enable them to provide leadership for the Revolution and to guide the people to set up a socialist society "devoid [of] political, economic, and social diseases."[182]

Despite Qaddafi's intentions, the Revolutionary Committees have developed a broad power to "intimidate both wavering citizens and official functionaries"[183] as they have become tools to weed out opposition and to rid the society of the enemies of the Revolution. In 1980, for example, the Revolutionary Committees held a convention in Benghazi and drew up a plan to expose corrupt citizens at home and to pursue Qaddafi's opponents abroad. In the following months, a campaign was conducted to round up individuals accused of corruption[184] and public, televised trials were held in an effort to discourage others from opposing the Revolution.

As preparations were being made to deal with opposition abroad, Qaddafi first gave his opponents a chance to redeem themselves; he called upon them to return home and promised protection against any retaliation by the Revolutionary Committees. He warned, however, that failure to do so would result in their "liquidation."[185] When his plea went unheeded, "hit squads" were sent overseas to eliminate some of his opponents who had been plotting to overthrow his regime. Such action has drawn sharp criticism from several governments where a number of Libyan exiles were murdered.

In the face of the people's apathy and of growing opposition, it might have been justifiable for Qaddafi to form the Revolutionary Committees to heighten political consciousness, to keep the revolutionary zeal alive, and to counter the conspiracies to overthrow his regime.[186] But the heavy tactics they have used to silence opposition have led to the alienation of several groups and to spreading dissatisfaction among many segments of the population. They have also undermined any meaningful popular participation in the political process and have stifled freedom of expression. Many citizens now fear that any criticism might be misconstrued as opposition to the Revolution and its leader.

Qaddafi, however, has gone out of his way to defend the controversial work of the Revolutionary Committees. He has repeatedly denied that they have had a negative influence on the political process. He has pointed out that they are not exploiting the Revolution to serve their own ends, that is, to seize power and direct the instruments of government. On the contrary, he insists that they are only a tool to instigate the masses to exercise authority.[187] As he put it: "The Revolutionary Committees incite the people to revolt and take power, after which their role continues, in inciting the masses to practice authority until power is consolidated and the popular masses are gradually raised to the level of the Revolutionary Committees, which then, of course, cease to exist."[188]

Despite his defense, the Revolutionary Committees have used extreme measures to combat opposition in order to protect the new order and to safeguard Qaddafi's leadership. Their arbitrary decrees and campaigns of intimidation have disrupted the political process as the Revolutionary Committees and the popular congresses are locked in a power struggle. It is reported that some Revolutionary Committees have intervened in the work of the popular congresses by putting forward their own candidates to serve on the People's Committees and by objecting to the choices of the people.[189] This is often done because Revolutionary Committees want to fill these positions with individuals who are enthusiastic admirers of Qaddafi and who are committed to furthering the goals of the Revolution. In doing so, they have prevented the popular congresses from exercising their authority without being subjected to outside pressure to influence their decisions. This situation has adversely affected the popular participation in the decision-making process.

Popular Militia

In the face of internal opposition and external threats, Qaddafi has urged that military training be made compulsory for all citizens. In a broadcast on March 19, 1978, Qaddafi told the Basic People's Congresses that general military training had become a necessity in order to protect the country. He cited the recent clashes with Egypt as an example to support his argument.[190]

In response, the General People's Congress decided in 1979 to make conscription and military training compulsory for all young people, including both male and female students in universities. Later, this was extended to include preparatory and secondary schools. To make such training possible and comprehensive, the academic year was reduced to six months. Furthermore, students in public schools now study Qaddafi's *Green Book* to learn the principles embodied in his Third Universal Theory. Such detailed study is intended to prepare them to fulfill the future roles that Qaddafi has envisioned for them, especially to defend the Jamahiriya system and uphold the Revolution. This is part of Qaddafi's strategy – to use education, which is now free at all levels, as a means to create a new Libyan who is dedicated to the Revolution and who can serve and promote Qaddafi's revolutionary goals.

Military training is not confined only to student groups. During the thirteenth anniversary celebrations of the Revolution in September 1982, Qaddafi stated that a total mobilization was necessary because there was no barrier between Libya and Israel. This situation had come about because "Egypt today is totally subjugated; it is an American-Israeli colony. . . It is now a crossing bridge for the enemies to reach Libya."[191]

Consequently, every adult – young and old – is now being trained in the use of a variety of weapons. In conversations with some Libyans in Tripoli in September 1982, they stated that "they are reporting to training camps every week to receive military instruction." Such training is an ongoing program aimed at enabling the masses to use weapons and at maintaining the population in a state of readiness to defend the Revolution and repel aggression. It is estimated that 45,000 Libyans have completed military training, in addition to 65,000 in the Armed Forces.[192] Qaddafi wants the military training to continue until every adult citizen has been trained. His ultimate goal is to create a popular militia that eventually will replace the conventional military establishment. This follows his theory of putting power, wealth, and arms in the hands of the people. They are to defend the country in case of aggression, protect his socialist-oriented society, and confront all enemies of the Revolution whether they are inside or outside the country.

Conclusion

Since 1969 Qaddafi has dominated Libya's policies by the sheer force of his personality and leadership, both of which have been instrumental in imposing his ideas and structure in Libya. In the early years, as chairman of the RCC, he controlled both the legislative and executive functions of the government. He also directed the RCC's efforts to mobilize the masses and to foster their active interest in the political process. After a brief experiment with the Arab Socialist Union (ASU), he dismantled the traditional organs of government and reorganized the country's political structure to follow his Third Universal Theory. He set up a direct democracy, in which the instruments of government are placed in the hands of the people as a whole. People's Committees and popular congresses have been formed at the local, regional, and national levels to ensure mass participation in the nation's decision-making apparatus.

Qaddafi has been disappointed by his people's apathy and failure to play the role he envisioned for them. Yet the success of his democracy depends on the average citizen, who is expected to play an active role in political discussions and in running the government. To overcome the people's passivity, Qaddafi has become increasingly dependent on the Revolutionary Committees to revive the revolutionary spirit and enthusiasm that seems to be dissipating. Their main task is to entice the masses to exercise authority and to get rid of his opponents inside and outside the country.

Although Qaddafi renounced all official posts and titles in 1979, he has continued to dominate the political scene in his capacity as the Leader of the Al-Fateh Revolution – a title that he has retained for himself. His new function is to guide the Revolution and ensure that it is not sidetracked or sabotaged. This task has given Qaddafi the power to instruct popular congresses on how to run the country in accordance with his theory and to use the Revolutionary Committees to supervise the implementation of the popular congresses' decisions by People's Committees.

Over the years, Qaddafi has become more isolated and less tolerant of criticism as he has become fully committed to the strict application of his theory. He has also moved to fill the void that was created by setting up a loose political structure for a state without government. As a result, he has continued to function as a head of state. This has led some critics to accuse him of establishing a system of government that is democratic in appearance but without real and effective popular participation in the political process.

SOCIALIST ECONOMICS AT A CROSSROAD

W HEN QADDAFI CAME TO POWER, HE HAD TO confront the state of economic underdevelopment in the country. In 1969, Libya was under-industrialized and the national labor force was ill-prepared for any major industrial initiatives. Appropriate technology was non-existent. Libyan businessmen generally lacked interest in industry, which had remained embryonic during the monarchy. Agricultural expansion was hindered by the desert-like and rocky conditions of Libya's soil and by its dry climate, with insufficient rainfall to support large-scale agricultural activities.

Libya's economy was heavily dependent on the West, especially the multinational corporations that had controlled its oil wealth. Libya's finances had relied solely on oil exports, whose prices were manipulated by major Western powers in the world market. Although the discovery of oil resulted in increasing revenues for the state in the 1960s, only a tiny minority of the population had benefited from the oil boom and the majority remained impoverished. What made the situation worse was that the oil revenues were not used for development. Consequently, Libya had become heavily dependent on foreign imports to meet consumer demands for essential goods and services.

From the outset, Qaddafi believed that socialism was the way to solve the country's economic problems and to improve the material conditions of life for all the people. He was instrumental in getting the RCC to proclaim the Constitutional Declaration in December 1969, which stated that:

> The State aims at reali[z]ing socialism through social justice that prevents all forms of exploitation and through sufficiency in production and just distribution of national wealth. The aim [also] is to dissolve peacefully class differences, and to march forward towards [a] prosperous society.[193]

Thus, Qaddafi's socialism was based on social justice through the elimination of economic exploitation, to be accomplished by wide redistribution of national wealth among the people, and by gradual elimination of class differences. He hoped to achieve this by actions

63

that would preserve national unity and the social fabric of the society without taking the nation through a class struggle. He sought to use socialism to guide development efforts and to move the country toward becoming self-sufficient. His objective was to reduce, if not eliminate, Libya's needs for imported goods in both the agricultural and industrial areas. To do so, he felt that it was necessary first to put Libyans in charge of the national wealth and then implement his socialism.

The purpose of this chapter is to examine Qaddafi's economic policies. It specifically looks at: (1) efforts to liberate the national economy; (2) policies to implement socialism as outlined in Qaddafi's Third Universal Theory; and (3) development programs for self-sufficiency in both the agricultural and industrial sectors.

Liberation of the Libyan Economy

Although Qaddafi's ultimate goal was to set up socialism in Libya, his immediate task was to liberate the Libyan economy from foreign influence in order to turn it into a productive national economy. For this reason, foreign-owned banks and insurance companies were the first to be nationalized in Libya. In November 1969, foreign banks were given the choice of either converting into joint-stock companies or closing down their operations and pulling out of the country altogether. Barclays, for instance, opted to close down. Libyans were allowed to own shares in the nationalized banks in amounts not exceeding £L5,000, while the government owned at least 51 percent of the capital in all banks.[194] To Libyans, such nationalization was a necessary step; first as a way "to gain control and direction of the banking activities" so that they could be placed in the service of the national economy, and secondly, to break the linkage between Libya's economic interests and foreign monopoly, and the consequent subjugation of its monetary system to decisions made abroad.[195]

In July 1970, all petroleum distribution facilities were taken over by the government, setting in motion the process of nationalizing the oil industry. In December of the same year, the British Petroleum Company was nationalized. Three years later, all oil companies were nationalized, allowing Libya to take control of its oil resources,[196] which accounted for 98 percent of its exports in the late 1960s. In addition, Qaddafi moved to raise the price of Libya's oil, upon which the country depends for its foreign exchange earnings. His tough bargaining with multinational corporations in the early 1970s resulted in higher prices for his country's oil and, consequently, sharp increases in revenues that gave Qaddafi the necessary capital to finance his plans for development.

Qaddafi also insisted that Libyan land could not be owned or monopolized by foreigners. Accordingly, in October 1970, he expelled 20,000 Italians from Libya and nationalized their 369 plantations totalling 37,000 hectares. The nationalization of these plantations eliminated the largest land-owning class in the country. The average Libyan had only 20 hectares, and only three percent of the population held as much as 100 hectares.

Because these plantations were the best agricultural land in the country, Qaddafi decided to put them to good use. In 1973, some of the nationalized land was distributed among worker-farmers who had large families, very little income, and some knowledge about farming. Each of these farmers was given 10 hectares[197] and was provided with government loans, subsidies, and technical assistance to avoid a drop in production, such as had happened in other developing countries following the nationalization of natural resources. Another reason was to help the farmers make a reasonable income to ensure a decent standard of living.

With the nationalization of these critical resources, Qaddafi began to tackle Libya's economic problems. He had a dual objective: first, to implement his socialism to benefit the masses, who had been deprived of wealth under the monarchy; and second, to make Libya a self-sufficient nation capable of meeting most, if not all, of its needs.

Dimensions of Socialism

At the beginning, Qaddafi had to rely on both the private and public sectors for his developmental and industrial initiatives, especially in solving Libya's acute problems in the flow of goods and services. Up until 1978, he encouraged private investment to accelerate the pace of development by providing the private sector with favorable opportunities to expand their activities in commerce, consumer manufacture, and real estate.

This situation changed in 1978, however, when Qaddafi began to carry out his socialism, which sought to wipe out economic exploitation through a wide and just distribution of wealth among the people.

His objective was to satisfy the material needs of man "through the liberation of these needs from outside domination and control" and "without exploiting or enslaving others."[198] This undermined the very existence of the private sector, which is based on the exploitation of market and labor conditions to maximize profits. Qaddafi instead stressed self-reliance by urging individuals to work to satisfy their needs but without exploitation of others, and insisted that all possessions beyond the satisfaction of individual needs should become the property of the people through joint ownership.[199]

Qaddafi argued that "limitation of property means that, whenever capital oppression arises, the state has the right to curb it" through appropriate measures.[200] Accordingly,

> some people . . . have had their properties expropriated . . . as anything they owned proved harmful to human society. On the other hand, we [have] left others [to] own what they had as long as this ownership has been beneficial to society and has not harmed others. We have also taken away a certain amount of property from others when it was prove[n] that their properties [had] reached the level of exercising harm to others.[201]

He favors public ownership, where all productive sectors of the economy are jointly owned and directed by a broad base of people.[202] In his view, it provides a sound base "for the development of society and for the realization of sufficiency in production."[203] This is largely because people are in charge of the economy and are in a position to influence the direction of development. He opposes the establishment of large corporations, whether they are owned by individuals or by the state. Instead, such conglomerate companies are converted into socialist corporations so that the people can own these enterprises.

In 1978, Qaddafi put his socialism in motion by calling upon workers to take over both public and private factories and companies and to start managing production units.[204] This measure was initiated to end the exploitation of workers, in which their wages were not commensurate with their efforts in production. His plan was to establish a new partnership where workers are considered partners, not wage-earners, in the production process.[205] His ultimate goal was to abolish wages.[206]

The response of labor was slow. Workers were accustomed to the traditional relationship between employers and employees. In fact, Qaddafi spent a whole year explaining his concept of "partners, not wage-earners,"[207] and delineating the new responsibilities under the new partnership in the production process. The workers then took over the management and administration of production units. They elected People's Committees out of their ranks to replace the capitalist or state bureaucratic management. These Committees were put in charge of the socialist corporations "whether [the tasks] are company concern, production matters, or workers' problems."[208] They were to promote the welfare of the working people rather than the interest of an individual or state. To ensure sound economic policies, production unit congresses were established to make collective decisions, which were carried out by People's Committees in each unit of production.

To ensure the success of the new partnership, Qaddafi urged the labor force to guard against reactionary elements who would seek every opportunity to destroy the new socialist system and "to recommence their oppression and tyranny of the workers."[209] He also called upon the people to work hard to maintain productivity and to manage well the productive units.[210]

Abolishing the wage system proved to be difficult and took a long time to implement. This was largely because workers were used to the flow of cash every month. To allow time for people's attitudes, values, and habits to change, a small experiment was developed to demonstrate that abolishing wages could work and benefit the workers in the long run.

In the outskirts of Tripoli today, workers in a couple of factories receive no wages but instead get a share in production that is equal to their effort, capacity, and efficiency. This means that their income fluctuates depending on their contribution to the production effort. It is hoped that such a system will not only eliminate labor exploitation by employers but will also put an end to labor unrest. Libyan workers will see themselves as an integral part of the production cycle and control their own destiny by working for themselves.

The success of this experiment will help determine whether it is practical to abolish the wage system. It is not clear whether workers are capable of taking advantage of the new opportunity provided by socialism. Another factor is that because Libya's national labor force is very small, its industrialization relies heavily on foreign skilled labor and technicians to fill manpower shortages. In late 1981, there were some 500,000 foreign workers in Libya.[211] So many foreign laborers in a country with about three million population might complicate the task of implementing socialism; non-Libyan workers are not allowed to become partners in production but continue as wage-earners in accordance with their contractual arrangements.

Despite these problems, Qaddafi has pushed his socialism forward by initiating several measures to limit capital accumulation and, thus, to narrow the gap between the rich and the poor. In May 1980, for example, bank deposits in excess of L.D. 1,000 were frozen. Banks issued receipts for depositors with any amount exceeding this limit. In addition, all currency bills higher than one dinar were nullified. People were given a week to change their money.[212] To discourage individuals from smuggling their wealth out of the country, a severe penalty was imposed for breaking currency regulations.

In 1981, the General Secretariat of the General People's Congress gave the state exclusive rights for all imports and exports.[213] Such action dealt a severe blow to the private sector's involvement in import-export activities, particulary in the retail and wholesale areas. Its purpose was to remove opportunities for profiteering in commerce.

Under Qaddafi's instigation, other measures have been taken to weaken the merchant class. This is largely because there is no room in his socialist scheme for businessmen, who always strive to maximize their profits by controlling prices and by manipulating the market to their advantage. They create artificial shortages in the market, for instance, by withholding the supply in order to push prices up. Although governments have taken measures to regulate trade, merchants have always managed to use loopholes and other means to avoid complying with these regulations. Qaddafi's solution is to abolish private trade and to replace it by "popular trading circuits in which people sell (commodities) to the people at cost price." It is only under such an arrangement that "speculation will disappear . . . once and for all."[214] Also, exploitation will be ended because no one will manipulate the market to get richer through monopoly or black markets. Prices are fixed with no room for speculation.

In Tripoli today, retail stores are boarded up; the centuries-old Turkish Suq (bazaar) in the Green Square looks like a ghost town with most of the privately owned stores closed and abandoned. New state-run supermarkets are now open for business and are stacked with a variety of imported goods from both eastern and western countries. Customers find it easy to shop in these trade centers because most of the goods are found under one roof and are sold at prices that are close to cost. In addition, prices are the same in all stores, which has eliminated manipulation of prices. Currently, a series of central and satellite supermarkets is being constructed throughout the country.

Businessmen were offered financial compensation for the loss of their private enterprises and were given the opportunity to work at the state-run supermarkets. The only private businesses allowed to continue are those that do not employ workers and are based on a technical skill, including barbers, carpenters, plumbers, etc. These shops are not considered exploitative in nature because they provide services rather than sale of goods. In the Jamahiriya today, man "works for himself to guarantee his material needs, or works for a socialist corporation in whose production he is a partner, or performs a public service to the society which provides his material needs."[215]

Housing Problems: A Socialist Solution

To make people "master in their own castles," Qaddafi believes that every citizen must have the opportunity to satisfy his basic needs without relying on someone else and without the accumulation of wealth, which is always done at the expense of others. In his view, housing is a basic need and every citizen should have the right to decent housing. From the beginning, Qaddafi directed a national effort to tackle Libya's severe housing shortages. On the eve of the coup in September 1969, there were 65,000 families without homes,[216] 53 percent of the existing dwellings were in bad condition,[217] and as many as 40 percent of the population were living in tents and huts.[218]

The Al-Fateh Revolution made the solution of the housing problems one of its top priorities. Under Qaddafi's guidance, numerous housing projects were developed throughout the country, both in the urban and rural areas, in order to prevent population shifts from the countryside to urban centers. Table 2 shows that, between 1969 and 1975, a total of 110,212 housing units were built by both the government and private sectors at a cost of L.D. 623.5 million.[219] In addition, substandard living places such as shanty houses were torn down and replaced by high-rise public housing. In fact, the last hut was ceremonially burnt to the ground in 1976.[220]

Qaddafi argues that, since housing is a basic need, it should not be rented or owned, whether by the state or by individuals. It is a necessity that "no one, including the society . . . is allowed to have control over."[221] He rejects the concept of rental housing because of the inherently exploitative relationship between tenants and landlords. Tenants are treated like slaves because they are under the whim of the landlords who can put them out in the street if the rent is late or for any other reason. Rents also can go out of control because the landlords are in the housing business for profits.[222] Because of this exploitative element, Qaddafi insists that "no one has the right to build a house, additional to his own or that of his heirs, for the purpose of renting it, because the house represents another person's need, and building it for the purpose of rent is an attempt to have control over the need of that man."[223]

Qaddafi's solution is that every occupant should have the right to own the shelter in which he or she lives. In 1970, consequently, government-owned houses were sold to the public. To encourage low-income families to purchase these units, they were only charged 10 percent of the cost if their income was less than $150 a month.[224]

TABLE 2
Completed Housing Units
Between 1969-1975

	Governmental Sector	Private Sector	Total
1969/1970	--	3,100	3,100
1970/1971	3,012	2,957	5,969
1971/1972	3,891	5,634	9,525
1972/1973	6,651	8,173	14,824
1973	4,650	12,754	17,404
1974	12,633	18,480	31,113
1975	10,595	17,682	28,277
Total	41,432	68,780	110,212

Source: *Al-Fateh Revolution in Ten Years*, p. 83.

TABLE 3

Completed Housing Units
Between 1976-1978

	Public Housing	Agricultural Housing	Sebha Housing	Private Housing	Total
1976	36,541	7,828	2,097	82,580	129,046
1977	39,526	8,332	4,532	88,981	141,371
1978	40,799	8,885	6,561	92,381	148,626
Total	116,866	25,045	13,190	263,942	419,043

Source: *Al-Fateh Revolution in Ten Years*, p. 83.

In addition, they received government grants to buy their housing units. Middle-class families were given government loans to purchase their homes, with the loans to be paid back in installments.

To regulate home ownership, the General Secretariat of the General People's Congress issued new guidelines in 1978, giving each family the right to own its dwelling unit, but allowing no one to own more than one.[225] The only exceptions were "widows whose only source of income is rent, and families with at least one son over eighteen years of age." Landlords were ordered to turn over the ownership of their rental units to their tenants. To make the acquisition of these properties possible for the tenants, these units were "deliberately under-valued . . . often by as much as thirty or forty percent." The new owners have a mortgage and pay monthly installments to cover the unit price over a long period of time. The monthly payments are based on the family income and "usually amount to a third of the former rent." In addition, low-income families with an income under $190 got their units for free.[226] In January 1981, the General People's Congress decided to provide free housing for the poor and to set up "a housing saving and investment bank to lend money to citizens and to companies in the housing field."[227]

All these measures were adopted in response to Qaddafi's announcement in September 1979, during the tenth anniversary of the Revolution. He announced that "the house belongs to the occupier. There is no freedom for a man who lives in another's house, whether he pays rent or not." This was in line with his theory that "man's freedom is lacking if somebody else controls what he needs. Need causes exploitation. The house is a basic need of both the individual and the family."[228]

Other measures have been taken to ease the housing crunch. Libya will continue to build new housing until the Revolution's goal of providing every citizen with his own dwelling is realized. Table 3 shows that there have been steady and substantial increases in the amount of housing completed between 1976 and 1978.[229] Vacant buildings have been distributed among families in need of housing, following recommendations of the People's Committees in each district. The head of each needy household was asked to submit an application and proof of marriage. The Committee verified that the applicant did not own another dwelling at the time or that his present housing was in substandard condition. The People's Committees have also distributed vacant lots and approved loans for newly wed couples to help them construct their own housing.

All in all, these measures have eased the country's housing short-age and have put Libya on the road of making proper housing available for all citizens. They have eliminated the inherent exploitation in rental housing by giving the occupier the right to own his dwelling unit. They have made it possible for poor and low-income families to acquire their dwellings without taking on an impossible financial burden. They have succeeded in eliminating the problem of the homeless and have im-proved the living condition for most, if not all, the people.

Agricultural Development

While socialism has been steadily implemented in Libya, Qaddafi has proceeded to use his country's oil wealth to make it economically self-sufficient in the long run. His ultimate goal, however, is to free the economy from the domination of crude oil production and to develop a diversified economic base that will ensure a healthy, pro-ductive economy after the oil is gone. This goal requires a compre-hensive plan for the enlargement and expansion of all sectors of the economy.

Qaddafi has given top priority to the development of the agricultural sector for the following reasons. First, he feels that no country can consider itself to be truly independent "if it [can] not feed its own people without recourse to imported food."[230] Second, that sector was neglected under the monarchy during the decade following the oil boom, which resulted in Libya's heavy reliance on importing foodstuffs from abroad. Third, agriculture is central to the population's livelihood: 70 percent of Libya's active labor force was engaged in agriculture in the late 1960s. For these reasons, Qaddafi announced the Green Revolution, which aimed at spreading agricultural produc-tion to all parts of the country.

Qaddafi has called for revolutionary measures to fully utilize all na-tional resources, among them to reclaim arid land, to increase the land under cultivation, to establish pasture land, and to develop animal resources. An ultimate goal is to make Libya self-sufficient in food production—that is, to feed the people without relying on foreign imports.

Qaddafi stresses self-reliance by encouraging all citizens to satisfy their food and consumption needs through individual effort. He believes that if a citizen wants to set up a farm for his own personal use, he should be entitled to do so because land is "the collective property of all Libyans" and does not belong to anyone.[231] Land therefore cannot be sold, it can only be used to benefit the people by farming or pasturing.

Qaddafi opposes land reform laws which fix the acreage that can be owned by an individual or a family. This is primarily because private land ownership leads to exploitation of farm workers and competition to increase individual holdings at the cost of someone else. He prefers to give "equal opportunities for all farmers" and to allow them to use as much land as they can toil by their own effort without relying on hired labor.[232]

To stimulate agricultural development, Qaddafi directed that one-sixth of the 1971-1972 development budget—a fivefold increase over 1966 figures—to be allocated to the agricultural sector. Most of these funds went to soil and water preservation and to loans and subsidies for farmers.[233] In October 1972, the Council of Land Reclamation and Development was formed to accomplish the following objectives:

- Preservation and proper exploitation of natural resources, including water, soil, and forest.
- Increasing agricultural production to promote self-sufficiency in cereals and meat.
- Establishment of residential communities in the rural areas.[234]

To achieve these objectives, several development plans have been undertaken since 1973. The commitment to realizing self-sufficiency in food was quite clear in the Three-Year Plan (1973-1975), which allocated L.D. 566.1 million to increase agricultural production, especially wheat, barley, and vegetables. It was followed by the Five-Year Plan (1976-1980), which allotted L.D. 781.3 million for continued agricultural projects and another L.D. 445.3 million for agricultural development.[235]

Land reclamation and development was given special attention in order to set up new farms that would use a maximum of rain and surface water and that would, in turn, minimize the use of underground water resources. The plan aimed at reclaiming and developing 1,624,591 hectares in different parts of the country, namely, Jefara Plain, Jabal Al-Akhdar, Fezzan and Kafra, and Al-Sarir and Soloul Al-Khodr. These were ambitious projects because only five percent of the arable land, totalling 165,000 hectares, was under irrigation.[236]

The Great Artificial River
The Socialist People's Libyan Arab Jamahiriya

Source: Al-Fateh, no. 25, November 25, 1984, p. 8.

By 1979, a total of 714,935 hectares had been reclaimed and developed, representing 44 percent of the total hectares targeted for development and reclamation. In addition, 1,945 wells had been drilled, about half of the 3,793 wells planned for drilling. Housing had also been constructed to establish residential communities in these areas. For example, 6,827 houses had been built by 1979, representing 40 percent of the projected 17,092 houses for farmers and herdsmen.[237]

To overcome water shortages, irrigation schemes have been undertaken to use underground water resources deep in the Sahara. In March 1981, the Secretariat for Agrarian Reform and Land Reclamation began a feasibility study for pumping subterranean water from the desert in the south to the northern coastal regions for both agricultural and domestic use. This is necessary to support large-scale agricultural activities in the heavily populated coastal areas, where underground water supplies have been overexploited.[238]

As part of the most recent plan, Libya is now building 1,140 miles of pipeline extending from the Tazirbu and Al-Sarir regions in the southeast to Bengahzi, Marsa Brega, and Sirte in the north. When it is completed in 1989, it will pump about two million cubic meters of water annually for domestic use and for irrigation of 50,000 hectares in the northern regions.[239]

The Al-Fateh Revolution has spared no effort to increase agricultural production. Farmers have received loans, subsidies, and technical assistance to transform conventional agricultural methods to modern ones. They have been given modern equipment and tools for mechanization of agriculture as well as improved quality seeds for vegetable and fruit crops. Experimentation with new varieties of crops has also been conducted in an effort to increase the range of agricultural products.[240]

Development plans have included the establishment of training centers and institutions to train farmers in modern agricultural methods as well as in the use and maintenance of new farming machinery. In addition, farmers have been encouraged to form cooperative associations. Consequently, 260 associations have been formed, with a total membership of 116,181 and a nominal capital of L.D. 1.8 million.[241]

As a result of these plans for agricultural development, Libya has been staying on course in reaching for self-sufficiency in foodstuffs. It should accomplish this goal in due time if Libya's financial and technical resources continue to be available to support the development plan.

Industrial Development

Under Qaddafi's leadership, economic activities have been directed toward the diversification of the country's economic resources. In particular, this has involved the development of non-oil sectors, which are expected to account for 53 percent of Libyan income by mid-1980s.[242] Industry, for example, received the second largest allocation in the 1971-1972 development expenditures, representing a sevenfold increase over the 1966 figures. Considerable attention was given to development of the domestic manufacture of primary goods that are suitable to the size of the local markets, economically justified, and involve everyday consumer goods.

The year 1973 marked the beginning of a major wave of industrialization, largely generated by the government with its active industrial promotion policies. It involved a combination of nationalized industries and the importation of needed technology and skilled manpower. Local businessmen were only marginally involved. The Three-Year Plan (1973-1975) allocated L.D. 300 million for the development of industries.[243]

As the leader of the Al-Fateh Revolution, Qaddafi has directed the developmental and industrial thrust in Libya, which has been focused on meeting the needs of the people and the country. Special emphasis has also been placed on the development of food processing industries in order to reduce the country's heavy dependence on imported food and consumer goods. Libya in fact has been making a steady progress toward food self-sufficiency. Domestic processed food output met 27 percent of consumer demand in 1981 and is expected to satisfy 35 percent by the mid-1980s.[244]

The Five-Year Plan (1976-1980) allocated L.D. 1,515.4 million for industrial development designed to accomplish the following objectives:
- To support the public sector in areas of vital strategic importance and in areas related to the daily life of the people.
- To define a proper role for the private sector in the overall development plan.
- To increase industrial production by using technical studies and research on problems of productivity.
- To set up new industrial projects throughout Libya, whenever technical and economic factors allow.
- To increase manpower capacity, both administrative and technical, and to provide training in needed skills.[245]

The public sector, under the supervision of the National Establishment for Industrialization (founded in 1970), emphasized import-substitution industries such as food processing, tobacco, textiles, construction materials, petrochemicals, and metallurgy. By early 1979, 58 industrial projects were completed. Another 36 factories were under construction, while 34 other projects were under study.[246] Thus, Libya has been able to build a solid base for industrialization in a relatively short period of time. This is largely due to the allocation of 21.9 percent of the development funds to industry throughout the 1970s, which resulted in an average annual rate of growth of 17.5 percent during that period.[247]

The most recent Five-Year Plan (1981-1985) placed top priority on industrialization, giving it the largest allocation in development expenditures. A total of $13,508.9 million, or 23 percent of the development funds were designated for industrial development. The plan's goal is to reach an average annual rate of growth of 21.6 percent during the first half of the 1980s.[248]

Development efforts have been concentrated on increasing the domestic output of food until Libya is no longer in need of imported food. Accordingly, the latest plan has also emphasized the development of agro-industry. Recently, the Netherland's HVA was awarded a $122.2 million contract to supply and manage a milk products and poultry processing plant at Ghat Sultan, near Benghazi. Denmark's Danfarm Contractors has signed a $168.4 million contract to construct a similar plant at Wadi Al-Hari, near Tripoli.[249] There is a shift in emphasis favoring "the establishment of integrated agro-industrial complexes for dairy products and poultry"[250] in order to meet the consumer demand for high protein food.

Libya has not forgotten the need to develop both light and heavy industries in order to make its economy self-sufficient. Several major industrial projects have been established in the heavily populated coastal regions. It was natural for Libya to develop large-scale industries in such critical areas as oil, gas, and related industries (e.g., petrochemicals and fertilizers). This has necessitated a total control of oil production facilities. In May 1980, for instance, Libya entered into negotiations with Esso Standard to acquire a 51 percent interest in Libya's Liquified Natural Gas (LNG), which previously had been exempted from the 1974 law which had given Libya 51 percent share in Esso's other Libyan interests.[251]

Currently, a major petrochemicals complex is under construction at Ras Lanouf, located halfway between Tripoli and Benghazi. Expansion of the petrochemicals facilities at Marsa Brega is also under way, with plans already drawn for a new plant at Sirte and a major new oil refinery at Misrata.[252]

Libya has made giant strides in developing the industrial sector. Industrial projects tend to be capital-intensive because of Libya's abundance of capital and relative shortage of skilled labor. Libyan officials have acknowledged that their developmental and industrial plans have sometimes fallen short of their stated goals because of shortages in skilled manpower. For example, Musa Abu Freiwa, Planning Secretary, told the General People's Congress in January 1981 that labor shortages had hampered the execution of the 1976-1980 development plan.[253]

The fragility of industrial development will continue as long as Libya relies heavily on imported capital equipment and on foreign technicians and skilled labor. There is no prospect of immediate relief for this problem. However, Libya has taken concrete measures to provide citizens with the technical know-how and training necessary to Libyanize these jobs in the near future. Thousands and thousands of Libyans have been sent to industrialized nations to study science and technology, and Libyan youths have also been encouraged to pursue their education in these fields at home. In December 1980, it was announced that a technical university, including colleges of petroleum and electronics, would be constructed at Marsa Brega, one of the major petrochemicals complexes in Libya. Three months later, South Korea's Daewoo Development Corporation was awarded a $82.4 million contract to build a college of science at Qar Younis in Benghazi. In April 1981, Austria's Voest-Alpine signed a contract worth $7.8 million to set up a vocational training center at Misrate steelworks. Also, 24 Libyans were dispatched to Austria for training in the company's facilities at Linz. In June of the same year, Yugoslavia's Energoprojekt received a $220 million contract to set up the first merchant marine college in the country. It was planned to accommodate about 600 undergraduate students plus 100 postgraduates. In May 1981, 480 Libyans were sent to Greece for training in telecommunications.[254]

Qaddafi himself has led the public campaign to stress "the need for high level technology to be introduced" in the country's educational institutions to play a key role in training Libyans to meet the challenges of development. In his view, "only by acquiring the necessary skills could the Libyan people exert meaningful control over their wealth and natural resources."[255] This is undoubtedly a prerequisite for making Libya economically independent and self-sufficient.

Conclusion

Qaddafi's economic policies have been guided by his socialism which has had dual objectives: first, to eliminate the economic exploitation that had led to the hegemony of one class over another; and second, to transform Libya from a consuming country, relying heavily on imports, into a production-oriented, possibly self-sufficient society.

Qaddafi has initiated several measures to distribute the nation's wealth among the broad spectrum of people and to diversify sources of income. He has, first of all, done away with capitalist enterprises in favor of the public sector. There has been a sharp decline in the private sector due to a ban on private investment, trade, and rental housing. The only private businesses allowed to exist are those that provide services.

Qaddafi has also ended labor exploitation in both the agricultural and industrial sectors. Land is no longer private property and any citizen has the right to use as much land as he can cultivate without reliance on hired labor. As for industries, Qaddafi has established a new partnership where workers are considered partners in the production cycle. Qaddafi's ultimate goal is to abolish the wage system in favor of giving workers a share in what they produce and manage.

His socialist policies have succeeded in improving the economic lot of many Libyans, who are better off today than they were under the monarchy. Per capita income has risen from $1,500 a year in 1969 to as much as $8,000 in 1984.[256] Qaddafi's goal is to set up a classless society. He has systematically initiated measures to move Libya in that direction without the accompanying upheaval of a class struggle.

Qaddafi has also directed development efforts toward reaching a self-sufficient economy. His development programs have sought (1) to broaden the base of the national economy by moving it away from its dependence on a single commodity–petroleum–and (2) to end the country's heavy reliance on imported goods to meet the daily consumption needs of the people. This is to be accomplished by placing major industrial and agricultural projects in the hands of the public sector.

Although Libya has made almost miraculous achievements in both agricultural and industrial development, it has a long way to go to become economically self-sufficient. Oil has continued to dominate the economy and has proven to be an unstable source of foreign exchange earnings. The oil glut in the world market and the U.S. economic boycott have sharply reduced Libya's revenues. Oil revenues dropped from $22 billion in 1981 to $10 billion in 1984, forcing Libya to dip into its reserves, which had been reduced by 50 percent and totalled only $4.5 billion in 1984.[257] Furthermore, Libya has been forced to barter oil for other commodities to satisfy consumer needs and to sell oil at reduced prices to finance its development programs.

The world oil glut, which is expected to continue for some time, will undoubtedly hinder Qaddafi's plans for making Libya economically self-sufficient. Reduced oil revenues have already forced Libya to initiate austerity measures and to scale down development projects. It has, for instance, begun to deport foreign workers and technicians, who constituted 40 percent of the labor force. During the summer of 1985, thousands of Egyptian and Tunisian workers were sent home, apparently for economic reasons (although political motives cannot be discounted). In August interviews in Alexandria, Egypt, some returnees reported that they were not allowed to take their savings or possessions out of Libya except what they could carry in suitcases. The deportation of foreign workers and technicians is likely to have major repercussions on Libya's development; despite massive efforts to train Libyans in technology and science, Libya cannot continue its current development efforts without reliance on a foreign labor force.

QADDAFI AND ISLAM IN LIBYA

I SLAM, THE DOMINANT RELIGION, HAS HAD A SPE-
cial place in traditional Libyan society, where the overwhelming
majority of the people are Sunni Muslims, accepting the Qur'an
and the Sunna as the primary sources of the Islamic faith. Religion
has dominated all facets of life, "significantly affect[ing] the structures,
values, and attitudes of Libyan society. It is a primary unit of loyalty
and identity."[258] Qaddafi, a devout Muslim, acknowledges that the
effect of Islam is "very significant on every one of us. We cannot deny
that religion is an essential factor in the lives of all peoples."[259]

Prior to the Qaddafi-led coup in 1969, religious organizations and
leaders played a major role in the educational, social and political life
of the country, particularly in the institutions that regulated the society.
Notable religious leaders dominated not only the judicial system but
also important political committees and advisory councils.[260] In this
respect, Libya was a typical traditional society where religion was en-
tangled in the web of national politics.

This has been evident throughout Libyan history. The Sanusiyyah
Brotherhood, a militant Suffi religious order founded in the nineteenth
century, played a crucial role in the national resistance against Italian
colonial rule and subsequently contributed to the shaping of the country's destiny in the post-independence period. Between 1951 and 1969,
religion was "a political symbol of crucial importance in controlling
and mobilizing the masses."[261] King Idris, who was trained in Islamic
theology and law *(Sharia)*, used his position as Grand Sanusi to bolster
his political power. His "official symbolism was largely limited to
religious justifications" of the monarchical form of government.[262]
Observers noted "an inevitable association between family prominence
and religious leadership."[263]

On September 1, 1969, the era of monarchy came to an end when
the army, led by Qaddafi, ousted King Idris and declared Libya a
republic. Having no religious legitimation for seizing power, Qaddafi
emphasized the humble origins of the Free Unionist Officers and later
declared that the ideology of the September Revolution "stems from
the eternal message of Islam and from the Holy Qur'an."[264]

83

This chapter examines Qaddafi's efforts to restore Islam to its proper place in Libyan society. The chapter is divided into three parts: (1) an examination of Qaddafi's measures to revive Islam in Libya with the cooperation of the religious establishments that were not affiliated with the monarchy; (2) an examination of Qaddafi's actions to weaken religious leaders when they interfered with implementation of his Third Universal Theory; and (3) an examination of his theory, which calls for a return to religion.

Revival of Islam

From the start, Qaddafi emerged as the strong man in Libya, controlling the actions and decisions of the RCC. To secure his political power, he had the RCC move against the Sanusiyyah, the power base of the royal family. Its privileges were taken away; restrictions were placed on the operation of the Zawaya and Sanusi religious instructions.[265] In October 1969, a supervisor was appointed for the remaining Sanusi property, mainly educational centers. A year later, the Sanusi-sponsored Islamic University at Baida was incorporated into the University of Qar Younis.[266]

To counterbalance the Sanusiyyah influence on the masses, the RCC appointed a Grand Mufti, Sheikh Zahr Alzawi, in January 1970 and restored non-Sanusi Ulama (religious leaders) to prominent positions in the society. The RCC threw its weight behind orthodox Muslim groups, hoping that these groups could rally the masses, who are fundamentally attached to Islam, behind Qaddafi's revolution and his planned reforms to modernize the country. Qaddafi had no difficulty attracting the support of most non-Sanusi Muslim groups, which had been denied a proper place in the society for decades under the monarchy. Such support would continue as long as Qaddafi was committed to revive Islam.

Under Qaddafi's orchestration, the RCC moved to restore Islam in Libya by getting rid of foreign elements that had been borrowed from Europe and had no place in a Muslim society. The sale and consumption of alcoholic beverages, allowed under the monarchy, were banned because they are forbidden by the Qur'an. Nightclubs and bars were closed along with adult, provocative entertainment, since their activities were contrary to acceptable Islamic practice and alien to Islamic culture. Churches and cathedrals were closed. In May 1970, pornography, "obscene and vulgar performances," and "provocation to fornication by word, sign or movement" were banned. Anyone found guilty of employing Libyan women for obscene performances was subject to a large fine and harsh jail sentence.[267]

Furthermore, the use of the Muslim calendar was made mandatory in all public communications. Arabic replaced Latin script on street signs and public places.[268] The use of Arabic was insisted upon in all documents, including passports. Beginning in January 1, 1973, foreign passports were required to be accompanied by an Arabic translation for admission into Libya. As Qaddafi explained:

> We do not require aliens to present passports written solely in Arabic. . . [S]ince Arabic has been considered an international language and has been used by the United Nations Agencies, we will insist, starting from January 1, 1973, that Arabic must be one of the languages used in the passports of aliens visiting Libya, particularly as more than one language is normally used in writing passports.[269]

This measure was taken in an effort "to assert and emphasize the Arabic identity and personality" of the Libyan society.[270]

Qaddafi made no secret of his plan to make the Sharia the Law of the land. In October 1971, he had the RCC initiate the first step to make the Sharia a chief source of legislation. A Legislative Review and Amendment Committee was established; it was headed by Sheikh Ali Mansour, the Supreme Court President, and composed of the leading legal experts in the country. The Committee was assigned two major tasks: first, to bring all laws—personal, civil, criminal and commercial—in line with the basic tenets of the Sharia, in order to avoid any conflict between secular and religious laws; second, to overhaul the court system in order to eliminate the traditional separation between religious and civil courts.[271]

To broaden the consultation on the Sharia, the Supreme Council for National Guidance invited Muftis from all over the Arab world to a conference in Libya to debate the Sharia, its interpretation according to the Qur'an, and its application in contemporary societies. Following this debate and the completion of their tasks by the Legislative Review and Amendment Committee, a new law was proclaimed in November 1973, which incorporated the Sharia in all facets of the Libyan legal system. A series of Islamic laws, including several Qur'anic criminal penalties, had already been promulgated. A good example was the reinstitution of amputation of hand and foot as a punishment for theft and armed robbery. They were to be administered by utilizing modern medical methods, including anaesthesia.[272] In addition, the civil and religious courts were merged into a single judicial system, thus ending the long-standing division between the courts.[273] These changes made the judicial system primarily Islamic in nature and eliminated the elements that had been borrowed from Europe over the decades.

Qaddafi and Religious Groups

With his demonstrated commitment to Islam, Qaddafi found the time opportune to move against religious groups which, in his view, served to breed sectarianism and factionalism. Libya's national experience has made Qaddafi suspicious of religious organizations since they often get too closely involved in politics. Such activities have led to divisiveness, schism and the undermining of national objectives. The way the Muslim groups cooperated with the Italian colonizers served as an important example. The Mufti had refused to declare Jihad (holy war) against the Italian colonizers and, instead, had chosen to acquire Italian citizenship in the 1930s. Another example was the Sanusiyyah support for the British military administration in the postwar period.[274]

Qaddafi's distrust of religious groups has led him to oppose the Al-Ikhwan Al-Muslimin (Muslim Brotherhood). He once explained that his opposition is based on the fact that

> [Al-Ikhwan Al-Muslimin] in Arab countries work against Arab unity, against socialism, and against Arab nationalism, because they consider all these to be inconsistent with religion. Colonialism [is] allie[d] and associate[d] with them because colonialism is against Arab unity, against Arab nationalism, and against socialism. So the [Al-Ikhwan Al-Muslimin] movement cooperated with colonialism without being aware of this, or perhaps colonialism had to choose one group or another, and thus it chose them.[275]

Qaddafi, a practitioner rather than a theologian, was against "the old tradition of the royal regime which says: this has to be in accordance with this sect or that *ism*." He made it clear that "we do not want to be the followers of any particular theory, or limit ourselves to one religious interpretation. . . We must not restrict ourselves to

one independent judgment in a legal or theological question."[276] His
objective is to "transcend sectarianism by going back to the origin"[277]
because sectarianism leads to differences which, in turn, lead to divisions and subdivisions in religion.[278] He says, "Sectarian tendencies
are responsible for many political movements and conflicts—something
which the Libyan people are not aware of."[279]

Qaddafi, in a major speech at Zwara on April 15, 1973, announced
the start of his Cultural Revolution which aimed, among other things,
to abolish all existing laws in Libya. To assure the masses of the direction of his Revolution, he stated that "we are Muslims and apply the
Islamic law. If you apply the law of God, it is impossible to wrong
any person or threaten his security."[280] As he put it:

> We are sure that we apply the sound ideology and the great
> humanitarian thought declared by the Prophet [Muham-
> mad]. . . We adhere to the Book of God, as we believe
> that there could not be any other ideology as solemn and
> as profound as the Book of God. . . Any different
> ideology from other books is regarded as misleading.[281]

Qaddafi also made it clear that religious leaders were no longer the
sole arbitrators on religion and their squabbles and disputes would not
be tolerated since they had political fallout, creating divisiveness and
undermining national unity. At Zwara, he promised that the law would
come down hard on any group engaged in clandestine activity. He said,

> Instructions will be given to the Minister of Interior to
> purge any group. . . If a member of the Muslim
> Brotherhood or the Islamic Liberation Party engages in
> clandestine activity, his activities will be considered
> sabotage against the Revolution which was triggered for
> the people.[282]

Qaddafi has successfully silenced independent sources of religious
interpretation because, in his view, it has been divisive for society
to have religious leaders advocate different views on religious matters. His main purpose, however, has been to limit their roles and
to weaken their influence in society in order to make himself the sole
arbitrator of religious matters. He took this stance primarily because
he was not happy with the different Islamic schools of thought. As
he explained, jurists "depended on the arguments of those people who
lived before them. . . Everyone claims that he is basing his judgment on what was said by such and such a man. . . If we adopt such
an extensive view, we would be transcending any difference and varia-

tion or divisions and subdivisions in religion."[283] He does not want sectarianism to exist in Libya because it affects politics. Instead, he advocates a return to the origin, the Qur'an, as the only source of the Islamic faith. This means that he rejects the Sunna, Prophet Muhammad's sayings and deeds as recorded in the Hadith, which are widely accepted by Sunni Muslims as the second primary source of the religion. His rationale is that there are disputes about the authenticity of some Hadith. In addition, Prophet Muhammad never intended to make his tradition replace the Qur'an, which is binding on all Muslims. As Qaddafi explained in 1978:

> If the Prophet had said: the Hadith is mine, follow its path, that would have meant that he was working to replace the Qur'an, but he continually insisted on taking the Qur'an alone. . . These words may seems strange. The reason is that we have strayed far at this stage, very far from Islam.[284]

He also rejected the Fiqh (jurisprudence) as a means for elaboration on the Sharia. In doing so, he left the Ulama with no role to play in Islamic jurisprudence, while making himself the sole souce of religious interpretation. This is evident in his rejection of the conventional date for the start of the Muslim calendar which began with the emigration of Prophet Muhammad and his followers from Mecca to Medina in 622. Instead, he ordered the Muslim calendar in Libya to begin with the death of Prophet Muhammad in 632.

The Third Universal Theory and Islam

Qaddafi's move against the Ulama was motivated by his desire to eliminate independent sources of power within society that could challenge the substance and direction of his domestic policy. Another reason was to facilitate the implementation of his Third Universal Theory in Libya – a theory that made no mention of Islam in the sections dealing with political and economic matters. The main reason is that Qaddafi never intended to limit the application of his theory only to Muslim states. His vision is to make it applicable anywhere since it provides solutions to human problems that neither capitalism nor communism has succeeded in solving. Qaddafi mentioned religion only in the third part, dealing with the social basis of his theory, and did not mention Islam but instead advocated a return to religion, any religion. As he later explained: "We do not present Islam as a religion in the Third [Universal] Theory. For if we do so, we will be excluding from the Third Theory all the non-Muslims—something which we evidently do no want."[285]

Qaddafi was also concerned about the power that the Ulama had on the masses who are fundamentally religious in nature. He was worried that such power might impede the implementation of his socialism. To eliminate their threats to his experiment, Qaddafi moved against their power base, the mosque, by calling on People's Committees to march on and take over the mosques. Qaddafi justified his action by accusing the religious leaders of hindering the march of the Revolution under a pretext of Islam, by fostering old ideas, and by distorting Islam in an effort to maintain their privileged positions in the society.

Socialism and Islam: A Controversy

There was religious opposition to his socialism. The Ulama objected to his move against private property, which, in their view, is in contradiction to the Islamic tradition. They had an interest in preserving private ownership to protect the Waqf—the endowment of private property for the upkeep of mosques and their personnel. Qaddafi rejected their argument and insisted that "Islam discussed justice and socialism before Marx or Lenin."[286] Thus, his socialism is consistent with Islamic teachings. He argues that land belongs to God and people can only use it. As he says, "Islam itself does not constitute an obstacle in the way of expropriation, nationalization or limitation of property." He adds that "Islam provides for the realization of justice and equity. It does not give the right [to] any rich person to use his wealth as a tool of oppression nor to exploit people." He argues that "limitation of property means that whenever capital oppression arises, the state has the right to curb it"[287] through appropriate measures. Regarding the rich, he states that the Qur'an "order[s] us" to "take away their money and give [it] to the poor."[288] He concludes that "Islam stands against poverty, and firmly stands by the side of the working classes. Likewise, Islam stands against exploiting capitalism."[289]

Qaddafi contends that "every man has the right to live free and not to be dependent on others in his livelihood."[290] Accordingly, every citizen has the right to own property or undertake any production or service through his own efforts to satisfy his needs without exploitation of others. Private ownership will only be expropriated when it is exploitative and harmful to human society.[291] Qaddafi insists that all properties that are beyond the satisfaction of individual needs should become the property of the people.[292] To him, "this is in full accord with the teachings of Islam. Islam teaches that one should support the poor and not allow the rich to tyrannize the poor by their wealth." He cites the following verse from the Qur'an to support his argument: "Verily, man oppresses man should he see him in a great need." He interprets this verse to mean that "if man becomes rich he oppresses others . . . politically, economically, socially and militarily, thereby harming them greatly."[293]

Qaddafi uses the Qur'an as a basis to achieve social justice and to satisfy individual spiritual needs. In the national context of Libyan society, his emphasis on Islam is natural because religion has always been strong in Libya and has been an important part of the Libyan search for self-identity as well as a national expression of the struggle against foreign domination and control.

Qaddafi believes that social relationships are best guided by an unwritten ethical code that cannot be enforced by law. This explains the emphasis he placed on the Islamic religion, which provides the general outline for the relationship between God and man, between man and man, and between man and society. In his view, the rights of parents, children, husbands, wives, elders, youngsters, individuals and society toward each other "are well defined in the Holy Qur'an." To Qaddafi, "all these rights are considered holy and are fostered by religion"[294] in Libya, leading to emotional and social stability. As he puts it: "We, here, do not need drugs or sedatives and we don't have to commit suicide. We do not suffer from psychological anxiety, we do not suffer from any confusion of mind."[295] In his view, these unhealthy conditions exist in other human societies because religion is not upheld in those communities. The lack of religion leads to emotional instability and social illness. To do away with these conditions, religion must guide people in their daily activity. It is only then that exploitation will be eliminated and the world we live in will be much better.

Qaddafi's revival of Islam is intended to liberate the Islamic heritage and to free the Arab mind from the destructive influences of alien cultures that were imposed during European colonialism under the pretext of modernization or Westernization. He argues that social classes were abolished by the Qur'an long before communism ever mentioned it. Classes are alien to the Islamic heritage and to Arab culture because there was no such tradition in Muslim societies prior to the coming of Europeans. Classes are un-Islamic because Islam is based on equality and brotherhood, allowing individuals to rise to power through ability and training. A return to Islam, he believes, is the fastest way to eliminate the alien and artificial classes that were a by-product of European colonialism. Thus, his pragmatism makes it imperative to liquidate class differences by merging classes peacefully and gradually in order to achieve an orderly transformation to a more egalitarian society. Unlike communists, he does not advocate class struggle, for fear that such action would disrupt the fabric of the society and hinder national development; instead, he favors a gradual elimination of class differences through evolution. He expects the masses and their popular organizations to act reasonably and responsibly to dissolve class differences harmoniously. He does not believe that law alone can do the job, for laws can be respected and obeyed only when people are in charge of their enactment and enforcement.[296]

Qaddafi also hopes that a return to the basic tenets of Islam will result in reawakening Arabs intellectually and politically and that this will help solidify national feelings and pan-Arabism by stressing their common origins and destiny. In his view, when nationalism and religion are compatible, harmony and stability can be achieved, and the nation is in a stronger position to meet the challenges of development.[297]

Women and Society

For Qaddafi, religion encourages morality and combats social problems, especially those arising from discrimination and segregation. In the Jamahiriya, there is no room for discrimination of any kind because Islamic values and principles are enforced. Qaddafi believes that "no people have the right to oppress other peoples . . . and no one may offend another."[298] He recites the Qur'an to support his argument: "We have created you males and females and made you into nations and tribes that you may know one another. The noblest of you in the sight of God is the best in conduct."[299]

Qaddafi considers sex discrimination to be "a flagrant act of oppression without justification"[300] because all human beings are descended from Adam and Eve. He cites the Qur'an to support his stance:

"Fear your God who created you from one being, and from this being he created his spouse and from these two he made many men and women go out." The Qur'an further states that "He created you, from ourselves, spouses so that you live together."[301]

Although there are biological differences between male and female, there is a role for each to play, matching their differences. In Qaddafi's view, women should not insist on performing men's duties in an effort to be equal in rights. Society must provide work for all men and women who want to work, "but on condition that each individual should work in the field that suits him [or her], and not be forced to carry out unsuitable work."[302]

From the beginning, Qaddafi paid special attention to the plight of women in the traditional Libyan society, which had denied them equal opportunities for education, employment or for playing any significant role in nation-building. As an initial step to remedy this situation, Qaddafi in 1970 got the RCC to invite all women to a special congress to air their problems and needs. He participated in the session and later saw that their resolutions were implemented. Subsequently, many laws were instituted to grant women equal rights. Women, for instance, have been given equal rights in legal procedures for divorce. They can now initiate court actions for divorce and can receive alimony and child support. It is now extremely difficult for a divorced man to marry a non-Libyan woman or for a single man to do so. In addition, the minimum age for marriage is set at 16 for females, who also have been given the right to choose their future husbands.[303]

Qaddafi has led the campaign to liberate women from past bondages. He has encouraged women to organize themselves politically and to actively participate in the political process as part of his drive to put the instruments of government in the hands of all the people. He also urged men, who traditionally have monopolized politics, to allow women to take part in his system of direct democracy because there can be no genuine democracy if half of the people are excluded from exercising their political and civic rights. He even suggested a separate chamber for women if the weight of tradition keeps them from full participation with men in a single assembly.[304] It is due to his persistent efforts that women are currently participating on equal footing with men in the popular congresses and People's Committees and some of them are occupying leadership positions at the highest levels of these organizations. This newly acquired status was evident

CHART 1

Development in the Number of Male and Female Students in the Public Elementary Education (1st Phase of Obligatory Education).

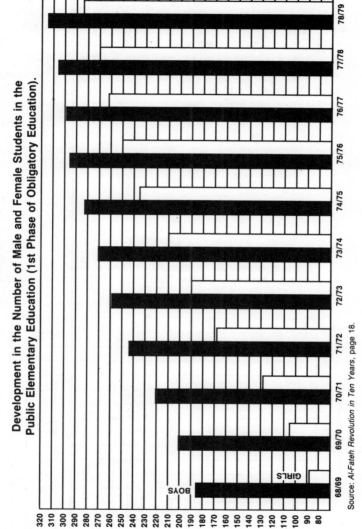

Source: Al-Fateh Revolution in Ten Years, page 18.

in the inclusion of three women in the Libyan delegation responsible for drafting a constitution for the ill-fated proposed union with Egypt.

Qaddafi has relied heavily on education as a means to provide women with the necessary training to become economically independent. This is certainly a long and difficult task because women had few educational opportunities in Libya's pre-revolutionary years. Since 1972 Libya has embarked on a campaign to eradicate illiteracy among women within twenty years. In addition, education is now compulsory through the end of preparatory schools. No expense or effort has been spared in providing free education to girls and young women as well as in training to prepare them to enter the job market in whatever profession or career they choose. Consequently, there has been a considerable increase in female enrollment in educational institutions from elementary through secondary schooling, as shown in Charts 1, 2, and 3.

CHART 2

Development in the Number of Female Students in the Public Prepartory Education (2nd Phase of Obligatory Education)

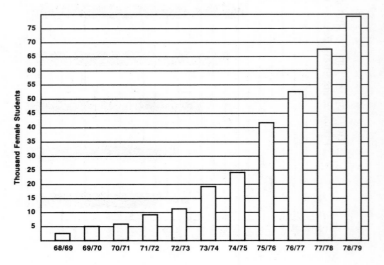

Source: *Al-Fateh Revolution in Ten Years*, page 20.

CHART 3

Development in the Number of Female Students in Public Secondary Education

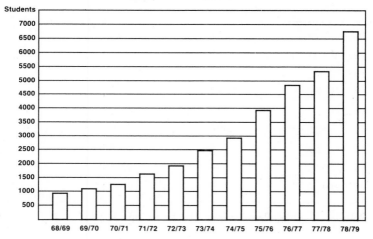

Source: *Al-Fateh Revolution in Ten Years*, page 24.

The same upward trend also existed in post-secondary education. Table 4 shows that female enrollment at the university level jumped from as little as 468 in 1968/1969 to as many as 2,661 in 1976/1977, representing a more than fivefold increase. Table 5 reveals that enrollment of Libyan women at Qar Younis University increased from 251 to 1,054 during the same period, representing a fourfold increase. As a result, a large number of women now graduate from universities every year. For example, 493 women graduated from the Al-Fateh University in 1981, compared with only 30 in 1971.[305] If this trend continues, Libyan women will soon be entering jobs that traditionally have been held by men.

As a result of Qaddafi's Revolution, women have made some important advances in Libyan society. All professions, including military services, are now open to them. For example, in 1973, eight women were trained as pilots. Some women are being recruited to serve in

TABLE 4

Number of Female Students
at Universities Between 1968/1969 and 1976/1977

	Al-Fateh University	Qar Younis University	Total
1968/1969	138	330	468
1969/1970	161	410	571
1970/1971	235	561	796
1971/1972	282	735	1,017
1972/1973	410	1,091	1,501
1973/1974	486	890	1,376
1974/1975	735	1,157	1,892
1975/1976	944	1,414	2,358
1976/1977	1,179	1,482	2,661

Source: *Al-Fateh Revolution in Ten Years*, pp. 38, 42.

TABLE 5

Number of Female Students
at Qar Younis University
Between 1968/1969 and 1976/1977

	Libyans	Non-Libyans	Total
1968/1969	251	79	330
1969/1970	294	116	410
1970/1971	386	175	561
1971/1972	496	239	735
1972/1973	719	372	1,091
1973/1974	615	275	890
1974/1975	831	326	1,157
1975/1976	971	443	1,414
1976/1977	1,054	428	1,482

Source: *Ibid.*, p. 38.

the Army and the Navy. In 1981, the first class of female cadets graduated from the Women's Military Academy in Tripoli. In addition, Qaddafi has several women from the military serve as his bodyguards,[306] and they usually accompany him on his overseas trips.

Qaddafi has also done much to bring greater participation by women in the economic life of the country. Many laws have been made to eliminate job discrimination against females and new regulations have been issued to help working mothers to meet both job and family obligations. Women are exempted from working night shifts or working more than 48 hours a week. They are given two breaks to nurse their babies and provided with a nursery at the work place if fifty or more women are employed. In addition, there is maternity leave as well as additional pay during the last five months of pregnancy. Also, women can retire with full pension at the age of 55.[307]

Since early 1970, women have been receiving equal pay for equal work and have had equal access to employment opportunities. This has led to the opening of many careers such as engineering, medicine, etc., that were traditionally closed to women. To eliminate disparities in wages, the General People's Congress in January 1981 approved a plan "based on equal pay for equal work and responsibilities, and agreed to link pay, allowances, and promotion to productivity." This was in line with Qaddafi's Third Universal Theory, which seeks to make "workers partners in their enterprise [and] to give them a voice in the management and control of their work."[308] Two months earlier, Qaddafi had urged the Basic People's Congresses to allocate 100,000 new jobs for women in the Five-Year Plan (1981-1985) in order to enable them to contribute to Libya's development.

Despite these formal gains, change is coming slowly as tradition maintains its hold on Libyan society. Many men have resisted Qaddafi's initiatives out of fear that they might disrupt family life and lead to poor child care. They have not yet accepted Qaddafi's repeated assurances that there is nothing to fear because the new laws protect the family while making it possible for women to assume a career. On the other hand, most older women are conservative and do not question tradition. They accept their supportive role in the family structure and see little to gain from changing their role. Sooner or later, they might realize that these changes promise a brighter future for their daughters. It is only then that some of them can be expected to lend support to the ongoing efforts to change the status of women in Libyan society.

Most married women still regard the family as the cornerstone of their lives, and consequently, family comes first. As Mrs. Rabab Adhams, an educator and principal of a girl's secondary school, put it, for example: "The family is my empire."[309] So far, she has managed to balance the family and her career but if there is a conflict, the job will have to go. Under no circumstances would she be willing to sacrifice the family. This attitude, which is grounded in traditional values, seems to be held by a good number of older educated Libyan women.

It can be expected, however, that, as younger women acquire university education and enter into professional careers in large numbers, prevailing attitudes will slowly change. Thus, economic independence and access to education should, in the long run, lead to concern for full equality. Clearly, giant strides have already been taken in the long march to liberate women; tradition has been challenged and the old ways have been uprooted in the Jamahiriya. All in all, women's emancipation has been pushed forward by Qaddafi and has been guided by his ideology. As a result, women's liberation and Al-Fateh Revolution have been inexorably bound together.

Conclusion

The Qaddafi-led coup in 1969 marked a decisive turn for Islam in Libya. From the outset, Qaddafi used Islam as a means to consolidate his power and to rally the masses behind his revolution. In the early years, he got the RCC to initiate measures that would eliminate foreign elements that had been incorporated into the country's culture over the decades and that would, instead, uphold the basic tenets of the Sharia (Islamic law). He also sought and received the support of Muslim groups that had previously been denied a prominent role in Libyan affairs under King Idris, the Grand Mufti of the Sanusiyyah Order.

This marriage of convenience ran into problems when Qaddafi began to implement his Third Universal Theory, which sought to carry out socialism in Libya. Qaddafi insisted that his socialism is in accordance with Islamic teachings:

> Islam discussed justice and socialism before Marx or Lenin, it called for humanism, it freed the Negro and encouraged learning . . . it upheld the rights of the oppressed before Marx, Lenin, or Mao, or Castro ever

uttered a word on the subject. It supported the poor and
the blind.[310]

His argument, however, did not convince the Ulama to change their
minds on his socialism. Their opposition put an end to his cooperation with religious groups and leaders. He weakened their positions
in the society by ending the role of the Ulama as the final arbitrators
on religious questions. He did so by making the Qur'an "the law of
the society."[311] This meant that he considered the Qur'an to be the
only primary source of the Islamic faith, thus downgrading the Sunna,
the other primary source for religious matters. In doing so, he
eliminated the role that the Ulama could play in religion, particularly
in the Fiqh (jurisprudence). He also made himself the sole arbitrator
on religious issues, thus putting both religious and secular power into
his own hands.

This outcome facilitated his relentless drive to shape Libyan society according to his theory, which did not mention Islam in its political
and economic sections. Furthermore, it was religion as a concept, not
Islam in particular, that was referred to in the social part, primarily
because Qaddafi did not want to limit the application of his theory
to Muslim societies. His objective was to spread it to other nations
as a replacement for both capitalism and communism, which, in his
view, have failed to solve human problems.

Although Qaddafi advocates that each nation should have a religion,
he recommends that the Qur'an should be read by non-Muslims
because it embodies all the guidance needed to run a state. In addition, the Qur'an was addressed to all people. This stance might explain the influence that Islam has had on his drive to create an
egalitarian society in Libya, where there are no classes or discrimination based on sex, color or creed. He has used Islam as a means to
eliminate social injustice and to strengthen the fabric of the society.
This is done in an effort to bring about stability, cohesiveness, and
harmony.

LIBYA:

A House Divided

ALTHOUGH QADDAFI HAS SOUGHT TO BRING THE masses into the political process and to redistribute Libya's national wealth among the people, something has gone wrong with the revolution, as there is evidence of growing opposition among the populace. Moreover, recent events revealed that this opposition is no longer confined to Libyans living abroad; it has also established itself inside the country.

This development has shaken the foundations of the Jamahiriya system, which Qaddafi has laboriously built to reflect his Third Universal Theory. It presents the first serious challenge to Qaddafi's leadership since he seized power in 1969 and reveals the fragility of his role in the face of opposition and the ongoing instability of the system as a whole. It has also raised doubts about whether his system will survive a change in the country's leadership.

This chapter examines the origin and development of the opposition to Qaddafi. It analyzes the extent of opposition and related incidents in order to shed light on the major problems he is confronting.

Qaddafi's Leadership: Popular Response in the Early Years

A revolution is generally influenced by the experiences and perceptions of the men who made it. Libya is no exception. Qaddafi, who engineered the 1969 coup, emerged as the leader of the Al-Fateh Revolution, and thereby provided the revolutionary process with its ideological, political, and organizational leadership. His humble Bedouin origin has led him to champion the cause of the poor and downtrodden; his country's anti-colonial struggle has made him ultra-patriotic and has caused him to reject ideologies from both the West and the East and to be determined to destroy foreign influence in Libya.

From the outset, Qaddafi employed his thought as the guiding prin-

101

ciple for a complete renovation of society. He moved to tear down the old order for the ultimate purpose of rebuilding on a different structure. But such a total transformation of Libya's political, economic, and social systems was a difficult and certainly long task. It required major changes in institutions and processes as well as in values and roles–changes that would not occur overnight nor would they be supported by everyone in the country. Certain groups were expected to object to the new order, especially those who had been privileged under the monarchy. These groups were largely ignored by Qaddafi, who sought to benefit the majority of the people who had been deprived of political power and national wealth in the past.

In the early years, Qaddafi made great efforts to rally the masses behind his plan to create a new Libya that would be free of foreign control, politically strong, and economically prosperous. He took the time to explain to people his actions to strengthen the country politically and economically. He led various efforts in political socialization. His objectives were to politicize the masses, raise their political consciousness, and develop new attitudes toward political participation–attitudes that would have political significance in the shaping of the revolutionary society.

Qaddafi was willing to share the decision-making process with other Free Unionist Officers in the Revolutionary Command Council (RCC), although he always stayed firmly in the driver's seat, especially in initiating substantial changes in the political, economic, and social fields. He generally influenced the outcome of any debate within the Libyan ruling circles. He guided the RCC efforts to lay the foundation of a new form of government where the people would play a central role in the political process. When his experiment with the Arab Socialist Union (ASU) failed to get the masses involved in political activity, he abandoned it in favor of a system of government modeled after his Third Universal Theory, which was still being developed.

In 1973, he announced the Cultural Revolution, which was intended to galvanize the masses and to set them on a long march toward the establishment of a democratic socialist society. He urged the people to dismantle the country's bureaucracy and to form People's Committees to run local government. Such action left many civil servants discontented as they struggled to perform their duties at a time of confusion and uncertainty. Most of them only grudgingly accepted the supervision of the People's Committees. Their grumbling could be ignored by Qaddafi, however, since his changes were viewed positively by the majority of Libyans. This change was especially welcome by many young people who were eager to participate in the new political process and saw opportunities to rise into the splendor of the public realm.

Split in the Leadership

Between 1969 and 1975, Qaddafi was quite popular in Libya. He often mingled with people in the streets and made numerous public appearances throughout the country. He also sought to broaden popular consensus about governmental activities by addressing the pressing problems that affected people's life from day-to-day. His domestic policies were widely acclaimed during these years. He initiated many programs aimed at meeting the nation's domestic needs and improving the flow of goods and services. He energetically used Libya's oil revenues to solve the country's acute housing problems, and to make education and health care free and available throughout the country.

Although he succeeded in mobilizing the masses behind his domestic programs, by 1975 he began to encounter opposition in the RCC over his foreign policy. This coincided with Qaddafi's shift toward closer ties with the Soviet Union, escalating expenditure on armaments, and increased support for revolutionary groups seeking to weaken Western influence in their regions or to overthrow pro-Western governments.

The first signs of opposition emerged in the mid-1970s and occurred among members of the ruling circles. Some members of the RCC objected to Qaddafi's costly foreign policy, particularly at a time when there was a decline in oil revenues. They wanted to reduce expenditures on arms purchases and to halt financial support for revolutionary groups in other countries. They also wanted to concentrate their resources and effort on economic and social development.

This opposition was so strong that it led to an attempted coup in August 1975. The attempt failed and Omar Muhayshi—one of the original 12 Army officers who mounted the 1969 coup that had brought Qaddafi to power—subsequently fled to Tunisia, to settle eventually in Morocco. Another member of the original group, Abdel Moniem Al-Huni, decided to stay in Cairo where he had been receiving medical treatment. Al-Huni had held different administrative posts in Libya's revolutionary government, including Minister of Interior and chief of counter-intelligence. He decided to remain out of Libya because he feared that he might be implicated in the coup.[312] The abortive coup left Qaddafi's leadership unchallenged and his foreign policy intact as the remaining members of the RCC continued–out of fear or loyalty– to support him. As Lisa Anderson, Assistant Professor of Government at Harvard University, put it:

> Soon the ruling circles were composed exclusively of Qaddafi's loyalists, some genuinely committed to his revolution, some merely sycophants, but few willing or able to stand up to the regime's principal figure.[313]

In the aftermath of the coup attempt, Qaddafi moved to consolidate his power, to combat opposition, and to make himself the sole leader of the country. Consequently, he emerged as an absolute ruler and was now in a position to impose his ideas and policies on the country. Qaddafi continued to be a benevolent ruler, however; he tried to attract public support by projecting himself as the leader of a great patriotic struggle to bring about Arab unity in the face of strong animosity from the U.S. and opposition from pro-Western governments in the Arab world.

With no opposition to speak of, Qaddafi proceeded to bring about radical changes in the very nature of government through the introduction of direct democracy. His *Green Book* became the guiding principle for nation-building as well as a symbol of ideological unity. Copies of his book were distributed and his theory was discussed widely in an attempt to turn the entire country into a great school of Qaddafi's thought.

Qaddafi proceeded to set up the political structure for his direct democracy–a political system that would reflect his revolutionary goals. This political system was completed in 1977 when the "Declaration of the Establishment of the People's Authority" was made and the era of the Jamahiriya began. Libya now is a state without a government. Qaddafi has put the people in charge of the government apparatus and has them directly involved in making and implementing public policy. They are now expected to rule themselves.

Between 1977 and 1979, Qaddafi served as the Secretary General of the General People's Congress, which is the highest political authority and the primary instrument of government in the country. In his new capacity, he was in a position to run the country and direct the government, allowing him to introduce radical changes in economic conditions and in the fabric of society.

In 1979, he relinquished his official posts except as the Leader of the Revolution—a position that let him continue as the undisputed leader who still calls all the shots in Libya. As the country's self-appointed thinker and the leader of the Revolution, he still sets limits and provides some opportunities for political participation. Yet he still orchestrates all major policies. He sets the framework for both legislative and executive decisions, for example, when he broadcasts his comments on the agenda of the popular congresses on the eve of their opening sessions.[314] He expects them to follow his directives in order to keep the revolutionary march on the right path.

Over the years, Qaddafi has functioned as Libya's president or head of state, even though there is no such position in the political structure. He has conferred with foreign envoys, decided on the levels of aid to give other countries, and determined Libya's relations with foreign powers. He holds the key to war or peace. An example is Libya's direct military intervention in Chad's civil war. It was Qaddafi's decision to intervene in Chad and the General People's Congress was not even allowed to debate the issue or react to the decision. Another example was Qaddafi's ill-fated attempt, in 1982, to become the chairman of the Organization of African Unity (OAU)—a position that is held by an African head of state.

His one-man style of leadership has gained him the animosity of many Libyans who had supported the revolution and had been sympathetic toward many of his ideals in the early years. Opposition has come from several groups, each harboring their own grievances. In large measure, this opposition is a reaction against Qaddafi's unlimited power even though he does not hold an official post and even though the people theoretically control and direct the government through popular congresses and People's Committees. It is also a response to Qaddafi's unwavering commitment to implement his Third Universal Theory in Libya even though some aspects have turned out to be controversial. As criticism to his ideology and policies has been voiced, Qaddafi has grown intolerant to different points of view. Consequently, he has become more isolated as he relentlessly pushes his theory forward and has become increasingly dependent on the Revolutionary Committees to safeguard the revolution and to entice the masses to follow his ideology. His foreign policy has also become a source of contention. Libyan officials have objected to his plundering of the country's oil wealth for financing his foreign ventures, especially at a time when there is a sharp drop in revenues resulting from the U.S. economic boycott and the oil glut in the world market.

Opposition to Socialism

Qaddafi's socialism, instituted in 1978, has affected a wide range of areas of economic life and overall development policy. The Libyan people have reacted in different ways to his programs to make income distribution more equitable, to do away with private businesses, and to ban rental housing. Workers and peasants, who are the main beneficiaries of Qaddafi's socialism, have supported these programs. Indeed, many of the new programs have benefited the working classes and have done little to appease the middle class, including representatives of the private sector.

Several groups have opposed the 1980 decision to "liquidate the middle class and its parasites."[315] This action had culminated in a virtual banning of private ownership and televised trials for persons accused of corruption. The outlawing of rental housing was viewed negatively by many people who have acquired apartment buildings to supplement their income and to guard against unexpected calamities. Such a ban also resulted in a setback for real estate development because it killed the incentive to construct new private houses. This might affect Qaddafi's long-term plan to provide decent housing for every Libyan. There also are signs of dissatisfaction among young people who cannot find housing when they are ready to get married and settle down. In conversations with some young professionals in Tripoli, it became evident that they have reluctantly put off marriage and are forced to live with their parents because of the housing shortage.

The middle class has been adversely affected by the decision to nullify currency higher than one dinar and to freeze bank deposits in excess of L.D. 1,000. These measures have created a liquidity crisis and have caused families to lose their life savings.

Businessmen have been sharply affected by the policy to end the role of the private sector in the Libyan economy. First, the private sector has been shut off from participating in the lucrative development projects, which are controlled and dominated by the public sector. Second, private companies and factories have been taken over by the workers who are now managing them. Third, merchants are no longer permitted to participate in export-import activities, which are now handled by the state. Fourth, privately owned retail department stores were closed to make room for state-run supermarkets.

Businessmen are discontented over the dissolution of these businesses and the loss of their economic independence as well, since some are now employed in the supermarkets. Some of these merchants have left the country; others are beginning to show a violent response to Qaddafi's socialism. A recent example, apparently, was the firebombing of one of the supermarkets in Tripoli.[316]

Religious Opposition

Muslim fundamentalists and religious groups are much opposed to the socialist changes that have taken place in Libya. In their view, socialism, especially the ban on private ownership, contradicts the teachings of Islam. This is coupled with their resentment of Qaddafi's campaign to weaken religious leaders, who have been popular and have had strong influence on the people. Qaddafi, for instance, has told the People's Committees to take over the mosques—the religious leaders' power base.

Qaddafi has justified his action by accusing the religious leaders of harboring old-fashioned ideas that hinder the march of the Revolution. His actions against fundamentalist groups were necessary to implement his Third Universal Theory, which made no mention of Islam, except a return to religion in general. He also wishes to eliminate independent sources of power that could challenge his ideology and leadership.

Qaddafi has met with stern opposition from religious groups, especially the Al-Ikhwan Al-Muslimin (Muslim Brotherhood), who objected to his drive to concentrate religious power in his own hand and to make himself the sole interpreter of Islam in Libya. They are critical of Qaddafi's promotion of his *Green Book* at the cost of playing down the Qur'an, his interpretation of the Sunna (Islamic tradition), and his changes in religious practices. For example, he has started the Islamic calendar in Libya with the date of the death of Prophet Muhammad in 632 rather than the date of the Hegira (the Prophet's emigration from Mecca to Medina) in 622, which is used throughout the Muslim world. He often puts Libya at odds with other Muslim countries when Ramadan (the month of fasting) begins in Libya a day later or earlier than other nations. In 1982, he denied exit visas to Libyans who had performed the Hajj (pilgrimage) once but wanted to go to Mecca again. Instead, he asked them to contribute the money to the "Nidal Fund." In a speech in June 1984 on the occasion of the Eid Al-Fitr, he urged the Libyans going for the Hajj to distribute the *Green Book* and to advertise the Jamahiriya system as well as to liquidate his opponents. As he put it:

> In Arafat and the Al-Jamarat you can say what you want, call for what you want, advertise for anything you believe is truthful and beneficial for Muslims: You can call for and show the Masses (Jamahiri) system.[317]

He added that "it is the duty of every able young person who goes to Hajj to take the responsibility [for] fighting and liquidating the enemy and stray dogs [opponents] if they are found there between Safa and Marwa."[318]

These are unprecedented actions and violate Islamic tradition. Such advocacy has added more fuel to the religious opposition, already aggravated by his campaign to wipe out the Al-Ikhwan Al-Muslimin in Libya. It will not be easy for Qaddafi to dislodge this group because it is highly organized, with small secret cells formed throughout the country. Its members are dedicated to upholding the Qur'an and Sunna—the main sources of the religion—and are willing to combat heresy by force. This group has attracted a lot of followers among Libyan youth, especially university students, who have become a target of a campaign of intimidation designed to uproot the Al-Ikhwan Al-Muslimin from university campuses.

Student Opposition

The latest groups to join the opposition are the college students, who are disillusioned by the excessive, "watch-dog" activities of the Revolutionary Committees. The founding of these handpicked committees are seen by students as a sign of the failure of Qaddafi's popular form of government; the main functions of these committees now appear to be to enforce his ideology and to prod People's Congresses to act in a way to promote his revolutionary goals.

Qaddafi has placed the Revolutionary Committees under his command and has become increasingly dependent on them to bring people closer to his ideology. Over the past few years, these committees, having become highhanded enforcers, have usurped a great deal of power, overshadowing and weakening the political structure that was modeled after Qaddafi's Third Universal Theory. Their activities are blessed by Qaddafi, who has given them a mandate to combat counter-revolutionary forces and reactionary elements, which, he believes, are waiting for an opportune time to dismantle his socialist revolution. Consequently, the Revolutionary Committees have worked to curb any disloyalty to Qaddafi. They have set up people's tribunals and have sent "suspected enemies of the Revolution" to public execution. In several cases, they have taken the law into their own hands, acting as both jurors and judges with complete disregard for the country's judicial system.

The most recent example was the public hanging of two students at Al-Fateh University in Tripoli on April 16, 1984 – an incident which caused a vocal opposition at home and an outcry of protest among Libyan exiles abroad. This incident triggered violence at the university; two members of the Revolutionary Committee, who were responsible for the execution, were found murdered on campus and the university auditorium was burned in protest.[319]

Overseas Opposition

In the early 1980s, some senior and middle-level government officials quit their posts and spearheaded the opposition to Qaddafi. They have formed a half dozen anti-Qaddafi groups abroad. The most vocal group is the National Front for the Salvation of Libya, which seeks to oust Qaddafi and dismantle his system of government in favor of a Western-style democracy. They are very concerned about his "reckless expenditures" of the country's oil revenues to support his policy of intervention and subversion. They accuse him of spending millions of dollars to impose his revolutionary ideology on neighboring countries, to finance his military intervention in such nations as Uganda and Chad, and to bankroll revolutionary activities of such groups as the Irish Republican Army (IRA) and the Muslim insurgency in the Philippines.[320]

The National Front organized a peaceful demonstration in front of the Libyan People's Bureau (embassy) in London to protest the April 1984 execution of students. A person inside the building opened fire, killing a British policewoman and wounding eleven demonstrators. This shooting resulted in the breaking of diplomatic relations between London and Tripoli and led to anti-Qaddafi demonstrations by Libyan students in Washington, D.C.[321] Shortly thereafter, the group initiated an armed struggle to end Qaddafi's rule.

On May 8, 1984, the National Front carried out a bold attempt on Qaddafi's life in Tripoli, resulting in a five-hour shootout with Libya's security forces less than a mile from his official residence and headquarters.[322] Although the plot was foiled, it led to a massive crackdown on opponents and to the arrest of about 3,000 persons, including government officials, army officers, and students. The Revolutionary Committees have been allowed to round up anyone who is suspected of being "an enemy of the revolution," a charge that may carry a death penalty or lead to permanent disappearance. A spokesman for the National Front commented that "The Revolutionary Committees, a law unto themselves, have been carrying out arbitrary arrests."[323]

Following the unsuccessful coup in May, "nine men accused of trying to overthrow the regime were summarily tried by Revolutionary Committees and later hanged. They were denied defense counsel and the right to appeal. Some were tortured before they died." A documentary film was made of the public execution and was shown every day on Libyan television in June and July "as warning to opponents of the regime."[324]

Thus, a drive to safeguard Qaddafi's revolution has led to further oppression and intimidation at the cost of sacrificing freedom. This fits well with Qaddafi's own definition of freedom, which he enunciated in his historic speech at Zwara in 1973. He said, "Freedom should be for all Libyan people and not for their enemies. If there are ten persons freedom must be for nine at the expense of one and not vice-versa."[325] To stamp out opposition, Qaddafi has relied on the secret police, which has become increasingly oppressive. "A lot of people are frightened," a foreign student has commented and "whatever is said about people's democracy, this is a rough, tough dictatorship."[326]

Qaddafi was angered by the May attempt on his life. He accused Tunisia, the Sudan, the U.S., and Britain as well as the Al-Ikhwan Al-Muslimin of being behind the plot to overthrow his regime. In retaliation, he has formed "death squads" to liquidate his opponents abroad, particularly in the U.S. and Britain. In an editorial on May 21, 1984, *Al-Zahf Al-Akhdar*–the Revolutionary Committees' newspaper–reiterated that "the Libyan people are ready to carry out the death sentence against the terrorists and stray dogs [Libyan exiles who oppose Qaddafi]." It added that "the Libyan people are also ready to carry the battle into America and Britain."

American and British officials take Libyan threats seriously because expatriates were assassinated in several European cities in 1980 in response to Qaddafi's call for physical elimination of his opponents. These threats have aroused anxiety abroad over the direction of the Al-Fateh Revolution, especially Qaddafi's policy of intervention, subversion, and terrorism that does not show respect for the sovereignty of other nations or the norms of international law. On June 11, 1984, for example, Qaddafi warned the Reagan administration that "we can assassinate and set fires inside the territory of the United States." He also gave American allies in the area "until September 1 to change, or 'revolution' will begin."[327] Three months earlier in a speech in Tobruk, Qaddafi threatened to "upset the balance" of power in the region unless the U.S. ended its support for Egypt and the Sudan. He admitted that Libya had been supporting "with all our strength" Egyptian and Sudanese "military and civilian revolutionaries" who were working inside these countries to combat their "treason and hireling status."[328]

Opposition in the Armed Forces

Qaddafi's adventurism has alienated the Army which was instrumental in bringing him to power in 1969. Dissension within the Armed Forces especially focuses on Qaddafi's unilateral decisions to employ Libyan forces to achieve foreign policy objectives. Signs of their disillusionment began to surface in the late 1970s, following Libya's military intervention in Uganda. His unsuccessful rescue mission to save Idi Amin's regime cost Libya 500 casualties[329] and the loss of large quantities of arms and ammunitions, including tanks and armored vehicles. Moreover, there was a strong public reaction, especially in the military, against the sending of Libyan troops into Chad to support one of the warring factions in the incessant civil war there. In their view, repeated intervention in that war-torn country has made Libya fully extended in terms of personnel and overextended financially at a time the country's oil revenues were dropping sharply. The presence of 5,000 Libyan troops in Chad has raised questions about Libya's vulnerability and the extent to which Qaddafi is willing to commit his country's forces to support the Goukouni faction.

Over the years, opposition in the military has been building up and has manifested itself in several attempted coups and assassination plots. The press has reported the following incidents since 1979:

- November 1979–[Qaddafi] escaped shooting by a soldier outside Tripoli.
- August 1980–Army coup crushed by [Qaddafi] forces in garrison in Tobruk.
- September 1981–[Qaddafi] wounded in the cheek by a soldier while reviewing Libyan troops.
- January 1982–Abortive coup against the [Qaddafi] regime and an attempt on [Qaddafi's] life.
- November 1983–[Qaddafi] disappear[ed] from the public view for three weeks amid rumors of [an] assassination attempt.[330]
- 1985–Some military officers twice attempted to assassinate Qaddafi during this year.[331]

The latest attempt took place in August 1985 when Qaddafi ordered some military units to move closer to the border with Tunisia, following the expulsion of thousands of Tunisian workers from Libya. Qaddafi was forced to back down because (1) there was a mutiny in the Armed Forces, which led to the execution of about 43 officers who had been implicated in the plot to oust him;[332] and (2) without the Armed Forces support, Qaddafi could not afford to have a showdown over Tunisia with the U.S. and its friends in the area. It was reported that, during the crisis, Algeria moved some troops to the joint border with Tunisia and Libya as a show of support for the embattled Tunisia. In addition, there were unusual diplomatic contacts between Tunis, Algiers, and Cairo to coordinate their plans to challenge Qaddafi if he decided to invade Tunisia.

The military establishment is not pleased with Qaddafi's costly foreign policy, which has isolated Libya and has led to deteriorating relationships with many of the Arab governments. Some officers have resented the growing Soviet presence in Libya, a result of Qaddafi's heavy reliance on the Soviet Union for armaments as well as his policy of confrontation with the U.S.

Qaddafi seems to be aware of the grumbling in the Armed Forces. This is evident in the fact that, in September 1985, the Armed Forces for the first time since 1969 did not participate in the celebrations of the sixteenth anniversary of the Revolution. They were replaced in the parade by the Revolutionary Committees[333]–Qaddafi's ideological shock troopers.

The growing opposition in Libya's Armed Forces has caught the attention of the Reagan administration, which has been trying to undermine Qaddafi's regime for years. American officials view Qaddafi as a threat to U.S. national interests because of his world-wide support for militant groups seeking to overthrow pro-Western governments or to weaken Western influence in various regions. In the fall of 1985, Reagan authorized the Central Intelligence Agency (CIA) to provide covert assistance to anti-Qaddafi groups, especially the National Front for the Salvation of Libya. The plan is to create an incident that will either encourage dissenting Libyan officers to stage a coup or will give a neighboring country such as Algeria or Egypt a pretext to intervene militarily in Libya.[334] The success of this plot depends on the cooperation of Qaddafi's neighbors who have so far been reluctant to participate in the U.S. destabilization campaign against Qaddafi.

Ironically, the CIA involvement lends credibility to Qaddafi's claim that his opponents are financed and supported by foreign governments, especially the U.S. The opposition's tie with the CIA is a liability and is likely to undermine any support from other Libyans. The U.S. is not seen as a friend of the Arabs, in view of its special relationship with Israel. Qaddafi has often used U.S. antagonism to rally the masses behind his leadership by projecting himself as a champion of Arab unity engaged in a bitter struggle against U.S. intervention and subversion in the Arab world.

Conclusion

Although there is growing opposition to Qaddafi, he is vulnerable but is in no immediate danger. This is largely because he has not allowed any organized opposition to exist. So far, he has managed to control and suppress opposition to his leadership or policies by expanding the functions of the Revolutionary Committees, by manipulating the flow of information through the media, and by developing an efficient intelligence apparatus in order to discover what people are doing and whether they are likely to revolt.

Over the years, Qaddafi has successfully stamped out internal opposition before it has mushroomed. He has relied on the Revolutionary Committees and the Bedouin-based secret police to round up and put behind bars suspected enemies. He has made it difficult to plot against his life: he resides and works in a well-fortified barrack on the out-skirts of Tripoli; he never stays long in one place; he keeps his movements and plans a secret, even from his close advisers; he reduces to a minimum his public appearances. He even has some people taste his food before he eats to avoid food poisoning. Moreover, he has beefed up the security around him, which is now handled and super-vised by East German experts.

Qaddafi has concentrated power in Libya's top leadership, typified by his role as the leader of the Revolution. He still provides the revolu-tionary process with its ideological and organizational leadership. He is the boss of the original group of officers who were involved in the 1969 coup. Currently, there are only four of them still active in public life and they serve at his pleasure. He has made sure that he is the sole power broker in the country by moving top-ranking officials in and out of various administrative posts. This constant shuffling ensures that they have to remain loyal to him if they would like to continue their employment. Their job security will depend on their willingness to perform any task they are called upon to carry out.

The same pattern can also be found in the military. He has fre-quently forced senior officers to retire from active service and has pro-moted young officers to higher ranks to guarantee their loyalty and minimize the possibility of a military coup. He has placed loyal of-ficers in charge of the military units around the capital and has sent wavering officers to remote areas of the country.

By using "hit squads," Qaddafi has succeeded in assassinating some leaders of the opposition abroad, thus weakening their rank and file. His heavy tactics have forced some leaders of the anti-Qaddafi groups to go underground and to avoid making public pronouncements. This situation has led to a slowing down of the tide against Qaddafi, at least for some time. The only group that has remained visibly active is the National Front for the Salvation of Libya. It has a regular radio broad-cast to Libya and a magazine—*Al-Inqad*—which exposes Qaddafi's op-pressive policies and his campaign to silence opposition inside and outside the country.

Qaddafi's systematic campaign of intimidation has so far succeeded in weakening the opposition overseas. Each group operates separately with no plan to pool their scarce resources together or to rally the estimated 50,000 to 100,000 Libyans living in exile behind their ef-forts to oust Qaddafi. Moreover, internal opposition is spasmodic and often a reaction to a specific event. This situation can be expected to continue unless there is a coordination of opposition activities inside and outside Libya to mount a serious challenge to Qaddafi's leadership. The real threat to Qaddafi, however, comes from the Armed Forces, which is the only organized group capable of ousting Qaddafi by force. Much will depend on the extent of opposition among the officers and on their willingness to take the risk to bring about change in the country's leadership.

PART TWO

FOREIGN POLICY

A Challenge and Response

QADDAFI'S RISE TO POWER IN 1969 MARKED A major shift in Libya's foreign policy. Qaddafi wasted no time in reversing his predecessor's policies that had placed Libya in the Western orbit and allowed the United States and Britain to maintain vital military bases in his country. He wished to have no part in the Western strategy of having a military presence in Libya in order to protect the southern flank of the North Atlantic Treaty Organization (NATO) against Soviet expansionism and to deter Soviet penetration into the Middle East.

From the beginning, Qaddafi was determined to end Libya's passive role in the international arena, a role that had placed it on the periphery of the Arab world and that had prevented it from any meaningful involvement in regional politics. To enable Libya to play the active role he envisioned in world and regional politics, it was urgent first to free Libya from Western domination and control. In formulating this new policy, he was influenced by the recent Arab experience under European colonialism and was inspired by Nasser's ideology: non-alignment, anti-colonialism, and Pan-Arabism. He therefore has championed the cause of Arab unity and the liberation of Palestine and has waged a bitter campaign against colonialism. Such a policy has brought separation from the U.S. and rapprochement with the Soviet Union.

This chapter examines Qaddafi's foreign policy because he, as the leader of the Al-Fateh Revolution, has continued to control and direct Libya's policy even though he is no longer holding an official post in the government. The chapter discusses his relations with the superpowers in the years following his coup as well as his subsequent policies toward the Middle East and Africa.

Superpowers: Alignment or Non-Alignment

Qaddafi's nationalism has dictated that he pursue a policy of non-alignment in which the rejection of alliances with cold-war parties[335] is augmented by a reaffirmation of Libya's right to deal with any

119

major power regardless of its own ideology. For Qaddafi, this policy represents more than simply a non-alignment in great-power conflicts or an attempt to balance blocs. It is also a commitment to fight against colonialism and to work toward Arab unity. Tied to these policies is Qaddafi's strong ambition to play a major role on the world stage.

Qaddafi's non-alignment is a political and psychological reaction against Anglo-American political control and economic domination in Libya under the monarchy. His foreign policy is influenced both by past colonial experience and by contemporary realities.

To Qaddafi, non-alignment is a way to assert his own independence by keeping Western influences and domination out of Libya and the Arab world.[336] It is also a vehicle to enhance Arab solidarity by keeping the Middle East region out of the cold-war competition between the U.S. and the Soviet Union. He is strongly opposed to any attempt by either of the cold-war contenders to drag the Middle East into the cold war or to intervene in the Arab world.

His non-alignment, a policy of enlightened self-interest, seeks to ensure political freedom and independence for Libya and contribute to national self-respect. While it keeps his small nation from getting involved in larger cold-war conflicts of no concern to it, this policy does not mean noninvolvement in the great issues of the day. Indeed, it rejects passivity toward, or disengagement from, difficult world problems. Nor does it advocate fence-sitting or attempting to escape international responsibilities. Rather, it means that Libya has not chosen sides in the East-West struggle and remains opposed to any such allegiance.

Between 1969 and 1974, Qaddafi pursued a policy of strict non-alignment by having no close ties with either the U.S. or the Soviet Union. In an early action, he asked the U.S. and Britain to close their military bases in Libya. They both complied without protest. Wheelus Air Force base, the largest American airbase outside the U.S. at the time, was closed. The Nixon administration did so because Qaddafi was seen at the time as "a sincerely religious man and an intense Arab nationalist." In addition, American diplomats in Tripoli suggested that "nothing should be done to interfere with what they saw to be Qaddafi's 'natural' anti-Soviet bias."[337] American officials mistakenly thought that they could take advantage of Qaddafi's anti-Soviet stance to entice him to maintain the traditional close ties between the two countries and to preserve the dominant position of American oil companies in Libya.

Qaddafi, however, soon initiated several measures to weaken Western influence in his country. In October 1970, he expelled 20,000 Italians,[338] left behind in Libya after the collapse of Italian colonialism at the end of World War II, who dominated Libya's commercial activities and owned large plantations. In addition, he nationalized all foreign banks, insurance companies, oil distribution facilities, and some oil companies.[339] Nationalization was deemed necessary for two reasons: first, it would enable Libya to gain control of its major economic activities and redirect them in the service of the national economy; second, it would break the bonds between Libya's economic interests and a small number of foreign monopolies. Such monopolies were said to subject Libya's monetary system to decisions made in Western capitals.[340] This move also allowed Qaddafi to put Libya's national wealth in the hands of the Libyan people and to use its natural resources for economic development.[341]

Qaddafi's systematic campaign to erode Western influence in Libya led to a gradual worsening of relations with the U.S. Finally, in 1972, Ambassador Joseph Palmer asked to be recalled because he could no longer talk with the revolutionary government in Libya.[342] In subsequent years, neither the Republican nor the Democratic administrations sent another ambassador back to Tripoli. Then, in May 1980, the last American diplomats were withdrawn.

The souring of U.S.-Libyan relations was caused by several factors. First, the special relationship of the U.S. with Israel made it difficult to maintain cordial relations with Washington.[343] Qaddafi felt that "the U.S. is hostile to the Arabs"[344] because it "is helping the occupier[s] keep hold of the land of the Palestinian[s],"[345] who were evicted by force from their homeland. The U.S. has continuously supplied Israel with massive economic and military assistance, including the most sophisticated weaponry in the American arsenal. In this way, the U.S. has ensured Israel's qualitative and technological edge over any combination of Arab states,[346] thus frustrating Arab attempts to recover Palestine from Zionist control.

A second factor was Qaddafi's view that the U.S. has deliberately kept the Arabs militarily weak by refusing to sell advanced weapons to the progressive and front-line Arab states that have been on a confrontational path with Israel. Since 1973, the U.S. has refused to issue an export license for the delivery of eight C-130 Hercules Transport planes Libya purchased from Lockheed. Nor has it returned the $60 million Libya paid in hard currency for the planes.[347] This action was taken, apparently, to show displeasure with Qaddafi's ideology and the conduct of his foreign policy. Washington also has continued its ban on arms sales to Libya and has lobbied among its NATO allies to block Qaddafi's attempts to purchase weapons in the open market in Europe. Ironically, such a policy caused Libya to move closer to the Soviet Union,[348] which has been willing to sell the arms Qaddafi needed to modernize his armed forces and strengthen their military capability to defend both Libyan and Arab interests.

A third factor was U.S. objection to Qaddafi's attempts to export his revolution and to intervene in the internal affairs of neighboring countries in an effort to bring about Arab unity. It should be noted that Qaddafi's revolutionary nationalism does not recognize the existing boundaries among Arab states, which, in his view, all belong to the Arab nation. It is within this context that Qaddafi has no qualms about his agitation of the Arab masses against their governments whenever they seem to stand in the way of Arab unity. He therefore does not understand the U.S. fuss about his intervention in Egypt, the Sudan, Tunisia, or Morocco. In fact, he has repeatedly called on the U.S. "to leave the Arabs alone to solve their own problems."[349] On the other hand, Qaddafi argues that, being an Arab, he has the right and duty to bring about Arab unity at any cost. In his view, U.S. opposition to Arab unity is an imperialist conspiracy to keep the Arabs weak by keeping them divided. Such an attitude has provoked deep friction with the U.S.

As for the Soviet Union, Qaddafi, being a devout Muslim, is naturally inclined to oppose Marxism and the Soviet Union. This was evident in his early decision to stay at arm's length from the Soviet Union, which he considered an "imperialist power."[350] In the early 1970s, he criticized the Soviet government for allowing Russian Jews to migrate to Israel[351] and for its failure to supply the Arab states with advanced weapons to match the armaments Israel was getting from the U.S. In October 1973, he called the Soviet Union "the arch enemy of the Arab world"[352] because he believed that Soviet bragging about the airlift of arms to Egypt and Syria in the midst of the October war caused the Nixon administration to initiate its massive arms airlift to Israel. Furthermore, while the U.S. supplied Israel with sophisticated weapons, the Soviet Union sent the Arabs "the most obsolete equipment."[353] In his view, Moscow had given the Arab states defensive rather than offensive weapons, making it impossible for the Arabs to win a war.

In 1974, Qaddafi was forced to change his attitude toward the Soviet Union in an effort to break the isolation that Libya found itself in and to obtain Soviet assistance for Libya's military buildup. This occurred after the U.S. refusal to sell him arms. Qaddafi was frustrated by his failure to convince Egypt and Syria to mount an all-out war against Israel in 1973 and by his inability to play a major role in the Arab oil boycott against the U.S. and the Netherlands because of their support for Israel during the war. Qaddafi's failure to bring about union with Egypt also led him to abandon diplomacy as a way of promoting his policy objectives.

To pave the way for better relations with the Soviet Union, Qaddafi, who was known for his anti-Soviet stance, volunteered to step down from the government and devote full time to the revolutionary task. This was a strategic move designed to persuade the Soviet leaders of the Libyan desire to improve relations and to give Major Abdul Salam Jalloud, Libya's second strongman, a chance to mend fences with Moscow. This was not hard to accomplish because both Moscow and Tripoli felt animosity toward Egypt's Anwar El-Sadat. Sadat had turned down Qaddafi's offer for a union; he also had expelled several thousand Soviet advisers from Egypt in June 1972 and moved his country closer to the U.S. In addition, both Libya and the Soviet Union were committed to weakening the American influence and presence in the Middle East.[354]

The Soviet Union saw some gains in Libya's overture. First, it would recover from the loss of Egypt, particularly the naval facilities in Alexandria along the Mediterranean Sea. Second, it would be lucrative for the Soviets to sell arms to Libya, which was in a position to pay in dollars. Such transactions would provide the Soviets with much-needed foreign exchange to purchase Western merchandise and technology. It was even beneficial for the Soviets to barter arms for oil since they could sell Libyan oil to Eastern bloc countries and generate cash needed to purchase goods from the West. Third, the Soviets could enlist Qaddafi's help in combatting the Western presence in the highly strategic regions of the world because of his commitment to promoting revolutionary changes by the use of force in the pro-Western countries.

The rapprochement with Moscow enabled Qaddafi to obtain Soviet weaponry and to pursue his revolutionary goals. Since 1974, the Soviet Union and its allies have supplied Qaddafi with a $20 billion arsenal[355] that is far beyond his country's security needs and the capabilities of his armed forces. A recent study reveals that, between

1974 and 1978, Qaddafi obtained quantities of Soviet arms four times higher than did Egypt during the same period[356] despite tremendous differences in the size of their armed forces and population.

The Soviet arms sales brought Tripoli and Moscow closer to each other as Libya continued to rely on Soviet and East European military advisers to train Libyan forces in the use of Soviet-made weapons. Despite these close ties, however, Qaddafi kept his distance form the Soviet Union. For instance, he did not permit the Soviet warships to pay visits to Libyan ports during the 1970s.[357] He also resisted pressure to grant the Soviets a naval base along the Mediterranean Sea which would have offset their expulsion from Egypt in 1972.

In essence, Qaddafi's non-alignment sought to refrain from aligning Libya militarily or politically with any of the antagonistic blocs. This was manifested in his call for the "immediate liquidation of all foreign bases, the rejection of military alliances, and [the] emancipation from all forms of influence and satellitization"[358] for all the countries of the Third World. These calls were manifestations of his nationalist opposition to foreign domination and his goal of putting an end to Western influence by steering clear of formal military ties with the West. He has continued to oppose the presence of military bases on Arab soil because, in his view, they are always used to further Western rather than Arab interests.

Thus, Qaddafi strongly objected to the U.S. decision to step up its military presence in the Red Sea and the Indian Ocean following the hostage crisis in Iran and the Soviet military intervention in Afghanistan. He was opposed to allowing American forces to use Egyptian airfields at Marsa Matruh on the Mediterranean and at Ghardaqah on the Red Sea as well as on the Oman coast and at Berbera in Somalia. He said,

> We consider the presence of the American troops in Egypt, Somalia and Oman as an invasion and a flagrant aggression against other independent states, even if this presence is at the request of the Governments of these states.[359]

He warned that, unless these U.S. moves were resisted, Americans would continue their advances in the Middle East until the Arab world lost its independence and became "an American-Israeli colony." He feared that these American bases were "only bridgeheads" in a grand military strategy "to occupy the Arab homeland." He thus called for "united action to drive the Americans out of the bases"[360] and urged neighboring governments to deny Americans access to these bases in order to keep the Arab world out of the cold-war sphere, stating,

> If a superpower such as the U.S.A. uses military force in the Gulf region, this will lead to another power opposed to the U.S. doing so, too.[361]

He feared that such development would drag the Arabs into big-power conflicts that were of no real concern to them. In his view, the American military presence was a threat to all Arabs and was designed to subvert progressive movements in the region. Furthermore, he contended that "so long as American forces remain on Arab territory the Arab people will not be free to determine their policies freely and in the interests of the Arab nation."[362]

Qaddafi also has opposed any U.S. show of force, whether it involved the presence of the Sixth Fleet in the Mediterranean Sea or naval exercises off the Libyan coast. He saw them as a threat and part of a campaign to destabilize his country and to overthrow his system of government. In response, then, Qaddafi ordered his Air Force to challenge any American intrusion into Libya's airspace or territorial waters. In September 1980, Libya's Air Force shot down a U.S. reconnaissance plane at the edge of Libyan airspace — an incident that led the U.S. to increase its protection for future flights.[363] A year later, two Libyan Jets were shot down by F-14 interceptors from the carrier *Nimitz* when the jets came near to challenge the U.S. naval exercises in the Gulf of Sirte off the coast of Libya.[364] This aerial clash over the Gulf led to further deterioration in Libyan-U.S. relations.

Although Qaddafi has tried to mend fences with the U.S. by urging U.S. administrations to send the American Ambassador back to Tripoli and to deliver the C-130 planes, his efforts have been fruitless. The U.S. has insisted that Qaddafi must cease his policy of intervention and his support for "international terrorism" and must join efforts to find a peaceful solution for the Arab-Israeli conflict. These conditions have been unacceptable to Qaddafi: they would mean a complete reversal of his position. Consequently, his relations with Washington have worsened further, as Qaddafi continues to oppose the active involvement of the U.S. in the Middle East.

Qaddafi's hostility also increased toward U.S. friends in the region, particularly Egypt and the Sudan, which had received American military assistance to beef up their capabilities to cope with Libya's threats. Libyan-U.S. relations took a turn for the worse when Egypt's

Sadat was assassinated in October 1981, because Qaddafi had advocated Sadat's assassination and had provided financial and material assistance to Egyptian dissident groups involved in clandestine activities to overthrow the pro-U.S. regime. The U.S. responded to the loss of Sadat by speeding up the delivery of weapons to Egypt and the Sudan and by expressing its readiness to act to uphold friendly Arab governments against external aggression. This development made reconciliation even harder to achieve because Washington and Tripoli had now taken diametrically opposed courses in the Arab world. The outcome has been a steady worsening in relations with the U.S. and, in turn, a steady improvement in relations with the Soviet Union.

Middle Eastern Policy

Qaddafi's policy has been greatly influenced by Nasser's ideology – Pan-Arabism, anti-Zionism, and anti-colonialism – ideas which have caught Qaddafi's imagination and have provided him with potent ammunition to agitate the Arab masses far beyond the borders of his country. Qaddafi is "determined to destroy the borders set up by colonialism between the children of the Arab nation."[365] He told the Libyan masses on the fifteenth anniversary of the Al-Fateh Revolution on September 1, 1984, that "the people of Jamahiriya bear a historic responsibility of uniting the divided Arab nation, mobili[z]ing its forces, liberating Palestine and destroying the hostile Zionist camp."[366] It is within this general framework that Qaddafi has formulated his Middle Eastern policies.

Arab Unity

Qaddafi has devoted his time and energy to bringing about Arab unification. He strongly believes that nationalism must be organized on a regional basis if it is to restore Arab dignity and liberate Arab land from foreign domination. He argues against the type of nationalism that militates against Pan-Arabism, a nationalism that has divided the Arabs into different political entities. For this reason, he does not accept a political sovereignty based on colonially drawn geo-political boundaries which have led to balkanization and gravitation away from Arab unity.[367]

Armed with his convictions, Qaddafi has initiated a Pan-Arab drive that has led to many conflicts with other Arab governments; most of these governments fiercely fought him to preserve their national sovereignty. This, however, has not discouraged Qaddafi from pursuing his Pan-Arab policy. As he said, "so long as [his] revolution continues, it will not stop seeking Arab unity."[368] In his view, Arab states cannot function and prosper in isolation from each other, nor can they advance in their development in the absence of regional unity. For example, Qaddafi argues that unity between Egypt, the Sudan, and Libya will be for "the long-term benefit of the peoples of the region." His plan is to convert "the barren desert [in the three countries] into a green paradise" by linking the Nile with the artificial river, which is under construction to bring water from the south to the coastal areas in northern Libya. Such a project will not only increase land productivity in his country but will also "save the Egyptian and Sudanese people[s] from poverty and hunger," He therefore sees the unity between these three countries as "the nucleus of the Arab unity and the weight and heart of the Arab nation."[369]

Since 1969, Qaddafi has tried many ways to bring about Arab unity. He has attempted to persuade several Arab leaders to form a union with his country. His quest has taken him to Egypt, the Sudan, Tunisia, Syria, and finally Morocco. With the exception of the latter, Qaddafi's efforts have been fruitless.

In the early 1970s, he was disappointed by the lack of progress on the proposed union with Egypt, which was initially discussed with Nasser prior to his departure.[370] For this reason, Qaddafi took advantage of his visit to Tunisia in December 1972 to issue a call for "the immediate establishment of Arab unity."[371] His call fell on deaf ears as Arab leaders continued to ignore his plea for a union with Libya. A few months later, he staged his Cultural Revolution, designed to revive the Islamic-Arab heritage as a means to free the Arab individual and nation. Notably, it took place at a time when Qaddafi was experiencing difficulties in convincing the Egyptian and the Sudanese governments to form a union with Libya. Thus, by stressing Pan-Arabism and their Islamic heritage, he hoped to arouse the masses politically; he believed that Arab governments were "in one dale and the people . . . in another."[372] He contended that people should take authority into their own hands because governments have too long directed policies and interpreted national interests, while the masses remained passive with no role to play in shaping their destiny or running their governments. His objective was to crush these forms of governments and to replace them by one dominated by the people in accordance with his Third Universal Theory. In December 1972, for example, he called for "the overthrow of the monarchical regimes, [and] the establishment of similar governments in all the Arab lands."[373]

Qaddafi repeatedly criticized Egypt's Sadat and the Sudan's Nimeiri for their refusal to form a union with his country and for their pro-U.S. policies. Indeed, Qaddafi openly encouraged revolutionary and dissident groups in both countries, urging them to oppose rapprochement with the U.S., to oust their leaders, and to support Pan-Arabism.

The result was that Sadat and Nimeiri shared hostility to Qaddafi. Both governments had strained relationships with both Tripoli and Moscow, having thrown out Soviet advisors and technicians, and then finding their countries flanked by pro-Soviet Libya and Ethiopia. They accused Qaddafi of engineering several coups against their regimes such as training and equipping the Sudanese National Front which attempted to overthrow the Nimeiri regime by force in July 1976.[374]

Given these circumstances, it was not surprising that Nimeiri and Sadat sided with each other against Qaddafi's threat and against the growing Soviet influence in the Middle East and East Africa. They were supported in this position by Saudi Arabia, which was critical of Qaddafi's attempts to spread his revolutionary ideas in the Arab world and of his close ties with the Soviet Union. The Saudi government also feared that its oil riches were threatened by the Soviet presence in South Yemen and Ethiopia. Partly in consequence, in the late 1970s, Saudi Arabia formed an anti-Soviet coalition among the countries located along the Red Sea, particularly those directly threatened by Soviet expansionist policy and flanked by the pro-Soviet countries of Libya, South Yemen, and Ethiopia. Saudi Arabia, Egypt, the Sudan, and Somalia were determined to weaken the Soviet presence along the Red Sea and adjacent areas as well as to prevent further growth of the Soviet influence in the region.[375] This situation has further fragmented the Arab world by dividing the Arab countries according to cold-war ideologies, a development that works against Qaddafi's drive to achieve Arab unity.

Qaddafi's failure to persuade the Arab governments to set up an Arab nation led him to abandon diplomacy in favor of working with opposition groups in these countries to remove their leaders who, in his view, stood in the way of Arab unity. Tunisia is a case in point. After Qaddafi had failed to convince President Habib Bourguiba to form a union, Qaddafi trained and armed some Tunisian exiles and sent them in January 1980 across the borders to start an armed rebellion at Gafsa in southern Tunisia that was to pave the way for Libya's military intervention.[376] The failure of the Qaddafi-supported insurgency resulted in a worsening of relations between Tripoli and Tunis; it also led Bourguiba to ask for and receive military assistance from the U.S. to cope with Qaddafi's threats.

This setback did not discourage Qaddafi from continuing his campaign to bring about Arab unity. His agreement to form a union with Syria came to naught. In August 1984, however, Qaddafi and King Hassan of Morocco agreed to merge their countries[377] despite their ideological and political differences: Qaddafi's Libya is revolutionary with close ties to the Soviet Union; this stance contrasts with Morocco's conservative monarchy, which has been a traditional ally for the U.S. It is too early to tell whether this merger will be able to overcome such contradictions and will stand the test of time.

Qaddafi has blamed the U.S. for his failure to bring about Arab unity. The U.S. has played up the Soviet threat as a means to divide the Arab world and to further its own strategic and economic interests in the region. Washington has never looked favorably on any drive to achieve Arab unity for fear that it might hinder Western interests in the area and, further, might place the U.S. in an awkward position because of its commitment to the survival of Israel.

The Liberation of Palestine

Qaddafi has vowed to "work day and night to destroy [the] hostile, racist, Zionist entity"[378] because, in his view, "the Palestinian issue is an Arab issue, and all Arabs must accept responsibility for it."[379] Another reason is that "Israel has no end at all and no limits."[380] He believes that Israel, with U.S. backing, plans to "swallow the Arab world state by state, with a view to forming a Zionist empire."[381]

Qaddafi is critical of Arab governments which have concentrated their efforts on the return of the Arab territories occupied by Israel since 1967. To him, this is self-defeating because the crux of the problem is Palestine. As he sees it, "The problem . . . started since Palestine was handed over to the Jews" in 1948.[382] In his view, "Western Jews . . . have their own countries in Europe and America. Their destiny is that of the resident colonialists when liberation is about to take place."[383] Qaddafi advocates the return of the European Jews to the countries they came from. As for the Arab Jews whom he considers to be "our cousins and brothers," they should be allowed to "live in our midst in peace as they did in the past."[384]

Qaddafi insists that "the solution is a military solution."[385] He adds, "We must not let the enemy remain [in Palestine]. There is no reason to cease-fire. There is no reason not to fight."[386] He argues that "the weapons the Arabs now have can liberate Palestine"[387] if the Arab states would enter into a full battle against Israel. He has criticized the Arab governments for their token support for Palestine and for their failure to mobilize their resources for a full-scale war against the Zionist state. He blames Arab leaders for entering into "a quarter of a battle, half of a battle or two-thirds of a battle"[388] – a situation that has contributed to their defeat. In wondering about "what prevents us from starting the war," Qaddafi argues that "we just need the systems of government that want to undertake the liberation duty."[389] This is why he advocates the overthrow of conservative and moderate Arab governments in favor of modeling these countries after his Third Universal Theory where power, wealth, and arms are placed in the hands of the people.

Qaddafi is in a key position in the confrontation with Israel. His radical policy will not endanger Libya's national security because it does not share a border with Israel. He can use his country's oil wealth to help the front-line Arab states build up their military capabilities to confront Israel. He can also give material and financial assistance to the Palestine Liberation Organization (PLO), which has been waging an armed struggle against the Zionist state, as well as provide sanctuaries and training camps for Palestinian fighters. This can all be done with little fear of retaliation because of Libya's location and distance from Israel.

It is no secret that Qaddafi has supported the Palestinian armed struggle because, as Ali Treiki, Libya's Foreign Affairs Liaison Secretary, says it is "the duty of the whole Arab nation . . . to arm the Palestinian people and directly defend it to deter aggression."[390] It is within this context that Qaddafi's relationship with the PLO has been influenced by the extent of its demonstrated ability to carry out an effective military campaign against Israel. Consequently, Qaddafi's support has shifted from one group to another among the eight groups that make up the PLO, depending on whether they are actively engaged in the battle against Israel.

Qaddafi has spared no effort to finance and train Palestinians willing to fight Israel and has approved the Palestinian strategy of establishing working relations with revolutionary groups in other countries to further the Palestinian cause. For example, he has been willing to provide material and logistical assistance to European radical groups to carry out commando attacks on Israeli targets on behalf of the Palestinians. To further this goal, Qaddafi has, since 1976, set up training camps for thousands of foreigners, including Palestinians and Europeans, in Libya.[391] Beginning with 1972, attacks are no longer confined to Israel proper but have been expanded to include Israeli targets anywhere around the world.

In 1972, Qaddafi called for an "upsurge of revolutionary will" among the Palestinians and expressed his country's readiness to train Palestinian fighters and to finance their operations. It was around the same time that Qaddafi developed close ties with the Black September Organization, which had been established in the aftermath of King Hussein's assault on the PLO forces in the early 1970s in an effort to get them out of Jordan. Shortly thereafter, Qaddafi provided "the clandestine material support for the Black September Organization's attack on the Olympic village in Munich in September 1972."[392] He gave a public funeral for the commandos killed in action in Munich and gave the PLO Chairman Yasser Arafat $5 million to expand his operation against Israel. In October 1973, the Libyan-backed Arab National Youth Organization for the Liberation of Palestine (ANYOLP) hijacked a Lufthansa plane and forced the Bonn government to free the three Munich commandos held in West Germany's jails. Upon their release, they headed to Libya.[393]

In December 1972, Black September commandos also stormed the Israeli Embassy in Bangkok, Thailand, and took several hostages, including Ambassador Shimon Avimor. The crisis ended 19 hours later when the hostages were freed in return for safe passage to Egypt in the company of some Thai officials.[394] These incidents marked the beginning of a world-wide campaign against Israel in an effort to attract world attention and to stress the urgency of finding a just solution for the Palestine problem.

In the early 1970s, Qaddafi became impatient with the lack of progress in the military campaign against Israel. He therefore parted company with Al-Fatah—the largest faction in the PLO and the traditional power base of Arafat—because of its failure to mount an effective campaign against Israel. In 1973, he suspended his annual subsidies to Al-Fatah but promised to reconsider his decision if there was an acceleration in the fighting against the Zionist state and a change in their ideological orientation. By mid-1974, Qaddafi and Arafat reconciled their differences and issued a joint statement in Tripoli, promising to escalate the "Palestinian armed struggle."[395]

Meanwhile, Qaddafi shifted his support to the more radical, Marxist Popular Front for the Liberation of Palestine (PFLP), which pulled out of the PLO in September 1974. Although Qaddafi opposed its leftist ideology, he saw an advantage in working with the PFLP whose leader–George Habash–had close ties with leftist revolutionary groups in Europe and elsewhere. Habash's European connection made it possible for Qaddafi to establish linkages with the international revolutionary network to solicit its services to expand the operations of armed struggle against Israel and its backers in the West. Qaddafi, for example, bankrolled not only the activities of the PFLP but also those of the notorious Carlos (Ilich Ramirez Sanchez), whose most famous operation was the kidnapping of the eleven OPEC Ministers at their meeting in Vienna in December 1975. The Ministers were taken on a hijacked plane to Tripoli, where most of them were released, and then to Algeria where the Ministers of Iran and Saudi Arabia were set free. During the flight, Carlos revealed to Saudi Arabia's Oil Minister, Ahmed Zaki Yamani, that "Qaddafi was deeply involved in the support and planning of the operation."[396] It was reported that Carlos received as much as $10 million for his service. These are but a few examples of Qaddafi's determination to work with any group willing to contribute to the battle against Israel. His financial and material support has been directed not only to the Palestinian factions but also to non-Arab revolutionary organizations which have been ready to expand the area of conflict with Israel beyond the Middle East.

War or Peace (1973-1979)

Qaddafi has always been ready to place Libya's manpower, oil, and financial resources at the disposal of the Arab states fighting Israel. For instance, he kept his promise during the 1973 war by providing the warring Egypt and Syria with oil, funds, and weapons to enable them to carry on the fighting against the enemy at a time when other Arab states provided only token or verbal support. He did so even when he was in disagreement with the Egyptian-Syrian war plans and goals. Qaddafi felt that they should not have limited their objectives to the liberation of the Sinai and the Golan Heights, both of which had been captured by Israel in the 1967 war, but must also strive for the complete liberation of Palestine.[397] He makes it clear that his country will not take part in any war unless its objective is the liberation of Palestine from Zionist occupation.

Qaddafi has criticized King Hussein for his refusal to join Egypt and Syria in the 1973 war against Israel to liberate the West Bank that was seized by Israel during the 1967 war.[398] His relations with Jordan have been strained further because of King Hussein's expulsion of the PLO from his country and his refusal to allow the PLO fighters to penetrate Israel from Jordan.

Qaddafi opposes any efforts toward cease-fire, negotiation, withdrawal or unilateral arrangements. He considers them to be "sedatives and tranquilizers" since they are not dealing with the crux of the problem. They are at best temporary solutions because "the clash is inevitable."[399] He does not see any way for the Arabs and the Israelis to co-exist because, in his view,

> in the Arab region are two nationalities, two entities, two religions, two civilizations, two nations and two heterogenous histories, neither of which can absorb the other and the relationship between them is that of hostility. Therefore, it is inevitable for the conflict to continue until one of the two entities is finished off.[400]

Since the region can accommodate only one entity, he urges the Arabs to maintain their military preparations and not to drop their guard because the big battle is inevitable. He supports "working for further preparation and determination because the conflict between Israel and us is natural and is one of the laws of nature." He advocates "real, radical solutions to the nature of the conflict rather than sedatives and useless solutions."[401]

Qaddafi thus strongly opposed Sadat's peace initiative, including his historic visit to Jerusalem in November 1977. He called for Egypt's ouster from the Arab League when the Egyptian delegation arrived in Israel for the final preparation for Sadat's visit, then broke diplomatic relations with Egypt on the day of Sadat's arrival in Jerusalem. He also objected to Sadat's planned meeting in Cairo for all the parties in the Arab-Israeli conflict (except the PLO), the U.S., the Soviet Union, and the U.N. in preparation for the Geneva conference. To undermine Sadat's plan, Qaddafi held a meeting with hard-line Arab states in Tripoli in December 1977. It was attended by Qaddafi and the presidents of Algeria, Syria, and South Yemen, while Iraq was represented by a low-ranking delegation. In addition, PLO Chairman

Arafat and the PFLP's leader Habash attended the meeting. After five days of deliberations, they agreed

> (1) to establish an Arab "front for resistance and confrontation;" (2) to "freeze" their relations with Egypt; . . . (3) to boycott all Egyptian individuals and firms dealing with Israel; (4) to challenge Egypt's membership in the Arab League and to seek the removal of Arab League headquarters from Cairo; and (5) to consider any attack on any member of the front as an attack against all.[402]

The Tripoli Declaration intended either to entice Sadat to change the course of his policy of reconciliation with Israel or to have him know that he would face tougher measures if he failed to do so.

In response, Sadat not only rejected their warning but also broke diplomatic relations with all five states. Further, he decided to go ahead with the Cairo meeting despite the boycott by Jordan, Syria, and the Soviet Union. The meeting was attended by Egypt, Israel, the U.S., and the U.N. – a meeting which resulted in Sadat's decision to work unilaterally with Israel and the U.S. toward a solution of the Arab-Israeli conflict. All of these actions provoked even deeper friction between Sadat and Qaddafi.

Qaddafi totally rejected the U.S.-engineered Camp David Accords, which he viewed as a unilateral peace treaty with Israel in exchange for the return of Sinai and for American military and economic assistance. In his view, it was a betrayal of the Arab cause[403] and an abandonment of the Palestinians. He therefore spearheaded a number of diplomatic offensives to punish Sadat for signing the accords. He was able to convince other Arab governments to impose sweeping political and economic sanctions against Egypt, to suspend Egypt's membership in the Arab League, and to transfer the League headquarters to Tunis. In addition, Qaddafi cut off Libya's economic assistance to Egypt and expelled several thousand Egyptian workers and technicians from his country.

He criticized Sadat for pulling Egypt – the foremost citadel of confrontation – out of the battle to liberate Palestine, thus weakening the unified Arab stand against Israel. Furthermore, he attacked the U.S. for trying to convince Jordan and Saudi Arabia to endorse the American peace process for settling the Middle East conflict and for trying to isolate the radical Arab states that are committed to the total liberation of Palestine.

To meet the new challenges, Qaddafi has joined Algeria, Syria,

South Yemen, and the PLO in forming the Steadfastness and Confrontation Front in order to solidify the struggle against Israel.[404] He has kept up his assistance to Syria and the PLO, both of which have been continuously engaged in the struggle against Israel. He also sought to shore up Arab support for the Rejectionists. In 1978, Libyan officials toured several Arab capitals to press for a united front against Israel following the Israeli attack on the Iraqi nuclear reactor. Secretary Treiki said that the reactor incident demonstrated that Israel's aggression is not confined to a single Arab country. He therefore urged the Arab governments to join the Confrontation Front because "when the enemy violated the territory of three Arab states to hit the Iraqi reactor, it did not differentiate between Baghdad, Damascus [and] Kuwait."[405]

Lebanon: A New Battlefront

Qaddafi continued his support for the armed struggle against Israel, which the PLO typically launched from southern Lebanon. Continuation of this military campaign depended on the PLO's ability to have access to Lebanon, especially after the PLO forces were expelled from Jordan and after Syria placed restrictions on the movement of the PLO fighters across the border. When the civil war broke out in Lebanon in the mid-1970s, the PLO sided with the radical Muslims against the Israeli-backed Christian Maronites.

During the 1975-1976 civil war, Qaddafi supplied the Palestinians with weapons worth $10 million.[406] His military assistance was intended to strengthen the PLO positions in southern Lebanon in the face of Israeli intervention. In May 1981, Arafat admitted for the first time that Libyan troops had been fighting side by side with the PLO since 1972.[407]

In the early 1980s, Qaddafi supplied the PLO with SAM-7 missiles, which were capable of striking deep inside Israel. In addition, he dispatched 150 Libyan volunteers to operate the missile bases in southern Lebanon.[408] These missiles were intended to discourage Israel from continuing its air raids in Lebanon. Qaddafi also offered Lebanon an anti-aircraft defense missile system worth about $2 billion to enable it to defend its territory against Israeli aggression, which had resulted in killing hundreds of civilians in many cities, including Beirut. His offer was a response to a plea from Lebanon's Premier Shafik Al-Wazzan, who had asked the East or the West to supply his country with a reliable air defense system to protect his country against the intensified Israeli air strikes. Treiki said that "the defen[s]e of Lebanon was an Arab responsibility."[409] It was in that spirit that Libya's offer was made.

Despite Qaddafi's military assistance, the PLO was forced out of southern Lebanon and Beirut following the Israeli invasion in June 1982. The PLO evacuation was supervised by American and European troops, which came to Lebanon to separate the warring factions – the PLO and Israel. This development was a major setback for Qaddafi's campaign against U.S.-backed Israel. One immediate result was a growing rift between Qaddafi and Arafat, stemming from a sharp disagreement over the conduct of the armed struggle and the new American peace initiative put forward by President Ronald Reagan in September 1982: Reagan reaffirmed the principle of "full autonomy" for the Palestinians in the West Bank and Gaza as set forth in the Camp David accords; he called for a freeze on Israeli settlements in the occupied Arab territories; he proposed that Palestinian self-government be conducted in association with Jordan.[410]

Qaddafi, who has rejected any Arab move to negotiate – directly or indirectly – with Israel, became irritated with Arafat when he showed signs of moderation in the spring of 1983 by conferring with Jordan's King Hussein "about the possibility, eventually rejected, of entering negotiations with Israel over the future of the occupied West Bank and Gaza."[411]

Since the PLO evacuation from Beirut, Qaddafi has become hostile to Arafat, launching a verbal campaign against him and fomenting dissent and division within the PLO. In May 1983, he financed and armed an open rebellion by the Al-Fatah against Arafat's leadership.[412] Qaddafi and these rebels shared a common objective, that is, to remove Arafat, who, in their view, has abandoned the armed struggle against Israel and has changed his stance on the U.S.-sponsored peace process in the Middle East.[413] Their objective was to install a more radical anti-Israeli and anti-American leadership.

The mutineers also had the backing of Syria's President Hafez Assad, who was interested in getting rid of Arafat because he was too independent. Assad, who would like a new, cooperative PLO leadership that would enhance Syria's claim as a regional power, was in a strategic position to influence the power struggle because the PLO forces in Lebanon now rely on Syria to keep open their supply lines. Without Syria's consent, the PLO would be in no position to receive new supplies or even to operate out of eastern Lebanon, which is controlled by Syrian troops. Thus, Assad, Qaddafi and the Al-Fatah rebels all wanted to oust Arafat but for different reasons. To accomplish this objective, the mutineers moved against Arafat's loyal forces in the Bekaa Valley in eastern Lebanon. They were assisted by Syrian tanks and troops, which surrounded the loyalists' camps, halted their movements, and turned away new supplies of arms and ammunition.[414] In addition, the Assad government declared Arafat *persona non grata* in Syria.

Although Arafat's forces were driven out of the Bekaa Valley and Tripoli in December 1983, the attempt to oust Arafat from the PLO leadership was not successful. The immediate result was an irreversible split in the PLO rank and file, thus weakening the unity and independence of the PLO. It also resulted in weakening the PLO's ability to confront Israel and has undermined the PLO's claim as the sole and legitimate representative of the Palestinian people. It has led to a further division in the Arab world as Arafat sought and received the backing of other Arab governments to preserve the independence and unity of the PLO under his leadership. For example, in June 1983, Iraq's President Saddam Hussein expressed his country's "readiness to back up the PLO with all available means to preserve its unity." He also "emphasized that the Arab countries should stand beside the PLO against any attempt aimed at harming its independence or weakening its unity."[415]

Arafat managed to stay in power by rallying the support of Saudi Arabia, Algeria, and the Arab League as well as the Soviet Union, Romania, and China. Although he failed to smash the rebels militarily, Arafat was able to rally support among Palestinians to retain the chairmanship. He did so by renewing his commitment to the armed struggle against Israel, by denouncing Reagan's plan as a basis for a Middle East settlement, and by agreeing to limit his power in favor of a more collective leadership.[416]

African Policy

Qaddafi moved his anti-Israel campaign into Africa in an effort to woo African support for the Arab position on Palestine. This was not an easy task because Israel had already established close ties with many African states which, in turn, opted to stay out of the Arab-Israeli conflict in order to receive Israel's economic and technical assistance. It was thought that Israel could not have undertaken such an aid program without external assistance because Israel has meager resources and cannot itself survive economically without the infusion of tremendous amounts of foreign aid and capital. Libyan officials therefore speculated that the U.S. must have supplied the aid given to Africa in order to deny African support for the Arabs in their long-standing feud with Israel.

Qaddafi was quick to realize the danger to Arab interests inherent in the activities of Israel in Africa and decided to take some action. Between 1970 and 1973, he initiated a counter-offense to tip the balance in Africa in the Arab favor. He thus intensified Libya's diplomatic activities in Africa. He visited Mauritania, and several African heads of state descended on Tripoli. In their conversations, Qaddafi drew a parallel between Israel and South Africa, both of which are settler states set up by European colonizers in the midst of the Arab and African regions. In doing so, Qaddafi was linking the Palestine problem with other problems of dependent peoples in Africa. He expected that such a context might encourage African support for the Palestinian armed struggle because the Arabs had supported (both materially and diplomatically) the liberation struggle in Africa. Qaddafi also stressed the historical ties and cultural linkages between the Africans and the Arabs.

On the economic level, Libya indulged in massive efforts to compete with Israel in providing economic assistance. Libya began to extend loans and grants to Muslim and non-Muslim governments in Africa to assist in financing economic development programs. In addition, student exchange programs for Africa were organized, and scholarships were granted for African students to come to Libya for Islamic and university education.

In dealing with Muslim African countries, Libyan officials emphasized the Islamic connection and provided financial assistance to build mosques and schools in an effort to turn them away from Israel. Libya's efforts met with some success. Following his visit to Tripoli in February 1972, Uganda's Idi Amin broke off diplomatic relations with Israel.[417] At the end of 1973, the Israeli presence in Africa came to a virtual end when almost all African states severed diplomatic relations with Israel following the outbreak of the October War. The rupture of relations with Israel also marked the beginning of a closer African-Arab cooperation in areas of mutual concerns.

Qaddafi's anti-Israel campaign in Africa was conducted in concert with his crusade against colonialism and imperialism. In the early years, he urged African countries to live up to the true meaning of non-alignment by closing foreign bases in their countries and by terminating their traditional ties with their former colonizers. During the summit of the Organization of African Unity (OAU) in May 1973, Qaddafi unsuccessfully recommended that the organization's headquarters be transferred out of Addis Ababa, the capital of Ethiopia, because Emperor Haile Selassie had placed his country in the Western orbit by allowing the U.S. to maintain a major communications base near Asmara and by letting Israel use Ethiopia as a base to penetrate Africa.[418]

Qaddafi has repeatedly criticized the African states that maintain close political and economic ties with their former colonial masters. Thus he told the African ambassadors in Tripoli in May 1980 that "imperialist policy is aimed at continuing to exploit Africa and keeping the Africans underdeveloped.[419] He warned that imperialists are determined to make the independence of African states a "fiction." He launched his severest attack on the French-speaking nations because, in his view, France still considers them as "colonies." He added that "it is a French tradition to convene these countries each year so that France may make sure they follow its policy." He threatened to reconsider Libya's aid to these states if France continues its assistance to this group. Thus he might decide to have Libya restrict its aid to those African countries which receive no assistance from France. This measure would be taken because, in his view, France is using its aid program as a means to further its own political and economic interests in Africa. He also threatened to remove all Libyan diplomatic representation to Paris if France continues to exercise leadership over the Francophone African states. As a follow-up to that threat, Libya decided to close its embassy in Dakar, Senegal, in June 1980 and to conduct its relations with Senegal through the People's Bureau in Paris. This step was initiated on the basis that Senegal had become "a country totally subservient to France."[420]

Qaddafi's anti-colonial stance dictates that Libya must sympathize with African national aspirations. Revolutionary Libya has always supported the right of dependent peoples to self-determination as well as their right to bear arms to overthrow colonialism and racism.[421] Such a stance has caused the U.S. to accuse Qaddafi of fostering and encouraging "international terrorism" and of financing terrorist activities in order to undermine international peace and security. This criticism, however, has not swayed Qaddafi from his support for national liberation struggles in Africa and elsewhere or from "making Libya a center of international resistance to imperialism.[422]

African National Liberation

Qaddafi recognizes the legitimacy of the liberation struggle against colonialism and racism; he upholds the rights of all peoples to self-determination and freedom as stated in the U.N. Charter. For this reason, he has provided financial and material assistance to a number of progressive African liberation movements to liberate their homelands and to attain independence.[423] His policy is guided by the following principles:

- Support of peoples' causes for liberation, security, inter-national cooperation on [an] equal footing and peace based on right and justice.
- Standing openly and unrelentingly against all forms of racial discrimination, exploitation and threats against the destiny of people.[424]

Qaddafi invited a number of African liberation movements to open their offices in Tripoli. He also set up several training camps for African freedom fighters who were engaged in armed struggles against colonizers and oppressive minority regimes, a fact which drew criticism from Western governments. In addition, he denied landing facilities or the use of Libya's airspace to Portugal, South Africa, and Rhodesia (Zimbabwe).

Qaddafi provided material and financial assistance to the Partido Africano da Independencia da Guine e Cabo Verdo (PAIGC) in Guinea-Bissau, the Frente de Libertação de Moçambique (FRELIMO) in Mozambique, and the Movimento Popular de Libertação de Angola (MPLA) in Angola—all of which conducted armed struggles to liberate their countries and to put an end to Portuguese colonial rule. These countries are now free and independent under the leadership of progressive nationalist movements.

As for Zimbabwe (Rhodesia), Qaddafi sided with the Patriotic Front—the Zimbabwe African People's Union (ZAPU) and the Zimbabwe African National Union (ZANU)—that waged an armed struggle against the Smith regime after it unilaterally declared Rhodesia's independence from Britain and set up a white minority government in 1965. Qaddafi continued to support the Front after Smith and the black internal leaders worked out an internal settlement. Then, following the signing of the Lancaster Agreement (1979), Qaddafi moved swiftly to recognize the newly elected Prime Minister Robert Mugabe of ZANU and promised material assistance to independent Zimbabwe. Qaddafi seeks to strengthen and expand political ties between the two countries,[425] emphasizing that both Libya and Zimbabwe are committed to socialism and share common views on the anti-colonial struggle.

Regarding Namibia (South West Africa), Qaddafi has continued to support the South West African People's Organization (SWAPO), which has been conducting an armed struggle against South Africa's illegal administration of the territory. He has recognized SWAPO's right to use force to free Namibia, which is governed by Pretoria, in defiance of the U.N. and of a ruling by the International Court of Justice. He has provided SWAPO with financial and material assistance as well as military training to enable it to put an end to South African occupation.

Qaddafi cannot be indifferent to the armed struggle in South Africa that is necessary to overthrow the white-minority government and to dismantle its system of apartheid – the most thoroughgoing system of official racism on earth. Under apartheid (separate development of races), the black majority not only are denied political, economic and social equality but also are denied citizenship in their own country. This is done in order to uphold white supremacy by maintaining white domination and control.

Qaddafi sees intrinsic linkages between the African struggle against the white rulers in South Africa and the Palestinian struggle against Zionist occupation of Palestine. This is largely because both Israel and South Africa are settler states and have helped each other militarily and economically to uphold their "colonial" regimes and to continue the subjugation of both Arabs and Africans with assistance from the U.S. and Western Europe. This situation has led Qaddafi to endorse the use of force to bring about revolutionary change in both countries.

Qaddafi's strident anti-colonialism has sometimes led him to initiate policies that have worsened Libya's relations with fellow Arab and African countries. An example is his support for the Frente Popular para la Liberacion de Saguia el Hamra y Rio de Oro (Polisario), which is conducting an armed struggle against foreign domination of the Western Sahara. When Spain terminated its control over the territory in 1975, Morocco and Mauritania annexed the Western Sahara, claiming sovereignty over the territory. Such a move was opposed by the Sahrawi people, who have been trying to establish an independent state in the tiny, phosphate-rich country.[426] For his part, Qaddafi has refused to recognize the sovereignty of Morocco and Mauritania over the territory and instead has advocated the right of self-determination for the Sahrawi people. Libya, along with 36 other countries, has recognized the Sahrawi Arab Democratic Republic (SADR), which has been formed in exile in Algeria. Libya, along with 25 other African states, also supported the SADR's application for membership in the Organization of African Unity (OAU)—a move that was opposed by Morocco and other pro-Western African governments. Libya and Algeria have become the major aid donors to the Polisario,[427] which is determined to continue its armed struggle until Morocco agrees to terminate its control over the Western Sahara, particularly since Mauritania has given up its claim.[428]

The recent union between Libya and Morocco raises questions about whether Qaddafi will terminate his financial and material assistance for the Polisario. This will depend largely on whether the union can endure their diametrically opposed ideologies and policy orientations. If the union is able to survive such contradictions, there is some likelihood that Libya's support for the Polisario will be ended. This will be similar to Qaddafi's decision to cease his support for the Eritrean liberation movements once the pro-U.S. regime of Emperor Haile Selassie had been overthrown and a pro-Soviet, Marxist regime was established in Addis Ababa.

Military Intervention

Qaddafi's anti-U.S., anti-Israel stance has led him to use Libya's wealth to provide military assistance, including dispatching Libyan troops, to friendly or revolutionary governments which were threatened by invasion from neighboring countries. An example was Ethiopia during the Ogaden War (1977-1978). Qaddafi provided material and financial assistance to hard-pressed Ethiopia when Somalia and the Western Somali Liberation Front tried to liberate the Ogaden desert, a region inhabited by Somali-speaking ethnic groups. Libya supplied aid against Somalia, a fellow Muslim country and a member of the Arab League, in order to help the Mengistu government fight to maintain Ethiopia's territorial integrity at a time when it was facing a serious threat of disintegration. In doing so, Qaddafi was denouncing Somalia's historical claims for large tracts of land in neighboring Ethiopia, Djibouti, and Kenya. Qaddafi's aid to Ethiopia was also a response to the support given Somalia by Qaddafi's arch-enemies—Egypt, the Sudan, Saudi

Arabia, and Iran—all of which were pro-U.S. governments and had strained relations with Libya.[429]

It should be noted that Qaddafi's military assistance paralleled concerted efforts by the Soviet bloc to help the Marxist government in Ethiopia restore its territorial integrity, which was being threatened by several secessionist movements. Aside from Libya's aid, the Soviet Union airlifted massive arms and military equipment worth $1 billion as well as military advisers to Ethiopia. Cuba increased its military personnel in Ethiopia from 800 in December 1977 to 12,000 in February 1978. South Yemen also sent a force of 2,000 men to aid Ethiopia in its counter-offenses to recover the Ogaden region.[430] Foreign military intervention was instrumental in turning the tide once again in Ethiopia's favor, forcing the Somali forces out of Ogaden in March 1978. These combined efforts led to an alliance between the revolutionary governments of Libya, Ethiopia, and South Yemen in August 1981 for the purpose of working together against what they perceived as American threats. This alliance was established in response to the increasing military activities by the U.S. in the Red Sea, the Indian Ocean, and the Mediterranean Sea, which Qaddafi viewed as a threat to the revolutionary regimes in the Middle East and East Africa. The alliance was designed to counter the presence of the U.S. Rapid Deployment Force in Egypt, Somalia, and Oman.[431]

Another example is Uganda's Idi Amin who was first faced with a destabilization campaign and then with an invasion by neighboring Tanzania and Ugandan exile forces. Amin's troubles began in 1972 after he had broken off diplomatic relations with Israel and moved to support the Palestinian armed struggle under the PLO leadership. This tilt resulted in criticism from the U.S. and praise from Qaddafi. As American hostility increased, Amin turned to Qaddafi for help to cope with U.S. threats. In response, Libya provided military training in 1973 to hundreds of Ugandan troops. Qaddafi also financed Amin's purchase of arms from France in 1973 and again from the Soviet Union in 1977. He also gave Amin economic assistance to ease the crisis stemming from U.S. sanctions against Uganda. The sanctions, taken because of Amin's record on human rights violations, were intended to discredit Amin's regime and to prepare the ground for his overthrow. In mid-February 1979, Qaddafi hurriedly dispatched 2,500 Libyan troops fully equipped with tanks and armored vehicles to help Amin repel a joint invasion by the Tanzanian and the Ugandan exile forces. Qaddafi's rescue mission failed and his troops, along with Amin, were forced to evacuate Uganda in April 1979.[432]

Qaddafi's intervention in Chad was quite different from that of Uganda and Ethiopia. Libya had had a territorial dispute with Chad over the Aouzou territory, 44,000 square miles of territory which might have large deposits of uranium. Qaddafi has claimed that this territory is an integral part of Libya [433] historically, politically, and culturally and has refused to recognize the 1936 pact between Mussolini and Laval which had resulted in the territory's changing hands. In 1973, he used force to capture and annex the territory.[434] This action marked the beginning of Qaddafi's involvement in Chad, which had been going through a civil war since the mid-1960s.

Qaddafi's anti-colonial stance led him to oppose the French military presence in Chad – a country that borders Libya – for he objects to great-power intervention in former colonies as well as to having foreign troops on African and Arab soil.

France put the southern Christian-dominated government in power in Chad on the eve of independence and gave it support during the civil war. Chadian Muslims, in contrast, were deprived of power, wealth and arms. This led to their rebellion, starting in the east and spreading to the north. As early as 1977, Qaddafi decided to intervene in the Chadian civil war by siding with one Muslim faction or another among the eleven warring factions. His intervention greatly increased after 1979, following the massacre of thousands of Muslims in the capital city, Ndjamena, by the southern army prior to its retreat to the south.[435] The massacre also coincided with the Muslims sweeping into political power; Goukouni Woddeye, chief of the Islamic Toubou tribe in the north, became an interim president of Chad in April. Goukouni, whose National Liberation Front (Frolinat) had been supported by Qaddafi at one time during the power struggle, turned against Qaddafi when he assumed the presidency in April 1979. In July, he accused Qaddafi of supplying military assistance and advisers to one or more of the factions fighting his government; he contended that Qaddafi wished to oust him because he was not receptive to Libya's territorial claims. To prove his allegation, Goukouni put on display three captured Libyans who confessed to "acting in an advisory capacity to Chadian dissidents opposed to [his] government."[436]

Subsequent events in Chad, however, caused Goukouni and Qaddafi to reconcile their differences. This took place when Goukouni was ousted by another faction headed by Hissene Habré, Goukouni's

Defense Minister, who was backed by Egypt, the Sudan, and the U.S. Qaddafi's military intervention in Chad in late 1980 was intended to restore Goukouni to power and to defeat the pro-Western faction of Habré. When the mission was accomplished, Qaddafi announced a merger between Chad and Libya in January 1981.[437] As Qaddafi put it:

> We tell France and the whole world that Chad is linked to Libya, Libya is linked to Chad by destiny, geographically, humanly, historically, futuristically, by security and economically.[438]

This announcement caused concern about Qaddafi's plan to set up a Pan-Islamic state in north Africa. Niger, for instance, felt threatened when Qaddafi announced, "We consider [Niger] second in line after Chad."[439] Niger and Mali accused Qaddafi of stirring ethnic animosities inside their countries and forcing military training on their nationals working in Libya with a plan to send them back home to overthrow their governments and to pave the way for Libya's military intervention. They were joined by other African governments, including Nigeria, in demanding Libyan troop withdrawal from Chad. In November 1981, Qaddafi responded by pulling his troops out of Chad; he had been asked to do so by Goukouni, who was seeking legitimacy for his government from African states and support from France. Another reason for Qaddafi's swift withdrawal from Chad was his desire to appease African states and to remove any hurdles that might stand in the way of holding the OAU summit in Tripoli in the summer of 1982 and of his assuming the chairmanship of the regional organization for a year.

In the summer and fall of 1982, Qaddafi attempted to hold the OAU summit in Libya's capital city to no avail. He failed because his aim became mixed up with the inability of African states to reach a compromise over the representation of the Western Sahara and Chad. In July, Qaddafi had insisted that the Sahrawi Arab Democratic Republic (SADR), which was fighting Morocco for the independence of the Western Sahara, be given a seat at the summit since it had already been admitted as the OAU's fifty-first member in February 1982. Morocco, on the other hand, objected to the SADR admission because the organization's membership is limited to independent African states.[440] Morocco was able to convince enough governments to stay away from the summit meeting planned for August in Tripoli if the SADR was allowed to take a seat at the summit. Qaddafi's failure to bow to the African demands resulted in a lack of a quorum so the summit could not be convened.

His second attempt to hold the conference – in November – ran into problems when Qaddafi refused to give Chad's seat to the Habré government, which had just ousted the Libyan-backed Goukouni. When Qaddafi declined to let Habré occupy Chad's seat at the summit, many African states boycotted the conference, thus denying him a quorum for the second time. This was his last attempt to hold the summit in Tripoli, and it meant that Qaddafi also lost his bid to become the OAU chairman.

This development angered Qaddafi and led him to renew his intervention in Chad to overthrow Habré and to restore Goukouni to power. In June 1983, Qaddafi not only provided the Goukouni faction with logistical and material assistance but also sent Libyan troops into northern Chad in an effort to topple Habré. His military intervention met with limited success due to timely French intervention. Goukouni, with the help of Libyan forces, took control of northern Chad but was unable to move further south to oust Habré from the capital. The cessation of hostilities gave France a chance to try diplomacy to convince Qaddafi to end his military intervention in Chad. These efforts paid off when Libya and France agreed to pull their forces out of Chad in fall 1984. Although the French completed their withdrawal, it has been reported that Qaddafi has not kept his part of the agreement and that Libyan troops have remained in the north. In response to these reports, Qaddafi suggested on December 20, 1984 that "an international commission . . . be set up to confirm that his troops have withdrawn from . . . Chad."[441]

Conclusion

Qaddafi's coming to power in 1969 marked a dramatically new phase in Libya's foreign policy. Qaddafi reversed his country's traditional ties with the U.S. and Britain which, in his view, had hampered its ability to act independently on regional and international problems. He formulated a new and more active policy that was designed to keep Libya out of big-power conflicts and to make it free to conduct its foreign policy independently from the super-power blocs. His policy of non-alignment is essentially a nationalist policy aiming at furthering Libyan and Arab interests and giving Libya the flexibility to act in any way it deems necessary and to cooperate with either of the two cold-war contenders as it sees fit.

Qaddafi is determined to finish the tasks started by Nasser, namely Arab unity and the liberation of Palestine. His relations with neighboring Arab countries are largely determined by the extent of their commitment to Pan-Arabism and their stance on Palestine. Such a policy has resulted in Libya's drifting away from Egypt, Nimeiri's Sudan, and Tunisia, all of which have resisted Qaddafi's attempts to form a union and have strongly opposed his maneuver to spread his revolutionary ideology over the Arab world.

Qaddafi's drive to achieve Arab unity has led him to intervene in the affairs of neighboring countries. This has often dragged the Middle East into the cold-war arena as Egypt has sought to counter Libyan and Soviet threats by throwing itself into the American orbit. Egypt, along with Somalia and Oman, has agreed to allow American troops to use its naval facilities and airfields to counter Soviet moves in the region. Such developments have led to a worsening of relations with Libya, thus putting obstacles in the way of achieving Arab unity.

Qaddafi has opposed the establishment of American military bases on Arab soil because, he argues, they are used to further Western rather than Arab interests. He is critical of the American military presence and its intervention in the Middle East because of the U.S. commitment to the security and the well-being of Israel. Such a commitment runs contrary to the Arab interests since the Arab states have sought to liberate Palestine from Zionist occupation—an action that cannot be accomplished as long as the U.S. maintains friendly relations with some Arab governments. Qaddafi feels that Western influence and domination in the Arab world must be eliminated in order to make the Arab governments free to act in a manner that is consistent with Arab interests. He believes that the battle against Israel can be won if the Arabs are willing to mobilize their resources and take unified action against Israel and its allies. He blames Arab misfortunes on their failure to throw all their resources into a full-scale war against Israel. He is willing to offer all of Libya's resources to the battle to liberate Palestine. However, he has indicated that his country will not participate in a war whose objective is limited to the recovery of the Arab land captured by Israel in the 1967 war.

His uncompromising support for the liberation of Palestine has led him to take his anti-Israel campaign to Africa. He sought African support for the Arab position on Palestine by drawing a parallel between Israel and South Africa. He expected African support for the Palestinian armed struggle since the Arab states had supported the wars of national liberation in Africa. His efforts met with some success as some African governments broke off diplomatic relations with Israel prior to the outbreak of the 1973 war.

His opposition to colonialism has led him to support the principle of self-determination for the oppressed African peoples fighting to liberate themselves from the yoke of colonialism and racism. His support is not limited to African Muslim countries – he has provided financial and material assistance for African liberation movements, particularly in southern Africa. This assistance has not been kept a secret despite open criticism by the U.S. and other states.

Qaddafi is also critical of his fellow African leaders who maintain close political and economic ties with their former colonial masters. He urges them to destroy colonial ties and break the dependence on the West which he considers as a continuation of the colonial past. In his view, unless this is done, these governments are not free to conduct their foreign policies in the best interest of their people or to make their own decisions. He seeks to eliminate all forms of Western domination and influence because, in his view, Africa's independence is threatened as long as colonialism and imperialism are alive. Qaddafi thus argues that Libya is not free until all others are free. Such an attitude might explain Qaddafi's relentless effort to support African liberation struggles and to provide military assistance to anti-U.S. governments whenever they are subjected to a destabilization campaign or foreign invasion. He has paid a high price for upholding his revolutionary ideas and sustaining his anti-colonial campaign. For example, he was unable to hold the OAU summit in his country in 1982 and to assume the chairmanship of the regional organization because of his support for the Polisario against Morocco's annexation of the Western Sahara and for Goukouni's faction in the civil war in Chad.

REAGAN'S RESPONSE TO QADDAFI:

Politics of Confrontation

SINCE 1969 LIBYA AND THE UNITED STATES HAVE been at odds with each other, taking conflicting stands based on their national interests, political ideologies and policy objectives. Qaddafi, a revolutionary, nationalist leader, has pursued a militant pan-Arab, pan-Islamic policy that has resulted in collision with the U.S. in the Middle East and Africa. His nationalism has led him to oppose American military bases or facilities in the region, especially the Rapid Deployment Force that is designed to increase the American military presence in the Persian Gulf and the Red Sea. He has also carried out a systematic campaign to turn the Arab masses against the U.S. and has blamed America's unlimited support of Israel for the lingering Palestinian problem and for the continuing occupation of Arab territories captured by Israel in the 1967 war.[442] Throughout his time in power, Qaddafi's activities have reflected an ingrained ideological hatred of the U.S. and a readiness to undermine Western interests and allies in the area.

Prior to 1981, both Tripoli and Washington managed to downplay their areas of conflict and stayed at arm's length from each other. They apparently did not allow political squabbles to interfere in their mutually beneficial economic relations. Business as usual continued despite major disagreement over foreign policy issues. Libya ranked third among U.S. oil suppliers, accounting for about 11 percent of U.S. oil imports. The U.S. was a lucrative customer for Libya, supplying nearly $12 billion a year in revenue for Libya.[443] Five American oil companies—Exxon, Mobil, Occidental Petroleum, Marathon, and Continental Oil—bought over half of Libya's oil output.[444] In fact, American technicians played a vital role in Libya's oil production.

U.S.-Libyan relations took a new twist after Ronald Reagan entered the White House in January 1981. Reagan interpreted his victory in the 1980 presidential election as "a mandate to do things differently."[445] In response to domestic pressures and global challenges, Reagan was determined to get tough with the Soviet Union and its friends, including Libya, which had been combatting American influence in the highly strategic regions of the world. Reagan's top

149

priority, therefore, was to arrest "a growing threat" from the Soviet Union and its surrogates in the Middle East and elsewhere.[446]

U.S.-Libyan relations have subsequently deteriorated. In view of the sharp contrast between Reagan's conservatism and Qaddafi's radicalism, a clash of minds may have been unavoidable. Events since 1981 have certainly put further obstacles in the way and would make any future reconciliation between Washington and Tripoli hard to achieve.

Politics of Confrontation

From the outset, the Reagan administration wanted to neutralize Qaddafi because his policies ran counter to U.S. interests and objectives in Africa and the Middle East.[447] Republican officials were angered by Qaddafi's rhetorical denunciation of the U.S. and by his systematic campaign to erode American influence in the region. They accused Qaddafi of fostering international terrorism, and financing terrorist organizations which had advocated the use of force to bring about political change. They rejected Libya's distinction between random acts of terrorism and support for national liberation struggles.[448] On July 8, 1981, Chester A. Crocker, Assistant Secretary for African Affairs, told the Senate Foreign Relations Committee that

> under Colonel Qaddafi, Libya has adopted a diplomacy of subversion in Africa and the Arab world. It is a diplomacy of unprecedented obstruction to our interests and objectives. Qaddafi has tried in every way he could think of to obstruct our efforts to achieve peace in the Middle East. He has sponsored subversion from Africa to the Philippines. He has actively supported international terrorism, using assassinations abroad as an instrument of his policy.[449]

Most American officials resented Qaddafi's close ties with the Soviet Union, his major arms supplier. They considered him a surrogate of the Soviet Union,[450] who would further the Soviet goal of destabilizing the region, particularly the pro-U.S. governments of Egypt, the Sudan, Morocco and Saudi Arabia.[451] Although some American observers disagreed with this view and argued that Qaddafi is his own man[452] and is using the Soviet Union to supply him with sophisticated weaponry, the dominant view within the Reagan adminstration has been that Libya is a Soviet surrogate.

The Soviet Union, on the other hand, has found Qaddafi a lucrative customer able to pay for arms in hard currency, for which Moscow is hard pressed. Since 1974 the Soviet bloc nations have supplied Libya with a $20 billion arsenal,[453] including surface-to-air missiles, tanks, fighter aircraft and self-propelled artillery. The Soviet arms sale has brought the two countries closer to each other and, consequently, has triggered continuing American accusations that Qaddafi is a Soviet surrogate, helping to combat American and Western influence in Africa and the Arab world.[454]

Qaddafi has publicly acknowledged that "almost all of our weapons are supplied by the Soviet Union, . . . whereas the U.S., with our money and funds, refuses to sell us even civilian cars."[455] He has adamantly denied that his country is becoming a "Soviet base" by recalling that he did not permit Soviet warships to enter Libyan territorial waters during the 1970s.[456] However, this situation changed following Qaddafi's visit to Moscow in April 1981. It was reported that

> on July 25, 1981, a Soviet naval task group visited Tripoli, with the simultaneous flight there of two IL-38 reconnaissance airplanes: the first Soviet naval or air visits to Libya since [Qaddafi] seized power. Since then visits have been frequent. In November 1982, the two states carried out a joint naval exercise, and in January 1983, a Soviet submarine paid a month-long call at Tobruk for maintenance purposes; another joint naval exercise was carried out in July 1983.[457]

Although Qaddafi has resisted pressure to give the Soviets a naval base along the Mediterranean Sea, which would offset their expulsion from Egypt in 1972, "the Soviets are slowly and quietly moving him toward granting them virtual basing rights in Libya."[458] This development would bring about a shift in the balance of power in the Mediterranean in favor of the Soviet Union, "significantly upset[ting] the calculations of Western strategic planners and Israel,"[459] according to the Congressional Research Service.

The CIA is concerned over the stockpiling of Soviet weapons and the presence of about 5,000 Soviet, East European and Cuban military advisers in Libya. It claims that this huge arsenal, which is beyond Libya's security needs, could be used at any time to launch a Soviet thrust into Africa and the Middle East. This led Alexander M. Haig, Secretary of State, to accuse Libya of being a Soviet "proxy force."[460]

In mid-1981, Francis J. West, Assistant Secretary of Defense, told the Senate Foreign Relations Committee that "Libya has been transformed, in effect, into a Soviet weapons depot and is able to promise and deliver Soviet-origin weapons to states and factions friendly to the Soviets and inimical to our interests."[461] American officials view the presence of Soviet advisers and weapons in Libya as a threat to NATO's southern flank and to the air communications lanes in the Mediterranean Sea and the Persian Gulf.

Qaddafi, on the other hand, has defended the presence of Soviet and East European advisers. He has argued that they are training Libyan forces in the use of Soviet-made weapons, which are needed to renovate his ill-equipped armed forces. He has also denied that there are Cuban military personnel in his country.[462]

Despite his explanation, the Reagan administration has continued to view Qaddafi as a danger that must be reckoned with. A senior American official called Qaddafi a "mini-imperialist and supporter of terrorism, an old-fashioned tribal leader who feels a mystical air about him and doesn't have much respect for a country's boundaries."[463] This is evident in Libya's military intervention in Chad late in 1980, which temporarily ended the long-running civil war and restored President Goukouni Woddeye to power. This action also defeated the pro-Western faction in Chad, led by former Defense Minister Hissene Habré and backed by Egypt's Anwar El-Sadat and Sudan's Jaafar Nimeiri.

Libya's swift military campaign in Chad caught many governments, including the U.S., off guard. Haig, in his first news conference, described Qaddafi's intervention in Chad as "a grave turn of events," which the administration was watching "very, very carefully."[464] The U.S., along with France, shared African anxiety about the security implications of Libya's military and political presence in Chad, especially because Chad's neighboring countries, being militarily weak and economically poor, were also vulnerable to external intervention. Egypt, Nigeria and the Sudan expressed alarm over Qaddafi's expansionism and, particularly, the presence of thousands of Libyan troops in Chad. They feared that Qaddafi might be tempted by his fresh victory in Chad to push his plan for a pan-Islamic republic under his dominance. Their fears were confirmed when a merger plan for Libya and Chad was announced in Tripoli in January 1981.[465] Sadat considered the planned merger as a threat to the Sudan, which shares a 600-mile border with Chad. He added that "what threatens [the]

Sudan threatens Egypt."[466] Nigeria, which had just closed the Libyan People's Bureau and ousted Libyan diplomats from Lagos, bitterly opposed the merger and spearheaded a diplomatic drive to get Libyan troops out of Chad.

Niger and Mali were directly threatened by Qaddafi's expansionism because they were "vulnerable to subversion."[467] Niger's President Seyni Kountche severed diplomatic ties with Libya, accusing Qaddafi of destabilizing his country by stirring ethnic animosities to pave the way for Libyan intervention.[468]

In response to this African uproar, Qaddafi decided to bow to the storm and to shelve his merger plan temporarily. This decision did little to reduce anxiety among the Africans, however, who still viewed the presence of Libyan troops in Chad as a threat to their security. They continued to demand that Libya withdraw from Chad, stressing that failure to do so would worsen Libya's relations with many African states and would threaten the scheduled OAU summit in Tripoli in the summer of 1982.

Although the Reagan administration was urged by many African leaders, including Sadat and Nimeiri, to initiate stern action against Qaddafi, Reagan did not move fast. He did not want to make a hasty move that might interrupt the flow of Libyan oil to the U.S. Instead, he ordered the State Department to review U.S.-Libyan relations and to recommend ways to deal with Qaddafi and what steps to take, if any, to show U.S. displeasure with his policy of intervention. It should be noted that the heavy U.S. reliance on Libyan oil at this time limited the policy options open to the U.S.

The State Department was divided on how to handle Qaddafi, although "nobody advocate[d] being nice to him."[469] The African Bureau, considering Libyan intervention in Chad as a regional problem, advised that the U.S. should stay out of it and discouraged taking any strong measures against Qaddafi. They argued that Washington should instead back any African decisions, since the African states were more familiar with the situation than the U.S. They also urged that African states and France (because of its close ties with Francophone Africa) should be encouraged to pressure Qaddafi to change his ways.[470]

These recommendations were rejected by Haig, however, who favored "a tougher and more positive response to Qaddafi's adventurism." He justified his stance on the ground that Libya's huge oil revenues are "almost exclusively diverted to the purchase of armaments, the training of international terrorists and the conduct of direct interventionism in the neighboring states of northern Africa,"[471] the most recent being the invasion of Chad.

In response to Haig's hard-line approach, the Policy Planning staff in the State Department argued that Libya's intervention in Chad made it essential "to draw a line on Libyan expansionism" lest Qaddafi's "delusions of grandeur" drive him farther into neighboring countries[472] to form a pan-Islamic empire of Saharan states. These analysts were determined "to oppose Libya and its militant, unconventional leader, Qaddafi,"[473] who was seen as "the world's premier exporter of subversion and terrorism."[474] Richard Kennedy, Undersecretary of State, told the Senate Foreign Relations Committee that "governments such as . . . Libya, which directly or indirectly sponsor, train, finance, and arm the terrorists, must be told their behavior is unacceptable. We will use all appropriate resources at our disposal, be they diplomatic, political, economic, or military, to respond to such acts of international intimidation and extortion."[475]

By summer 1981, the Republican administration was pursuing a two-track policy to force Qaddafi to change his policy of "international terrorism and subversion." First, it decided to provide military and economic assistance to countries threatened by Qaddafi. American objectives were to deal with their troubled economies – which gave Qaddafi the opportunity for intervention and subversion – and also to strengthen their defenses as a way to offset Qaddafi's destabilization campaign in the region. American officials said, "Adequate aid is essential to prevent economic instability and Libyan adventurism from damaging U.S. interests."[476]

On June 2, 1981, Assistant Secretary of State Crocker announced that "the U.S. [would] support all African nations that want to resist 'interventionism' by Libya."[477] To implement this policy, Washington moved to strengthen the military capabilities of its Arab and African friends in an effort to check, if not to halt, Qaddafi's promotion of revolutionary change in neighboring countries. During the same month, Frank Carlucci, Deputy Secretary of Defense, toured North African capitals and conferred with these governments about additional military sales that would strengthen their defenses in ways that would head off Qaddafi's threats. As a result, military assistance has been increased substantially to Egypt, to the Sudan and to Tunisia, all of which have been directly threatened by Libya's location along their borders. In July 1981, for example, the State Department announced a plan to sell M-60 tanks to Tunisia "in order to deter further Libyan adventurism."[478] In the following year, the Congress was asked to approve $10 million for Tunisia and $20 million for Morocco in order to "provide substance to our past assurances that we would be a dependable friend."[479] The Reagan administration also increased its military assistance to both Morocco and Somalia to assist them in their own confrontations with the Qaddafi-backed Polisario in the Western Sahara and the Somali National Salvation Front in Somalia, respectively. American officials have acknowledged that "our assistance helped [the] Sudan, Morocco and Tunisia to face threats of subversion or aggression emanating from Libya."[480]

As a second step, the Republican administration decided to make Qaddafi's life "less comfortable."[481] It initiated a series of measures intended to make it clear that the U.S. would not tolerate any new military ventures by Qaddafi.

A scrutiny of Reagan's get-tough campaign will shed light on the measures taken by the U.S. to demonstrate its displeasure with Qaddafi, and illustrate the limitations imposed by diplomacy on U.S. ability to do harm to Qaddafi, who has committed himself to weakening Western influence and to fighting U.S. penetration into the Middle East and Africa.

Closing of the Libyan Embassy

The Reagan administration, like its predecessor, has expressed alarm at Qaddafi's advocacy of "the physical and final liquidation of the opponents of popular authority . . . at home and abroad."[482] This was the context surrounding U.S. reaction when several Libyan expatriates were mysteriously murdered in several European cities in 1980. Western sources claimed that the assassination campaign was encouraged by Qaddafi to eliminate his opponents inside and outside Libya. American officials feared that the campaign might spread to the U.S. and, for this reason, expelled four Libyan diplomats in May 1980, arguing that they were linked with a campaign of intimidation to silence Libyan dissidents in the U.S. Despite this precautionary measure, a Libyan student dissident, Faisal Zagallai, was wounded in Colorado in October 1980. This incident attracted nationwide attention because the convicted assassin—Eugene Tafaya—was a former member of the U.S. "Green Beret" Special Forces, and his trial was widely covered in the American press.[483]

The Republican administration feared that such an incident might mark the beginning of an assassination campaign in the U.S. and decided to take immediate action. On May 6, 1981, the Libyan People's Bureau was closed and Libyan diplomats were ordered out of the country because of "a wide range of Libyan provocations and misconduct, including support of international terrorism."[484] Libya reacted angrily to the closing of the embassy and the ousting of its diplomats and challenged the U.S. State Department to produce evidence to support the allegation that Libyan diplomats were intimidating Libyan dissidents in the U.S.[485] Despite this denial, another Libyan student was killed in Utah in June 1981 by a Libyan who was known to be pro-Qaddafi.[486]

Reagan's action fell short of a full break in diplomatic relations between the two countries. It should be noted that the U.S. embassy in Tripoli had already been closed since May 1980 when the last American diplomats were withdrawn, six months after the embassy had been sacked and burned by pro-Iranian demonstrators. In fact, Qaddafi had repeatedly tried to get the U.S. to send its diplomats back to Tripoli by turning down numerous American requests to use a third country–Belgium–to represent U.S. interests in Libya.[487] He failed, however, to convince the Reagan administration to restore normal relations.

Another instance of Reagan's new stance is reflected in the fact that the administration successfully lured Edwin P. Wilson, a former CIA agent, out of Libya. He was accused of helping to train and equip Libyan terrorists as well as supplying explosives to Libya. The Justice Department vigorously prosecuted Wilson on several charges, ranging from shipping "four handguns and an M-16 rifle" to the sale of "20 tons of explosives" to Libya.[488] His trial was widely covered by the media, paving the way for further measures against Qaddafi.

Aerial Clash over the Gulf of Sirte

In August 1981, the U.S. conducted a naval exercise in the Gulf of Sirte, an area that Libya considers to be part of its territorial waters. The U.S. and Libya disagree over the status of the Gulf. Since 1973 the U.S. has refused Qaddafi's declaration of sovereignty over the Gulf,

The Gulf of Sirte

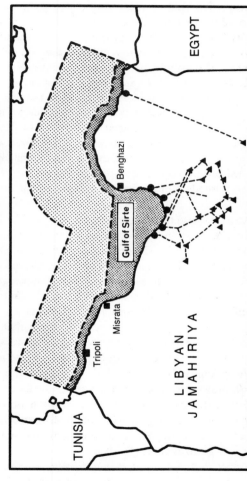

To justify American actions against the Libyan Jamahiriya, Washington and the press have said that Libya claims this 200 mile territorial limit.

■ Major oil ports, concentrated on the Gulf of Sirte, would be US targets if Washington's planned invasion ever materialised.

The real extent of Libya's territorial waters, based on a twelve-mile limit and the 'historic waters' of the Gulf of Sirte.

——— Oil pipe lines   ▲ Main oil fields

Source: "Battle in the Gulf of Sirte: Special Report," *Jamahiriya Review*, no. 16, September 1981, p. 13.

which extends from the coastal cities of Benghazi and Misratah. Instead, Washington has accepted the international standard of three miles, although it has informally observed a 12-mile limit claimed by Libya for other coastal regions.[489]

The naval maneuver off the Libyan coast was decided at the highest level in the Reagan administration. It was decided upon by Reagan at a National Security Council (NSC) meeting in late July. In anticipation of some reaction by Libya, the commander of the Navy Task Force was recalled to Washington prior to the exercise and had meetings with both the Joint Chiefs of Staff and the NSC to go over the details. American troops were told to be "on their toes"[490] and were instructed to return fire in expectation of a shoot-out with the Libyan Air Force. Consequently, on August 19, 1981, two Libyan jets were shot down by F-14 interceptors from the carrier *Nimitz* after they had fired a missile at the planes. Despite this aerial clash, American officials insisted that they did not go in looking for a fight "but rather to establish freedom of navigation and movement" in the Gulf.[491]

Since the U.S. naval exercise took place only 60 miles off the Libyan coast, some observers concluded that Reagan's intention was to provoke an incident[492] as part of a stepped-up get-tough campaign. Although Secretary of Defense Caspar W. Weinberger denied that the exercise, which was described as "routine," was a challenge to Qaddafi, it is clear that it was a direct challenge to Libya's territorial claim of sovereignty over the Gulf of Sirte and a reaffirmation that "we don't go along."[493] It was intended to warn Qaddafi that the Reagan administration, unlike its predecessor, was ready to use force if necessary to protect American and Western interests in the area. It was also a move to appease Arab and African leaders who had repeatedly urged Washington to take action against Qaddafi's adventurism and to translate its rhetoric of opposition into concrete measures that would show its opposition to Qaddafi's policy of intervention. Furthermore, it was a test of the Soviet reaction, to see how far Moscow was willing to go to defend Qaddafi.

The aerial clash over the Gulf resulted in a further deterioration in U.S.-Libyan relations. The Reagan administration warned Qaddafi that "any further attack against U.S. forces operating in international water and airspace will also be resisted with force if necessary."[494] The Libyan government, on the other hand, condemned the U.S. naval exercise as an "uncalled-for-interference and provocation" and reserved Libya's right "to take all measures to safeguard its airspace and territorial waters."[495]

American officials interpreted this statement as a threat of possible retaliation against the U.S. They were confident, however, that Qaddafi would not interrupt the flow of oil to the U.S. because he needed the $12 billion annual sales from U.S. purchases to support his costly armament and development programs. Nevertheless, they did not take lightly Libya's public threats against American officials. On August 13, the Free Unionist Officers in Libya threatened to respond to any harm to Qaddafi by striking against U.S. interests anywhere, and seeking the physical liquidation of American top officials.[496] This was in response to a report by *Newsweek* on August 3, 1981 that the CIA was covertly planning a destabilization campaign in Libya aimed at removing Qaddafi from power, possibly by assassination.[497] Although the State Department was quick to deny that report, Libyan officials decided not to take any chances. Security around Qaddafi was strengthened out of fear of a plot to assassinate him or to overthrow his government. He secretly left Libya before the U.S. naval exercise began off the Libyan coast and arrived in Aden, South Yemen, a few days ahead of schedule for a summit with pro-Soviet leaders of Ethiopia and South Yemen.[498] On August 19, the three leaders signed a Treaty of Friendship and Cooperation that American officials described as "a Libyan-bankrolled pact to confront American-allied countries in the area."[499]

Sadat's Assassination

The Reagan administration blamed Qaddafi for the negative turn of events it was witnessing in the Arab world, particularly his campaign to isolate Egypt's Sadat in the Middle East and Africa and his destabilization campaign in Egypt and the Sudan. Qaddafi did not forgive Sadat for his failure to live up to Nasserism, for turning down the merger plan with Libya, and for his conduct of the 1973 Middle East war. He opposed Sadat's policy that brought Cairo closer to Washington even as American policy remained firmly committed to the security and well-being of Israel.

On its part, the Reagan administration has conducted a systematic campaign to discredit Qaddafi, with increased momentum for this campaign since Sadat's assassination on October 6, 1981. American

officials accused Qaddafi of being behind the assassination[500] because
he had been suspected already of funding anti-Sadat groups in Egypt
and of supporting attempts to overthrow or assassinate Sadat because
of his pro-U.S. policy and capitulation to Israel, particularly after Sadat's
signing of the Camp David Accords in 1979.

Republicans were quick to blame Qaddafi even prior to the completion of the official Egyptian investigation on the nature and the
extent of the plot. Egyptian officials later insisted that there was no
outside involvement in the assassination, which was the work of
Muslim extremists who belonged to *Takfir wa Hijra*, a fundamentalist
group that opposed Sadat's internal and external policies, which, in
their view, deviated from Islam.

The Reagan administration responded to Sadat's assassination by
a show of force in the region. The Airborne Warning and Control
System (AWACS) aircraft were sent to Egypt to monitor Libya's troop
movements along the Egyptian and the Sudanese borders, following
Libya's call to overthrow the new Egyptian government.[501] When
Haig arrived in Cairo for Sadat's funeral, he announced that the U.S.
would speed the delivery of military equipment to Egypt and the Sudan
to enable them to cope with Libya's threats. He also promised additional military assistance to both countries to reinforce their defenses
against both Soviet and Libyan threats. He made it clear that the U.S.
would come to the aid of its friends in the region if there was a threat
from outside. He stressed that the U.S. was committed to preventing
the overthrow of friendly governments in the Arab world. His
announcement was intended to put Qaddafi on notice that the U.S.
would not tolerate any venture by Libya into neighboring countries
and that Qaddafi should not take advantage of the turn of events in
Egypt following Sadat's assassination. Reagan also decided to keep
in Saudi Arabia the four AWACS surveillance planes, which had been
dispatched by his predecessor in 1980. In addition, a U.S. Navy aircraft carrier task force was kept in the Arabian Sea, and a permanent
group of three destroyers was stationed at Bahrain in the Persian
Gulf.[502]

In November 1981, the U.S. conducted joint military maneuvers –
Operation Bright Star – with Egypt, the Sudan, Somalia and Oman.
It provided an explicit demonstration of the striking capability of the
U.S. Rapid Deployment Force and was intended to warn Qaddafi
against military moves on Egypt or the Sudan.

Economic Boycott

Following Sadat's assassination, American officials accused Qaddafi of a plot to assassinate President Reagan and top American officials. They went so far as to accuse him of sending "hit squads" to carry out these acts. Although Qaddafi persistently denied the American allegations and challenged the Reagan administration to produce evidence to support their claim,[503] Republican officials took measures to prevent any assassination attempt inside the country. Pictures of the members of the hit teams were flashed on television screens and in newspapers, and were distributed "to about 2,000 Customs and U.S. Border Patrol officials around the country"[504] who were ordered to keep a lookout for members of the hit squads. American embassies were given instructions to screen carefully all applicants seeking entry to the U.S.

Many observers thought that the publicity surrounding the alleged Libyan hit teams meant that the Reagan administration was considering initiating punitive measures against Qaddafi to put an end to his "lawless behavior"[505] in the international community. On January 18, 1982, Haig confided off the record to his senior staff that the administration might be moving to "phase II" of the anti-Qaddafi program. Possible measures might include a U.S. boycott of Libyan oil and an embargo on American exports to Libya.[506] He cautioned, however, that the administration first wanted to give Americans a chance to get out of Libya before initiating any measures, in order to prevent another hostage situation, similar to the one in Iran, that might prove embarrassing to Reagan.

The Republican administration had already taken several measures to pave the way for a boycott of Libya. In May 1981, following the closing of the Libyan embassy in Washington, the State Department had a meeting with U.S. oil corporations operating in Libya and advised them "to begin an 'orderly drawdown' of their personnel on the ground that the U.S. government was not in a position to protect and assist Americans if trouble came."[507] Two months later, another meeting took place at the State Department, which gave "a clear indication that something sensitive is brewing." As one official said, "The companies won't get another warning. We're playing confrontation politics and we want them out, whether there is a coup in the works or not."[508]

In response, oil firms reduced their American personnel from 2,000 in May to 1,500 in mid-August.[509] They were reluctant to cut further, however, because any additional reduction in manpower would be harmful to business and might violate their contractual obligations.

Because American response to the administration's call was slow, Reagan, backed by the NSC's decision in December 1981, ordered all Americans to leave Libya on the grounds that their lives were in danger because of the threat of another hostage crisis. He also banned travel by Americans to Libya.[510]

Reagan's objective was to take American technicians and executives out of Libya as a way of causing economic hardship for Qaddafi since they worked in Libya's oil fields and petroleum industry. Their sudden departure was expected to disrupt Libya's oil production, at least for the time being. An immediate result would be to reduce Libya's oil revenues, which Qaddafi relied on to generate hard currency to finance his development programs and arms purchases. Pulling Americans out of Libya would thus prepare for other retaliatory measures by the U.S., eventually including a ban on U.S. imports of Libyan oil.

In response to the President's order, many Americans left Libya, with about 400 persons remaining behind because they were still reluctant to depart. Americans in Libya were taken aback by the President's order to return home because they felt that there was no danger to their lives and there was no likelihood of a hostage crisis.[511] On the contrary, they insisted that they were treated well and their work was appreciated by Libyans. In addition, there were no signs of hostility toward the Americans working there. Qaddafi personally reassured the Americans about their safety [512] and encouraged them to stay but, at the same time, expressed a readiness to facilitate travelling arrangements for those who wished to depart.

The Americans, highly paid in Libya, were reluctant to leave because of the recession and high levels of unemployment at home. Some Americans sent their dependents back to the U.S., however, not out of fear for their lives but in response to the President's order. Others loudly wondered why the Reagan administration was ganging up on Libya. Some observers argued that Reagan, having avowed his conservatism, needed to act tough with a country with close ties with the Soviet Union. Libya was the logical choice because it is tiny, it is in no position to retaliate against the U.S., and it has few friends among America's allies. It was easier to pick on Libya than to have a showdown with Moscow, something Reagan certainly could not afford to do during his first year in office.

On February 26, 1982, the NSC decided to impose a ban on imports of Libyan oil and to halt the sale of American oil-production equipment to Libya, although without naming a specific date. This decision was easy to reach because the Reagan administration had steadily reduced its dependence on oil from Libya, which was once ranked as the third source of U.S. oil imports. At the end of 1981, Libyan oil accounted for only 3.5 percent of imported oil to the U.S., totalling about 150,000 barrels a day compared to 700,000 barrels a day in 1977. This minor degree of reliance—as well as the existence of an oil glut in the world market—meant that a Libyan oil boycott would not affect U.S. oil supplies or prices. The U.S. could easily find oil supplies from other countries because, with the world's surplus at the time, many oil-producing nations were ready to sell oil at reduced rates to generate the funds they needed for their own development.[513] These circumstances had already resulted in a cutback in production of Libyan crude oil by several American firms. For example, Occidental Petroleum, a major oil operator in Libya, had cut back its production "by almost half" and had reduced its staff.[514] In November 1981, Exxon made it known that it would cease operations in Libya and would "turn over its remaining holdings to [Qaddafi]." Mobil had also suspended production altogether.[515]

In preparation for the oil boycott, the Reagan administration quietly conducted a wide range of consultation with European allies. Their endorsement was essential for Reagan, who felt that such a boycott "would have to be worldwide. No one country could affect [the Libyans] by having a boycott."[516] European participation in the boycott would offer a clear signal to Qaddafi that continuation of his policy would mean trouble with both the U.S. and Western Europe.

Washington failed to convince the European allies to cease buying oil from Libya, however. In mid-December 1981, NATO foreign ministers, meeting in Brussels, flatly rejected Haig's appeal for their "understanding and support" of the U.S. stance.[517] Their rejection stemmed from their failure to view Qaddafi as a pariah and from their disagreement over the extent of the Libyan threat. Economic considerations also played a role. A Libyan oil boycott would cause economic hardship for many European nations, probably causing a sharp reduction in their exports to Libya. Italy, for instance, has a lucrative commerce with Libya; its exports to Libya more than doubled in 1981, reaching a total of $3 billion during the first nine months of that year. Italy therefore had no intention of joining a boycott against Libya. On the contrary, it wished to establish "a permanent and significant relationship with the Libyan people, economically, politically and all the rest,"[518] as an Italian official in the Foreign Ministry reported.

Moreover, Britain felt that a boycott would "do more harm than good."[519] Lord Trefgrane, Undersecretary of State in the British Foreign Office, told the House of Lords that

> we do not believe that the way to make our views known would be to boycott or isolate Libya. We believe it to be more effective to encourage the Libyans to adopt acceptable policies by maintaining a dialogue with the Libyan government and trying to develop as near-normal relations as possible.[520]

Similar views were expressed by France, which feared that a European boycott might push Qaddafi deeper into Soviet arms. French officials argued that "Libya is not yet a satellite of the Soviet Union, but cutting it off from commercial contacts with the West might turn it into one by forcing [Qaddafi] to rely on the U.S.S.R. for money and technical help as well as arms."[521] France also announced that it was planning to resume normal relations with Libya, following the withdrawal of Libyan troops from Chad the previous month.

In the face of European objections, the Reagan administration decided to act alone. In March 1982, it banned imports of Libyan oil and imposed on Libya the strictest categories of export controls available.

It was generally acknowledged, however, that the U.S. oil boycott would not cause major economic difficulties for Libya because of the sharp reduction of U.S. oil purchases since 1981. Libya would have little difficulty finding new markets for this small share of its oil.[522] The major impact was expected to be the dislocation caused by the loss of American technicians who were running Libya's oil fields. The Reagan administration was unaware that Qaddafi had prepared a contingency plan to offset such a departure of American oil-workers.[523] Since the U.S. threat to boycott Libyan oil began to surface in the fall of 1981, Libya had been shopping around for replacements for American workers. An option for Libya was to use European technicians to maintain the current level of production.[524] Furthermore, Italian oil companies were ready to replace Americans in Libya. Under these circumstances, it was unlikely that Libya's oil production would be seriously affected by a sudden exodus of American workers.

The only effect, perhaps, was psychological since it meant that the U.S. was serious about backing up its threats against Qaddafi. The U.S. hoped to make Qaddafi's life more difficult if he continued his course of action and to encourage internal opposition to take advantage of his political embarrassment.

At the same time, there was little that Qaddafi could do to retaliate against the U.S. boycott because he had few friends in the Arab world who would join him in an all-out oil embargo similar to the one that was imposed against the U.S. in 1973. Such a measure was particularly unlikely because of the oil glut and the conditions in the world market. The forthcoming summit of the Organization of African Unity (OAU), to be held in Tripoli in the summer of 1982, was another reason for a restrained Libyan reaction. Qaddafi would wish to avoid any retaliatory action that might cause alarm among African states at a time when he was planning to assume the chairmanship of the OAU in the coming year.

The OAU Chairmanship

In an attempt to spoil Qaddafi's bid to assume the OAU chairmanship for 1982-1983, the Reagan administration conducted a quiet, intensive diplomatic campaign throughout Africa to ensure that the scheduled summit would not come off. American diplomats toured African capitals and distributed a secret document discussing the implications of Qaddafi's becoming the OAU chairman. It stated,

> Qaddafi's unprincipled behavior would make it impossible for us to work with him as OAU chairman. If OAU members follow tradition and elect Qaddafi chairman, we hope something will be done to limit the damage he could do to the organization by bending it to serve his purpose. How this might be accomplished is for the members to decide, but we trust Qaddafi's support for disruptive and subversive forces throughout the continent and beyond has left OAU members without illusions about his ambitions.

It added that

> If Qaddafi is to become OAU chairman, it is more important than ever that the next secretary-general be someone

truly representative of the continent, someone who will have the international respect and access which Qaddafi does not. With Africa's economic problems becoming more acute in a world buffeted by economic distress, it would be unfortunate if the premier African organization were represented by individuals who were impediments to dialogue with the rest of the international community.[525]

American officials urged African leaders to deny Qaddafi the opportunity of becoming the spokesman of the continent. They found a receptive audience among conservative and moderate African states that strongly opposed Qaddafi's radical policies, particularly his intervention in Africa and his world-wide support for revolutionary groups which they viewed as "international terrorists." Consequently, it did not take much for Washington to convince a good number of African leaders to stay away from the scheduled OAU meeting in Tripoli.

Qaddafi twice failed to obtain quorums in Libya for the nineteenth African summit in August and November 1982.[526] This circumstance was primarily due to the failure of the African states to reach a compromise over two major issues, the Western Sahara and Chad. At the end of July, the dispute over the admission of the Sahrawi Arab Democratic Republic (SADR), championed by the Polisario which has been fighting Morocco for the independence of the Western Sahara, prevented the OAU ministerial meeting in Tripoli from completing arrangements for the summit of African heads of state to be held on August 5.

Qaddafi, who had been providing financial and material assistance to the Polisario, insisted that the SADR should be given a seat at the summit since it had already been admitted as the OAU's fifty-first member in February 1982. Morocco, on the other hand, lobbied among the nineteen countries that had walked out of the February meeting in protest over the admission of SADR; it had argued that the organization's membership is limited to independent African states. Moroccan diplomats toured African capitals in an effort to convince these governments to boycott the Tripoli summit unless the question of Polisario's admission was first settled. The Moroccan position was backed by the U.S., whose officials made it clear to African leaders that

> [The U.S.] continues to believe that the admission of the
> SADR to the OAU would be a grave mistake. Not only

it would frustrate the OAU's laudable efforts to resolve
the Western Saharan conflict by negotiation, it also would
violate the charter's principles by admission of an entity
which is a political organization rather than a state as commonly defined by international law and practice. It would
set a precedent which would haunt the OAU in the future,
and it could prompt the withdrawal of several members
from the organization.[527]

As a compromise, Nigeria proposed that the Polisario be allowed
to participate in the ministerial meeting but not be allowed to attend
the meeting of heads of state.[528] This compromise, however, did not
get enough support. Consequently, twenty governments stayed away
from Tripoli, causing a lack of a two-thirds quorum for the summit
that would have elected Qaddafi the OAU chairman for 1982-1983.
This outcome angered Qaddafi who "accused the U.S. of bribing
African leaders to boycott" the summit "in order to humiliate him."[529]

To make the best out of a bad situation, Qaddafi held informal
meetings with African leaders who had turned up for the Tripoli summit in August. His purpose was to search for a compromise that would
make it possible to convene the OAU summit later in the year.[530] He
hoped that a cooling-off period might solve the controversy over the
Polisario, thus paving the way for a summit in Libya that would allow
Qaddafi to assume the chairmanship of the organization for the next
year.

At the end of November, Qaddafi tried again to hold the summit
in Tripoli. However, this time the thorny issue was the representation of Chad. Qaddafi refused to allow the pro-Western Hissene Habré,
who had just ousted the Libyan-backed government of Goukouni
Woddeye, to occupy Chad's seat at the summit. Several African states
disagreed with Qaddafi's stance and demanded the seating of the current Chad government. If these states were not satisfied, they might
boycott the summit, thus again denying Qaddafi the quorum needed
to open the summit. This was particularly true because Egypt, the
Sudan and Somalia had already announced their boycott of the summit in protest over Qaddafi's policy of intervention.

To end the stalemate, it was suggested that the OAU recognize
Habré's government which, in turn, would "absent itself from the conference in deference to the Libyan hosts." This compromise was
"categorically rejected" by Habré.[531] Furthermore, Qaddafi was in no
mood to compromise. A Kenyan official commented that "there's no

way Qaddafi can admit Hissene Habré," considering that "many Libyan troops were killed by [Habré's] guerrillas before Qaddafi pulled his forces out of Chad." Yet, the same official admitted that "there's no way we can get a quorum" without the seating of Habré's delegation.[532]

Under these circumstances, the second attempt to convene a summit had to be aborted because of lack of a quorum. Qaddafi again blamed the U.S. and France for this turn of events. He also praised some of the African leaders for coming to attend the summit, "despite pressure put on them by Washington and orders from Paris,"[533] which, he claimed, were applied throughout the continent. Qaddafi's views were shared by several African leaders who acknowledged that the U.S. was "responsible for wrecking two attempts" to hold the OAU summit in Libya in 1982.[534]

At the end of the fall, it was evident that it was no longer possible to convene the OAU summit in Libya. A general consensus emerged, however, that a summit should be held somewhere else, probably in Addis Ababa, the OAU's headquarters, to prevent the organization from being permanently divided into rival camps and to keep Africa from becoming a theatre of East-West conflict. Unless the OAU remained strong, there would be an erosion of African influence in international forums, particularly with regard to African issues. It was hoped that the selection of Addis Ababa would attract enough heads of state to provide a quorum.

In June 1983, the delayed summit was opened in Addis Ababa and Ethiopia's Mengistu Haile Mariam was elected as the new chairman of the OAU. Such a choice left Qaddafi frustrated by his repeated failure to find enough support for holding the summit in Libya and becoming the OAU chairman. Undoubtedly, it was a major setback for Qaddafi, particularly his ambition to become the spokesman for Africa. However, it was also true that, having failed to become the OAU chairman, Qaddafi was now free to renew his intervention in Chad to end Habré's rule and to restore Goukouni to power.

1983: Chadian Crisis

When the civil war erupted again in Chad in June 1983, the Reagan administration became obsessed with giving Qaddafi "a bloody nose" because of his backing of the insurgents led by former President

Goukouni, who had recently been ousted by a pro-Western faction led by Habré. Goukouni, who fled to Libya, reorganized his army and, in late June 1983, overran the strategic northern town of Faya Largeau. However, when Goukouni's rebel forces marched south toward Abeche, 400 miles away from the capital, Ndjamena, Habré took command of his army in the field, drove the rebels back and recaptured Faya Largeau on July 31.

The Reagan administration was concerned about Libya's involvement in this anti-government insurgency in Chad and was determined to stop Qaddafi. Washington decided to let France take the lead in backing the Habré government, however, in recognition of France's responsibilities toward a former colony. A stronger reason, however, was that Reagan had his hands full in Central America and there was strong opposition in Congress to the U.S. getting directly involved in the incessant civil war in Chad.

To demonstrate America's resolution to stop Qaddafi, the Reagan administration airlifted military supplies to help Habré repel the Libyan-backed insurgency:

- On July 18, Reagan authorized as "urgent" a $10 million airlift of supplies to Chad, which included rifles, machine guns, ammunition and vehicles. Furthermore, the aircraft carrier USS *Eisenhower* was positioned off Libya in a show of force to discourage Qaddafi from continuing his air raids in Chad.

- On August 1, in response to Habré's appeal for American and French help to bolster Chad's air defense system, the Reagan administration decided to airlift 30 shoulder-fired, heat-seeking Redeye and Stinger anti-aircraft missiles and three military instructors to Chad.

- On August 4, Reagan authorized an additional $15 million in emergency military aid to help the embattled government fight an intensifying war against the rebels, who were supported by heavy Libyan air raids deep into Chad.

- On August 4, the administration also announced that the aircraft carrier USS *Eisenhower* would remain off the Libyan coast despite Qaddafi's threats to destroy American ships that would enter the Gulf of Sirte. In addition, two AWACS surveillance planes were dispatched to Egypt six days in advance of joint military exercises scheduled there.[535]

The U.S. airlift of military equipment and the additional military assistance was intended to strengthen Chad's defense system in the face of France's failure to comply with Habré's requests for air support. It also reflected Washington's concern about Libyan military involvement in Chadian civil war. As an American official commented, "Habré has nothing in terms of anti-aircraft defense and his people are being pounded on a continual basis by the Libyans."[536] The State Department hoped that these anti-aircraft weapons would give Habré's army "a better opportunity to defend themselves against continuing attacks by Libyan warplanes."[537]

On August 5, the U.S. reaffirmed its "strong strategic interest" in preventing Qaddafi from succeeding in his military venture in Chad or any other African country. This reaffirmation came at a time when the Chadian army was retreating from the eastern towns of Oum Chalouba and Kalait following heavy bombing by Libyan planes. John Hughes, a spokesman for the State Department, described the situation as "serious" and as something "we are concerned about."[538] Such concern was heightened as the rebels prepared their final assault to recapture Faya Largeau. It was reported that 200 Libyan armed vehicles were closing in on that town, while a column of tanks was spotted about 150 miles northwest of Faya Largeau.

The Reagan administration continued to press France for a stronger response to Libya's escalating involvement in Chad, particularly in the form of air power that might force Qaddafi to back down. As an American official put it: "He's a bully but he's a chicken."[539] Larry Speakes, White House Spokesman, said that "the United States has a strong strategic interest in assuring that Qaddafi is not able to upset governments or to intervene militarily in other countries as is currently happening in Chad." He added that "if Libya or Libyan-supported forces were to gain control of Chad, close U.S. allies such as Egypt and [the] Sudan would be seriously concerned about their own security. Other states in the region would also be deeply worried."[540]

American officials were disappointed by President Mitterrand's initial response, that is, the airlifting of French weapons and other military supplies to the Habré government. Mitterrand ruled out sending French troops or fighter planes to support the embattled government against Libyan-backed insurgents. The Republican administration, on the other hand, felt that France must do more to convince Qaddafi of the West's resolve to keep him out of Chad. It continued to press Mitterrand to increase French involvement by answering Habré's appeals for French aircraft to counter those of Qaddafi's.

Mitterrand, however, resisted American pressure and responded by sending anti-aircraft weapons to Habré's army, bringing the total of French military assistance to $45 million since the fighting had broken out in June. He insisted that the 1976 military cooperation agreement did not obligate France to get directly involved in a civil war, and thus refused Habré's repeated appeals for French troops and fighter planes and ignored mounting U.S. pressure for France to get militarily involved in Chad.[541]

In the face of France's reluctance, the Reagan administration announced that it would replace equipment lost by Habré's army in recent fighting. In addition, it dispatched to the Sudan two AWACS surveillance planes, accompanied by eight F-15 fighters, to monitor Libyan air attacks on Faya Largeau. American officials hoped that the dispatch of the AWACS would persuade France of American determination to stand up to Qaddafi's "aggression" and encourage Mitterrand to do the same. [542]On August 7, 1983, Senator John Tower (R-Tex.), Chairman of the Senate Armed Services Committee, said on "Face the Nation" that "what we are trying to do is not involve ourselves in a civil war but to prevent the intrusion into that war of Colonel Qaddafi, who is of course very hostile to the United States and very hostile to our interests."[543]

The U.S., along with African states, continued to pressure France to provide air support for Habré's army to counter Libya's air support for anti-government forces. However, Mitterrand was still reluctant to intervene directly in the Chadian civil war. He was critical of, and in fact, had campaigned against his predecessor's interventionist policies in Africa. In addition, some elements in his Socialist Party opposed direct military intervention in the ceaseless civil wars in Chad that appeared to offer a no-win situation. In response to Washington's pressure, however, France's Foreign Minister Claude Cheysson said in a television interview in Paris that "if Libya pursues its intervention in Chad, internationalizing the conflict, there will be consequences." He added that France "cannot be indifferent."[544] Such a statement was interpreted as a warning to Qaddafi that further Libyan involvement in Chad could lead to direct French military intervention.

To demonstrate its seriousness, on August 8, France sent about 180 military advisers to Chad in response to renewed heavy bombing by Libyan planes against government forces in Faya Largeau. French

officials made it clear that French instructors "are not going to participate in any fighting," which was centered on Faya Largeau. France
came under heavy pressure from American and African governments
when it was revealed that Libya was providing ground support to the
rebels in addition to carrying out almost daily bombings over Faya
Largeau. Diplomatic sources in Tripoli reported that 4,000-5,000 Libyan troops and one or two tank battalions had crossed into Chad in
preparation for the final assault on Faya Largeau.[545]

On August 10, Faya Largeau fell into the hands of the rebels whose
drive was supported by tanks, heavy artillery, and aircraft. The fall
of Faya Largeau coincided with the arrival of a small contingent of
French instructors in Ndjamena. In response to the news, France's
Defense Minister Charles Henru said that "France did not take the
initiative to internationalize the conflict; the Libyans did." He added
that "everything the Libyans do, we will also do, except the bombing
of civilian populations."[546] His statement led to speculation that
France might soon escalate military action.

The fall of Faya Largeau resulted in intensified pressure on France
to become directly involved in the fighting. Zaire's President Mobutu
Sese Seko, on his way home from the U.S., paid a short visit to Mitterrand in Paris. He said that "Chad must be able to [count] on its
friends to reestablish its territorial integrity." As he put it: "The
aggressor is Libya and the victim is Chad, which must not be left alone
in this affair."[547] In Washington, Senegal's President Abdou Dioufi
called on the U.S. and France to increase their military aid to Chad
"rapidly." He told editors and reporters at the *Washington Post* that "we
must stop the Chadian adventure. Otherwise, we shall see it being
repeated in other countries." He also warned against the partition of
Chad, saying that "if you choose the easy way out, there will be no
territorial integrity for any African state."[548]

The fall of Faya Largeau was a turning point in French involvement in the Chadian civil war. Mitterrand decided to meet Qaddafi's
challenge head-on by increasing the number of French troops to more
than 2,000 and by stationing 12 Mirage F-1 and Jaguar fighter bombers
in Chad.[549] The French drew a "red line" along the 15th parallel,
showing their determination to block Libya from moving its forces
any further south in the direction of the capital. French troops were
deployed in four key locations—Abeche, Biltine, Arada and Sallal.
These towns are located along the main routes that Libyan-backed
rebels would have to use to attack the capital. In addition, General

Jean Poli, with combat experience in Africa, was appointed to command French troops in Chad. These French moves, designed to bring an end to the fighting, accomplished their purpose. Between August and January, there was an undeclared cease-fire and several diplomatic moves by France to solve the conflict.[550]

The cease-fire was temporarily shattered in late January 1984 when Libyan-backed rebels attacked government positions at Ziguey behind the French lines. During this fighting, a French Jaguar jet was shot down and its pilot was killed. In retaliation, French troops moved their defensive "red line" to the 16th parallel, another 60 miles north, which was closer to the Libyan and rebel forces. This move was intended to show Qaddafi that France was determined to prevent the rebels from moving farther south toward the capital in an effort to oust the Habré government. To underscore that determination, France kept a 3,000-man force, 16 Jaguar and Mirage fighters, and tons of military hardware in Chad. As Chad's Ambassador to Washington, Mohamat Ali Adoum, said, the French gave Qaddafi a "clear signal that they were serious, too, and mean to defend themselves and have the means to do that."[551] France's strategy was to persuade Qaddafi to abandon his plan for a military solution in Chad, and, instead, to get him to work with France through the OAU to find a negotiated settlement.

Qaddafi, however, showed no immediate sign of abandoning his military campaign in Chad. In fact, he took advantage of the cease-fire to spread Libyan influence in northern Chad. His *Green Book* was widely distributed, and an administrative structure along the Libyan model was set up in the territories now controlled by the Goukouni forces and backed by a Libyan force of about 7,000 troops. The Libyans thus appeared to be preparing for a long stay. They were not only consolidating their control over the territories but they were also bringing in new reinforcements and military equipment to augment their troop strength. There were indications that the Libyan- backed war of attrition against Habré would continue, in an effort to discourage France from staying in Chad indefinitely.

The stalemate in Chad continued as both French and Libyan troops dug in. France, however, continued its diplomatic effort to end Libya's military involvement in Chad and to encourage the OAU to become increasingly active in the search for a peaceful solution for the long civil war. France was determined to prevent Qaddafi from overthrowing the Habré government and did everything in its power to avoid a military showdown with Qaddafi. The French effort paid off in

September 1984 when France and Libya reached an agreement on foreign troop withdrawal.[552] Shortly thereafter, the joint commission that was set up to monitor troop pullout reported that both countries had taken their forces out of Chad. It was soon revealed, however, that Libyan troops continued to be present in northern Chad even though French troops had totally withdrawn.

There was strong reaction to Libya's failure to comply with the agreement. The U.S. urged the French government to send its troops back to Chad and to take tougher measures against Qaddafi to get his forces out of the war-torn country. Mitterrand, however, decided to tolerate the Libyan presence in northern Chad as long as no move was made to oust Habré. This situation changed in February 1986 when Libyan-backed rebels attacked a government outpost at Ziguey. This incident resulted in renewed French intervention in Chad.

From Destabilization to Gunboat Diplomacy

The Reagan administration has been frustrated by its failure to force Qaddafi to change his foreign policy, as well as by his continuous intervention in Chad and other neighboring countries. During his second term, Reagan decided to step up his campaign against Qaddafi, taking advantage of the growing opposition in Libya's Armed Forces to Qaddafi's leadership. In the fall of 1985, Reagan approved a plan to destabilize Qaddafi's rule in Libya. He authorized the CIA to provide covert aid to groups seeking to oust Qaddafi by force. It was hoped that such action would solidify the opposition in general and might encourage dissenting officers to mount a coup to get rid of Qaddafi. If this did not work, it was expected that Algeria or Egypt might take advantage of some pretext to intervene militarily in Libya.[553]

The success of this CIA plan will depend on the willingness of either Algeria or Egypt to participate in the scheme. Yet so far, both governments have been reluctant to take part in this destabilization campaign. Algeria has flatly stated that it has no plan to intervene in Libya's internal affairs. Egypt's Hosni Mubarak, on the other hand, is preoccupied with his country's mounting economic problems. Furthermore, Reagan's orders in October 1985 to intercept the EgyptAir 737 carrying the four Palestinian hijackers of the cruise ship Achille Lauro humiliated Egypt and strained its relations with Washington.[554] One immediate reaction was a week of violent anti-American demonstrations in Cairo. Moreover, Mubarak would find it difficult to take part in Reagan's policy of intervention because, after the overthrow of the Nimeiri regime in the Sudan, Egypt is alone in North Africa in its opposition to Qaddafi.

Despite such a poor response, Reagan has pursued his campaign to make Qaddafi "a pariah in the world community."[555] His administration has seized every opportunity to provoke a confrontation with Qaddafi, who is accused of training and equipping militant Palestinians who have spilled Middle East violence into Europe, subjecting Americans to terrorist attacks abroad. The latest incidents were the coordinated attacks on Rome and Vienna Airports on December 27, 1985, which left 19 people dead, including five Americans. American officials did not wait for the Italian and Austrian authorities to complete their investigations. They immediately blamed Qaddafi for the attacks on the airports and hinted of swift retribution to make Qaddafi pay a high price for his active support of international terrorism. Pentagon officials proceeded to draw contingency plans for a military reprisal against Libya.[556] Reagan, however, decided against any immediate use of force. In a televised news conference on January 7, 1986, Reagan announced an end to all trade and economic activities with Libya, except for humanitarian reasons. He also ordered the 1,000-1,500 Americans working in Libya to return home. He warned that failure to do so would result in criminal charges and prosecution. The following day, he put a freeze on Libya's assets in the U.S.,[557] which are estimated to be several hundred million dollars.

The U.S. boycott is unlikely to have serious economic impact on Libya. Lloyd N. Cutler, Carter's White House Counsel, predicted that it "will have virtually no effect."[558] This is largely because, since late 1981, there has been a sharp drop in U.S. trade with Libya, resulting from Reagan's get-tough-campaign with Qaddafi and the 1982 ban on U.S. imports of Libyan crude oil. Libya has only $2 million in direct investment in the U.S. and has kept only a fraction of its $4 billion reserves in American-controlled banks.[559]

Moreover, the sudden departure of American technicians and executives may have little or no impact on the level of Libya's oil production. Qaddafi can easily replace them with Europeans, who have always shown a readiness to expand their economic ties with Libya.

Reagan is aware of such a possibility. For this reason, he once again urged European allies to join in the U.S. economic sanctions to isolate

Qaddafi. He also made it clear that "Americans will not understand other nations moving into Libya to take commercial advantage of our departure."[560]

There is little likelihood that Libya's major trading partners in Europe will impose economic sanctions because they have extensive commerce with Libya and rely on it for oil supplies. Second, they doubt that sanctions are an effective means to accomplish the desired results. As Margaret Thatcher, the British Prime Minister, put it: "I have never known a case in which sanctions have effectively worked."[561] Third, they do not see eye-to-eye with the U.S. about Qaddafi's threats. There is no definitive proof linking Qaddafi to the airport attacks and in the absence of concrete evidence, they are not ready to initiate punitive economic measures that would mean the loss of billions of dollars in investment, trade, and employment. By Qaddafi's account, there are currently 45,000 Europeans working in Libya and 230 companies doing business there worth about $13 billion.[562] Libya's trade with Europe is estimated to be about $4 billion a year.[563]

These facts diminish the prospect that American officials will persuade their allies to join in international sanctions against Libya. European investigators have concluded that the attacks were carried out by Palestinians who had been trained in the Syrian-controlled Bekaa Valley in Lebanon and who belonged to the Abu-Nidal faction, which broke away in 1974 from Arafat's mainstream Fatah organization. Consequently, European governments are not interested in joining U.S. sanctions that are motivated by Reagan's obsession about Qaddafi's menace, especially at a time when some of them are having economic difficulties that would surely be aggravated if they were to cut off economic ties with Libya. Europeans, acting out of self-interest, have thus far ignored U.S. appeals to mount a coordinated response against Qaddafi.

U.S. sanctions are doomed as long as such European allies as Britain, France, and West Germany are unwilling to join in them. Italy has halted exports of dangerous weapons to Libya but has refused the sweeping measures advocated by the U.S. However, it has promised that "no Italian workers would be allowed to take up jobs abandoned by Americans now working in Libya."[564]

An argument could be made that Reagan imposed sanctions against Libya because he felt he needed to do something to fulfill his promise of swift retribution against terrorism. His resort to sanctions as a political weapon is merely symbolic of his frustration in dealing with

Qaddafi, especially his inability to force Qaddafi to change his policies.

It should be noted that Reagan has not ruled out the use of force against Libya. He has promised to take "further steps," if economic measures "do not end Qaddafi's terrorism."[565] To increase pressure on Qaddafi, the USS *Saratoga* joined the USS *Coral Sea* in the Mediterranean Sea in mid-January. The stationing of these two aircraft carrier battle groups, totalling 28 ships, off the coast of Libya gives the Reagan administration a readily available capability to strike against Libya on a short notice. Moreover, the departure of American citizens from Libya "clear[ed] the decks" for possible military actions without fear of another hostage crisis.[566]

American officials are still trying to convince their European allies to join the U.S. in a concerted effort to force Qaddafi to abandon his support of international terrorism. They apparently put off military retaliation in an effort to avoid a rift with their NATO allies over Qaddafi. They are willing to give the Europeans more time to come up with a plan to counter Qaddafi's threats but, if they fail to do so, the U.S. would still be free to act unilaterally. This might lead to the use of air strikes against suspected terrorist camps in Libya.

In response to American threats, Libyan officials have considered Reagan's call for international sanctions against their country as "tantamount politically to a declaration of war."[567] Qaddafi has warned European envoys in Tripoli that "we will drag Europe into [the war]," if the U.S. uses their bases in Europe to launch an attack on Libya.[568] Qaddafi has also taken several steps to avoid being caught by a surprise attack and to ensure military preparedness in case of a military confrontation with the U.S. For example, anti-aircraft SA-5 missiles are now fully operative and manned by Soviet technicians – a situation that will prove to be problematic for any U.S. air strikes. Some Soviets might get killed inadvertently. Also, in a move to support the embattled Qaddafi, the Soviet Union has increased its fleet in the Mediterranean Sea to 28 ships and has stationed "the flagship of [its] Mediterranean fleet, a submarine tender packed with electronic gear, in Tripoli harbor."[569] These moves are intended to counter the deployment of American warships off the Libyan coast and to discourage the Reagan administration from ordering military actions against Libya. It should also be noted that many Muslim and Arab governments have condemned the U.S. economic and military moves against Libya.

These developments, however, did not discourage Reagan from

pressing on with his campaign against Qaddafi. In January and February 1986, the U.S. conducted a series of air and sea maneuvers off the Libyan coast, just north of the disputed Gulf of Sirte. This show of force was intended to demonstrate U.S. resolve to compel Qaddafi to cease his support for militant Palestinian factions and other revolutionary groups. Reagan, however, was careful in avoiding a military confrontation with Libya—a confrontation which might drag the Soviet Union into the squabble with Qaddafi. The U.S. did so by keeping the two aircraft carrier battle groups well north of the 32nd and 33rd parallels drawn by Qaddafi as the limits of his country's territorial waters. Qaddafi called it "the line of death" and threatened to go to war if the U.S. carriers crossed it.[570]

Qaddafi accused the U.S. of "aggressive provocation" for conducting these exercises so close to Libya. In response, he put his armed forces on "total alert" and sent his Air Force to patrol the skies over the Gulf. When Libyan planes headed toward the U.S. carriers, they were immediately challenged by U.S. jets. The crisis was averted when Libyan pilots turned back.[571]

In a show of defiance, Qaddafi sailed aboard a missile-carrying patrol boat to "the line of death" where he was planning to "stand and fight."[572] His action was intended to show that he was not afraid of the U.S.

Qaddafi turned the crisis to his advantage by talking tough in the face of the U.S. threats and by urging the Arab states to back his tiny country in its confrontation with the super-power. He managed to avoid a military showdown with the U.S., thus escaping the trap set up by American strategists who had expected him to challenge the U.S. military presence off the Libyan coast. By doing so, Qaddafi did not provide Reagan with a pretext to strike inside Libya without appearing as the aggressor.

The U.S. failure to provoke a military response from Qaddafi led Reagan to send the USS *Saratoga* and the USS *Coral Sea* back near the Libyan coast. In March, they were joined by the USS *America* and conducted another maneuver in the Gulf of Sirte south of "the line of death." Such action was a direct challenge to Qaddafi and, in turn, led to a skirmish with the U.S. It resulted in the sinking of two Libyan gunboats, the disabling of two others and the destruction of an anti-aircraft radar site at Surt.[573] Shortly thereafter, the Reagan administration ended the naval exercises off Libya ahead of schedule.

In response, Qaddafi announced that his country would conduct naval exercises in the Mediterranean 100 miles north of Sirte. In addition, Libyans began repairing the damaged SA-5 anti-aircraft missile site at Surt as well as completing another one at Benghazi.[574] These two sites would enable Qaddafi to better protect the Gulf of Sirte in the face of new American intrusion in what he considers to be his country's territorial waters.

Reagan, however, decided to keep up the pressure on Qaddafi to abandon his support for terrorism. In mid-April 1986, Reagan ordered an air strike against Libya in retaliation for the bombing of a Berlin discotheque earlier that month. That bombing had killed two, including an American, and wounded 230. American officials accused Libya of being behind that incident as well as of orchestrating a "campaign of terror directed through the Libyan diplomatic channels and missions specifically targeting Americans."[575]

On April 14, F-111 fighter bombers and A-6 attack planes dropped tons of explosives on five military and intelligence targets in Benghazi and Tripoli, including Qaddafi's official residence and headquarters at the Bab Al-Azzizia barracks. Reagan defended the raid as "necessary and appropriate" pre-emptive action "directed against the Libyan terrorist infrastructure and designed to deter acts of terrorism by Libya."[576]

It was evident, however, that a primary objective was to kill Qaddafi because at least one F-111 bomber dropped four bombs, each weighing 2,000 lbs., on Qaddafi's residence.[577] Although Qaddafi survived the attack, his infant daughter was killed and two sons were seriously wounded. In addition, residential areas in Tripoli were bombed by U.S. warplanes, killing dozens of people[578] and injuring more than 100. The raid has aroused anger among Libyans, who took to the streets in demonstrations against the U.S. Notably, the attack did not touch off a coup to get rid of Qaddafi—something that the Reagan administration had hoped would occur.[579] Neither did it halt terrorism as Libyan threats of retaliation were echoed. Consequently, reprisal attacks against Americans have been reported in the Middle East and Europe.

The American military action was condemned by all Arab states, except Tunisia, and by non-aligned nations. It was supported only by Israel, Canada and Britain. Margaret Thatcher, Britain's Prime Minister, was the most supportive. She had allowed the U.S. to use its warplanes based in Britain for the raid on Libya. Other European countries were indifferent. France and Spain had denied U.S. planes the permission to use their airspace en route to Libya; Italy and West Germany criticized the U.S. military action against Libya.[580]

Ironically, on the day of bombing, the twelve members of the European Community decided to: (1) reduce the number of Libyan diplomats and restrict their travel outside the cities in which they serve; (2) limit the number of Libyans entering their countries and deny entry to Libyans expelled from another country; and (3) scrutinize closely Libyans living in their countries.[581]

It should be noted that these measures were adopted in part to meet America's anger that Europe did not join the U.S. economic sanctions or back its military actions against Libya. European governments hoped that these actions would forestall further U.S. retaliatory strikes against Libya and thwart further reprisal attacks on American citizens and installations in Europe.

The Reagan administration, however, has continued to pressure its European allies for more coordinated punitive actions against Qaddafi's Libya. In response, at the economic summit in Tokyo in May 1986, the seven industrialized nations decided to fight terrorism "relentlessly and without compromise." They singled out Libya for action but failed to agree on economic sanctions. Instead, they expanded on the measures already adopted by the European Community. They agreed to "improve extradition procedures for bringing to trial those accused of terrorist acts" and to have "more restrictive rules of entry for persons suspected or accused of terrorist acts." In addition, they placed "restrictions on arms sales to nations sponsoring terrorists, limits on their diplomatic missions and personnel, and closer cooperation between law enforcement authorities."[582]

Reagan's efforts to line up Western Europe behind his get-tough campaign with Qaddafi have led to further deterioration in the relationship between Libya and the U.S. This is largely because neither Reagan nor Qaddafi is willing to back down: both have stuck to their rigid positions. While Reagan insists that Qaddafi must abandon his support for international terrorism, Qaddafi has vowed to continue his support for the Palestinian armed struggle and other revolutionary groups. Consequently, the stalemate is like to continue for some time.

No improvement in relations can be expected until there is a change in leadership in either country. Reagan is counting on driving Qaddafi out of office by using U.S might to embarrass him and to erode his influence inside Libya. In doing so, he hopes that Libyan opposition in the Armed Forces might be tempted to move against Qaddafi.

Time will only tell whether such a strategy can work in Libya, where Qaddafi has so far managed to eliminate opposition before it becomes a threat to his revolution and his system of government.

Conclusion

The coming of Ronald Reagan to the White House has marked a decisive turn in U.S.-Libyan relations. From the start, Reagan has pursued a policy of confrontation toward Qaddafi, whose policies have clashed with American interests in the Middle East, Africa and beyond. He has chosen Libya to demonstrate his tough anti-communist stance, in part because Qaddafi has maintained close ties with the Soviet Union and has purchased a huge Soviet arsenal. Qaddafi also has pursued an anti-Western policy, which has led him to support revolutionary groups seeking to overthrow pro-Western governments or to weaken Western influence in the highly strategic regions of the world. The Republican administration has been determined to meet Qaddafi's challenges in the Arab world and Africa directly and to frustrate his drive to set up a pan-Islamic or pan-Arab state. As Secretary of State Haig privately put it, Qaddafi is a "cancer which must be cut out."[583]

Since 1981, the Reagan administration has initiated a series of actions to make Qaddafi's life less comfortable. First, it closed the Libyan embassy in Washington and expelled Libyan diplomats from the U.S. Second, in August 1981, it conducted a naval exercise in the Gulf of Sirte, which Qaddafi has claimed as part of Libya's territorial waters. This exercise resulted in the downing of two Libyan planes and significant deterioration in U.S.-Libyan relations. Third, the administration urged American oil companies operating Libyan oil fields to pull out American technicians and executives. Shortly thereafter, it imposed an economic boycott against Libya, denying Qaddafi about $12 billion a year in the sale of oil to the U.S. Fourth, at Washington's urging, several African governments twice boycotted the scheduled OAU summit in Tripoli in 1982. In doing so, the Reagan administration successfully blocked Qaddafi from becoming the OAU chairman for 1982-1983.

When the Chad civil war broke out again in 1983, the Reagan administration airlifted military equipment to help the embattled Habré government repel the attack by the Qaddafi-backed faction of Goukouni. It also pressured France to provide air coverage to Habré's army in the face of intensified air raids by the Libyan Air Force. When France finally intervened, the fighting came to a halt but only after the Goukouni forces had already established themselves in northern Chad. The cessation of hostilities eventually led to an agreement in September 1984 to withdraw foreign troops from Chad. Although the French did so, the Libyans have continued their military presence, causing a *de facto* partition of the country and increasing the possibility of another round of fighting which did occur in February 1986.

Reagan's policy of confrontation has been counterproductive. It has failed to force Qaddafi to change his ways of conducting his foreign policy and has, in fact, caused Qaddafi to defiantly vow to continue his support for the Palestinian struggle[584] and other revolutionary groups. Qaddafi has consistently made U.S. adversaries his friends. The Sandinista government in Nicaragua, for instance, has been provided with weapons and material support to stand up against the U.S.-backed Contras. Qaddafi scored a success recently when the pro-U.S. regime of Nimeiri was overthrown in the Sudan. The new government not only restored diplomatic relations with Tripoli but also signed a defense pact with Libya.

Reagan's hostility has also led Qaddafi to move closer to the Soviet Union. Since 1981, he has paid frequent visits to Moscow to confer with Soviet leaders in the Kremlin. During his most recent trip in October 1985, he signed several agreements to increase cultural, economic, and scientific cooperation between the two countries.[585] Qaddafi has also allowed the Soviet Navy to pay visits to his country as well as to conduct joint maneuvers off the Libyan coast, the latest of which took place in May 1985.[586] It is reported that Qaddafi has been under pressure to grant the Soviets a naval base in Libya. So far, he has resisted this pressure but recently has threatened to sign a pact with Moscow if the U.S. continues its aggression against his country.

In early 1986, U.S.-Libyan relations took a turn for the worse when Reagan blamed Qaddafi for the bloody attacks on Rome and Vienna airports at the end of December. Although no proof was found of direct Libyan involvement in these attacks, American officials have hinted about possible military retaliation and have taken punitive measures against Qaddafi for his support of international terrorism. Despite the fact that Reagan's 1982 economic boycott was ineffective in causing serious economic hardship for Libya, Reagan decided, in January 1986, to reimpose economic sanctions against Libya. Americans who had previously ignored the President's 1982 directive about not working in Libya were now ordered to quit their jobs and return to the U.S. This was intended to tighten economic sanctions and to deny Libya access to American technology and personnel.

The Reagan administration is also trying to get its European allies to join in the sanctions. This might prove to be rather difficult. Yet they have resisted such moves ever since the 1982 U.S.-imposed economic boycott against Libya. Their failure to join the sanctions will leave the U.S. alone in its confrontation with Qaddafi and will certainly undermine Reagan's plan for using the economic weapon to bring about changes in Qaddafi's foreign policy. Although there has been a sharp drop in Libya's oil revenues in the past four years, this was not due to the U.S. economic boycott as much as to the current oil glut in the world market and falling oil prices.[587]

The current atmosphere is charged with tension, with a distinct possibility of further military confrontation. Aside from conducting air and sea maneuvers in the Gulf of Sirte, Reagan has already ordered one air strike against Libya and has persuaded European and Japanese allies to impose some restrictions on the Libyan diplomatic missions. On the day of bombing, Reagan said, "Today, we have done what we had to do. If necessary, we shall do it again."[588] This attitude is not conducive to turning the relationship around since neither Reagan nor Qaddafi has shown any sign of compromise. Qaddafi has vowed to continue his support for revolutionary causes. As he put it, "We will not abandon our incitement for popular revolution, whatever raids they carry out."[589] As a result, U.S.-Libyan relations are expected to move from bad to worse as long as Reagan and Qaddafi remain in power in their countries. Any improvement in relations will have to wait until there is a change in leadership in either Tripoli or Washington.

Excerpts from the Historic Zwara

Speech made by Muammar Qadhafi on April 15, 1973. *

The Five Points for the Continuation of the Revolution

If we want the Revolution to continue, we have to start anew. But how?

First: To Abrogate All Laws

All laws at present should be cancelled while revolutionary work will continue to lay down new measures. The new measures will be based on laws which are compatible with what is actually taking place. This does not mean any threat to the life and security of the people. That will never happen because we are Muslims and apply the Islamic law. If you apply the law of God, it is impossible to wrong any person or threaten his security.

Second: To Purge the Country of the Sick Persons

It is inevitable to purge the country of all sick people. Three years have gone by since the inception of the First of September Revolution, and I have forbidden the arrest of any person who stands against the people. I tried with all means not to pay attention to such persons, hoping that they might be cured naturally although they have been intriguing against the people and against the revolutionary transformation. They intrigue against the revolutionary cause in one way or another. The person who stays at home and neglects his work, and the one who is appointed to a project and shows reluctance to take up his post . . . those persons intrigue against the people. This is a kind of intrigue as well as a sort of hindrance to the revolutionary transformation and betrayal of the people.

We have promulgated various laws which have not been carried out for no other reason but the desire to forget and forgive the past.

What we do is different from what is taking place secretly under the Arab regimes. If we talk about Islam, it is because no other country adheres strictly to the essence of Islam like the Libyan Arab Republic. Likewise, if we talk about progressivism, the Libyan Arab Republic is more progressive than both the East and the West. The communists themselves testified that the popular progressive rule in our country does not exist in the communist world which claims progressive, popular rule. A delegation from North Korea said on visiting us: *"Your popular, progressive rule is unique in the world. It exists neither in Korea, nor in Russia or China."*

Third: Freedom of the People

I think that freedom should be for all Libyan people and not for their enemies. If there are ten persons, freedom must be for nine at the expense of one and not vice-versa. This is the right rule and this is the "Shariat." One of the principles on which democracy is based all over the world is that the minority must yield to the will of the majority.

Those people whose relatives died in the aeroplane event (the Libyan civil aeroplane shot down by the Israelis) which left no less effect on us, those people started to spread rumours, curse and call bad names everywhere. The right thing for those people to do, in my opinion, is to accept the challenge. They should be trained, armed and sent to join any Arab army or front . . . Three or five persons can be infiltrated into Palestine, if they want revenge, let them accept the challenge. But I know that they will not do that, for they only want to sit in cafes and spread rumours. Such logic is not accepted. I shall not allow anybody who is not able to accept the challenge to poison the people's minds.

Instructions will be given to the minister of interior to purge any group of those sick people. If a member of the Muslim Brotherhood or the Islamic Liberation Party engages in clandestine activity, his activities will be considered sabotage against the Revolution which was triggered for the people.

There are some people whom I knew and forgave what they had committed. But they will not be allowed to continue poisoning the people's minds.

Freedom should be for the oppressed masses rather than for those who look down on the people, therefore we shall distribute arms among many sectors apart from the armed forces and the popular resistance. It is for the masses that we revolted, because they were deprived of freedom for more than 400 years. Arms will be distributed among the masses who believe in the First of September Revolution. This will be a new experiment.

While regimes are usually afraid of their peoples and recruit armies and police for their protection, I, on the contrary, shall arm the Libyan masses who believe in the First of September Revolution. But whoever stands against the Revolution will not be given arms. Arms will be used against him.

The whole people will, thus, become a popular resistance. I tell you that you should not depend on the armed forces to protect the Libyan soil. Libya is only protected when all the people carry arms and stand against any aggressor.

Fourth: Revolution Against Bureaucracy

Those who stay at home and become a barrier between the Revolution and the masses; those who leave their work if there is not a head to supervise over them; those who close the doors in the face of the citizens and put off their needs . . .   all those belong to the bourgeois class—such a bureaucratic class necessitates the declaration of the administrative revolution. The masses whom I shall arm will destroy bureaucracy and do away with the barriers.

Every one of us is ready to carry arms, as we did on the First of September, and we are willing to take to the streets to defend the Revolution and to achieve Arab unity. We are ready to start anew so that the Revolution may continue as we planned. I do not care if all the masses become a force that destroys whatever stands in its way. I want the masses, for whom the Revolution took place, to come out victorious and be close to us.

Thus a revolution starts. Any bureaucratic person who says to any citizen, "come tomorrow," or neglects his work, should expect a man from the street to come and revolt against him. What is really important is that the masses should eventually come out victorious.

I am aware of the fact that there is an administrative organ that stands as a barrier in the face of the masses. It grows day after day. Revolution should be declared against such a structure. Accordingly whoever wants to join our march should become a revolutionary but he who stands against us will be trodden by our feet. The First of September

Revolution was not triggered for the mercenaries, but for the poor and oppressed Libyan masses.

If the people's interests are lost in the offices, such offices should be destroyed for the sake of the people's interests. If those interests are threatened by the government, down with that government, and long live the people.

Fifth: The Cultural Revolution

We declare to the whole world that the ideology of the First of September stems from the eternal message of Islam and from the Holy Quran. We are sure that we apply the sound ideology and the great humanitarian thought declared by the Prophet Mohammed, Peace be upon His soul, who took the people out of darkness and led them to the light of Faith. We adhere to the *Book of God*, as we believe that there could not be any other ideology as solemn and as profound as the *Book of God*. I do not think that there is any thing more trusted by Man all over the world than the *Book of God*. That is why we apply that Book. Any different ideology from other books is regarded as misleading.

Those who are called Beatles are sick. From where did they get the disease? From misleading and reactionary readings, be they Western or Eastern, Communism or Capitalism. The misleading reactionary readings have changed our young men into Beatles.

Those who want to stand against the revolution must be aware of the fact that the revolution will be as it was in the First of September Revolution.

This means that we can accomplish all the revolutionary projects in the shortest possible time through the working forces of the people who are really interested in the revolution. Thus, the Libyan people will be the first people in the world to have triggered a unique revolution in history to carry arms, build themselves and reorganise their life on their territory.

The masses to whom I addressed the First Statement of the Revolution will march and take over responsibility. That necessitates that you stand by the leaders of the revolution to do away with the bourgeoisie, bureaucracy and corrupt thought; to carry arms; to build factories and roads; to farm the plantations, and be ready to sacrifice everything for the revolutionary transformation. That means that the people should bear the responsibility of ruling.

Only through your efforts can all these things be achieved and the battles won. If you fail to achieve them, our main objectives will not be realized.

Rabi Alawal 12, 1393 H.
(Corresponding to April 15, 1973 A.D.)

The Arab Socialist People's Libyan Arab Jamahiriya: The Basic Facts. Ottawa, Canada: Jerusalem International Publishing House, 1982, pp. 60-65.

Declaration on the Establishment of the Authority of the People*

The Libyan Arab people assembled in the general conference of the People's Congresses, the People's Committees, and the Professional Unions (The General People's Congress/The National Congress);

Having reviewed the recommendations of the People's Congresses, the Constitutional Declaration of Shawal 2, 1389 H. (corresponding to December 11, 1969 A.D.) and the resolutions and the recommendations of the General People's Congress which met during the period from Muharram 4-17, 1396 H. (corresponding to January 5 through 18, 1976 A.D.);

Believing in the establishment of the direct democratic system heralded by the Great First of September Revolution and regarding it as the absolute and decisive solution to the problem of democracy;

Embodying the pioneer experiment of the popular rule on the soil of the Great First of September Revolution which established the authority of the People, who alone should have the authority;

Declare their adherence to freedom and willingness to defend it on the Libyan land and on any other land in the world.

Declare their preparedness to protect the persecuted freedom-seekers.

Declare their adherence to socialism as a means of achieving People's ownership.

Declare their commitment to spiritual values to safeguard morals and human behavior.

Support the march of the Revolution toward complete popular authority and consolidation of the people's Society where only the people control leadership, authority, wealth and arms—to realize the Society of Freedom.

Declare their total commitment to blocking the way in face of all forms of traditional instruments of government—be they individual, family, tribe, sect, class, representative, party, or group of parties.

191

Declare their readiness to crush forever any undemocratic attempt.

The Libyan Arab People, have regained–through the Revolution–total control over their affairs, and controlling their present and future potentialities with the help of Allah and adherence to His Holy Book as the everlasting source for guidance and as the ordinance of society.

Issue this declaration proclaiming the establishment of the People's authority and announcing to the peoples of the earth the emergence of the era of the masses:

Article I

The official name of Libya will be "The Socialist People's Libyan Arab Jamahiriya."

Article II

The Holy Kuran is the constitution of the Socialist People's Libyan Arab Jamahiriya.

Article III

The People's direct democracy is the basis of the political system in the Socialist People's Libyan Arab Jamahiriya, where the authority is in the hands of the People alone. The People exercise their authority through the People's Congresses, the People's Committees and the Professional Unions. The regulations of the congresses, committees and professional unions as well as the dates of their meetings are defined by Law.

The authority of the People is comprised of the following:

1. People's Congresses
2. People's Committees
3. Professional Unions
4. General People's Congress

People's Congresses

1. People are divided into basic People's Congresses.
2. All citizens register themselves as members of the basic People's Congress in their areas.
3. Every basic People's Congress shall choose from its members a committee to lead the congress.

People's Committees

The masses of the People's Congresses shall choose People's Committees to administer all the services. These Committees are responsible to the People's Congresses.

Professional Unions

Members of each profession shall form their own union to defend their professional rights.

General People's Congress

The General People's Congress is the national conference of the People's Congresses, People's Committees and Professional Unions. The General People's Congress shall have a General Secretariat to execute the general policy of the State as defined by the People's Congress, as well as drawing up the agenda of the General People's Congress and executing its resolutions and recommendations. The General Secretariat shall consist of a Secretary General and a number of secretaries; each shall supervise one of the sectors of activities in the State.

Article IV

The General People's Congress shall choose a chairman to preside over its sessions, to sign the laws by order of the Congress and to accept the credentials of the representatives of foreign countries.

Article V

In the case of absence of the Chairman of the General People's Congress or if something hinders him from performing his duties, the Secretary General will temporarily replace him.

Article VI

The General People's Congress chooses the Secretary General and the Secretaries, dismisses them and accepts their resignations from their posts.

The Secretary General and the Secretaries are jointly responsible to the General People's Congress, while every secretary is responsible for the sector he supervises.

Article VII

The General Budget of the State is issued by a law and the General People's Congress endorses the balance sheet of the State.

Article VIII

Law regulates the establishment of public departments and appointments and dismissals of government employees.

Article IX

Defending the country is the responsibility of every citizen. Through general military training, the People shall be trained and armed. Law regulates the method for preparing military cadres and the general military training.

Article X

The terms "Council of Ministers," "Prime Minister" and "Minister" are to be replaced, wherever mentioned, by the terms "General Secretariat of the General People's Congress," "Secretary General" and "The Secretary."

Libyan Papers No. 12. Published by the Mission of the Libyan Arab Jamahiriya to the United Nations, 1979.

LIBYA
Daring to Hope Again*

Blood, Tyranny, Subversion

Martyrs' Day

The seventh of April is a significant day in recent Libyan history. In 1977 three Libyan citizens were hanged publicly in the main square in Benghazi. One was left to die slowly and agonizingly over the course of two days. To prolong their amusement his executioners ensured that the rope was just long enough for his toes to reach the ground. But only just; gradually, in the desperate struggle for life, he weakened and finally choked and died.

There have, of course, been many martyrs in Gaddafi's Libya. In April that year 21 army officers were put to death while, on 7 April 1983, a student, imprisoned for ten years without charge or trial, was hanged at Tripoli University. Crowds of students and schoolchildren were brought along to watch the event. After the execution the student's body was dragged around the university precinct by "revolutionary committees" members. In Egdabia, on the same day, four teachers, two of them of Palestinian origin, were hanged at four different schools in the presence of their families and pupils. Small wonder that 7 April has come to be known, both inside Libya and without, as martyrs' day.

Relentless Ambition

The coup which brought Muammar Gaddafi to power in September 1969 overthrew both king and constitution. Libya, since, has been subjected to the whim and will of one man, determined whatever the cost to pursue relentlessly his own ambitions. Accepted codes of conduct – human dignity, truth, honour – form no part of the master plan. Instead a hotch-potch of ideas have been imposed on the Libyan people by the "Green Book" and the "third universal theory." Gaddafi is the self-appointed "thinker" and "legislator," dictating all

195

policies and taking all major decisions. Through a system of no government he extricates himself from responsibility, which he leaves collectively to "revolutionary committees," his own brainchild and instrument of government. The country exists in a state of tension and fear. There is no constitution. In 1973 a "popular revolution" abrogated all laws and abolished the administrative system, thus paving the way for Gaddafi's "third universal theory" under the guise of a so-called "cultural revolution."

Exporting Revolution

Libya is a small country with a population of just over three million people. With freedom dearly won from Italy in 1951, there was at least a hope of stability and prosperity. Certainly the Libyan people had not demonstrated any other aggressive intent and enjoyed cordial relations with the outside world. They had not shown any desire to subvert, undermine or otherwise seek territorial advantage over any of their neighbours or more distant Arab and African brethren. Yet, in Gaddafi's years of power they have been drawn into prospective unity or federation with the Sudan, Egypt, Syria, Algeria, Tunisia and Chad – all madhatter schemes which collapsed in disarray and precipitated more discord and strife as Gaddafi sought to export his own brand of revolutionary violence.

When his attempts to unite with Egypt failed, Gaddafi sent thousands of Libyans across the desert to the Egyptian border – only to see them stopped and turned back. When he was rebuffed by President Bourguiba of Tunisia in 1974, he dispatched an assassination squad to Tunis to murder the Tunisian president but the terrorists were intercepted in time. In 1976, Gaddafi organized a full-blown invasion of the Sudan using West African mercenaries and dissident Sudanese as his task force. Enormous damage was done to Khartoum before the invaders were routed. No credence can ever be given to any statement he makes. In short, he is totally untrustworthy or, as recently described by King Hussein of Jordan: "The Libyan regime has never adhered to any sacred promises and has not respected the rights imposed by brotherly ties. It abrogates in the morning the agreement it approved the previous evening."

No less serious have been Gaddafi's direct military interventions in Chad and Lebanon where he has contributed in full measure to the continuing misery in those unhappy countries. His soldiers have fought in Uganda in support of Idi Amin. He has helped to overthrow democracy in Ghana and actively conspired against the recognized governments of perhaps nine other African countries. He has financed terrorism far from any area which could remotely be called his sphere of influence – in Italy, West Germany, Northern Ireland, the Phillippines and Central and South America.

Humiliation

What has he gained for himself and his country apart from the fear and contempt of so many? Humiliation certainly. For the first time in its history the Organization of African Unity (OAU) refused to hold its annual summit in 1982 in a selected host country – Libya – and repeated the refusal on a later occasion. By the same gesture Gaddafi failed to become the Chairman of the OAU and caused a yawning split in the ranks of OAU members by his actions over Chad and Western Sahara. He can also be held in large measure responsible for the splitting in two of the Palestine Revolution, for which he will never be forgiven by the Palestinians and the great majority in the Arab world. Arab countries – notably at Fez in 1982, and again in 1983 – while preserving certain courtesies, keep him at arm's length.

His failures predominate: the retreat from Uganda; the loss of hundreds of his men in Chad; the sacrifice of his pilots in a futile mission against the U.S. Sixth Fleet; the bombastic instructions to the PLO, beseiged by the Israelis in Beirut, while not lifting a finger to help them. Failure, however, does not make him any less dangerous.

Libya's immense oil wealth has been a bottomless well from which Gaddafi has drawn at will to finance his adventures both at home and abroad. At independence Libya was one of the poorest countries in the world. Now, thanks to oil, it has the highest per capita income in Africa. But this most precious resource has been squandered by futile and reckless expenditure, and the Libyan people are the last to benefit from it, if at all.

Reorganization of Government

Typical of the extravagance has been continual reorganization of government and the administrative infrastructure. During the years after the 1973 "revolution," the system of local administrative rule which prevailed under the monarchy was changed more than four times. The first change came in 1973 when local administration was divided into ten governorates. Within three years this system was changed into an administration of 55 zones under the direct control of central government ministries. This was then converted into an administration of 48 municipalities and, later again, to one of 28 municipalities. With each alteration of the administrative structure there was a total turnover in terms of personnel and resources, throwing an intolerable strain on a bureaucracy already short of skilled man-power. Increasing [in]efficiency and creeping corruption, pervading all corners of the system, have been the predictable results.

The Myth of Development

The administrative chaos has been compounded by the frequent changes made to the texts of laws and regulations governing financial practices. With the huge revenues from oil being pumped into the economy, development leapt ahead without legal guidelines or constraints. Fortunes were made by a few, while grandiose and im-plausible agricultural schemes were launched, often without preliminary investigation. Overall the sums spent on development actually fell to less than 40 percent of the total revenue from oil after 1974, despite the law passed in 1970 stipulating that the development budget should be 59.5 percent of revenue from oil. Part of the tragedy of Libya is that the country had a unique opportunity to develop a productive economy as a hedge to the day when the oil would dry up. Instead, even when oil was showing its highest returns, Libya was facing an acute liquidity crisis with enormous budget deficits.

Massive Arsenal

A continual strain on the economy has been the expenditure on the armed forces which has swallowed up annually well over fifty per-cent of the revenues generated by oil.

According to the International Institute for Strategic Studies (1983/1984), Gaddafi's army now stands at 58,000 men and women, compared to 20,000 in 1971. His airforce has 8,500, his navy 6,500. To help compensate for the national shortage of manpower, Gaddafi formed a so-called "Islamic Legion," consisting of over 10,000 irregular soldiers of mixed Arab and African nationality. This force, wholly funded and equipped by Libya and functioning as an integral part of the Libyan armed forces, has been used as a spearhead for Libyan aggression in Chad, the Sudan and elsewhere.

As an indication of the almost incredible expenditure on armaments, the ratio of armour per serving soldier has been estimated as greater in Libya than in any other country in the world. The army has 2,600 tanks, 2,000 armoured personnel carriers and armoured cars and over 1,000 conventional artillery pieces. It is fully equipped with long-range surface to surface missiles. The airforce has 533 combat aircraft and 30 combat helicopters; the navy with 23 missile carrying craft, corvettes and eight submarines (6 Soviet F-class, 2 midget submarines) will soon be the largest and most modern in North Africa and the Middle East.

Most of this extraordinary arsenal, replenished on a continual basis, has been purchased from the Soviet Union and 4,000 Soviet bloc military personnel are involved in Libya's training, logistics and maintenance programmes, including a large number of East Germans. The East Germans advise Gaddafi's intelligence and security services. They are undoubtedly a vital prop for the regime and have acted swiftly to deal with any serious threat to Gaddafi. There are also Poles and Cubans in service with the airforce and the armoured corps. It is notable that Gaddafi has always publicly supported Poland's military regime in its confrontation with Solidarity.

Other more shadowy figures have flitted across the Gaddafi stage as he has conspired with underworld characters to circumvent arms embargoes and import sophisticated equipment for terrorist activity. He has even sought to buy an atomic bomb from the People's Republic of China and tried to persuade the Indian Atomic Energy Commission to build a plant that could give Libya access to plutonium.

Soviet Commitment

The strength of the Soviet commitment to Gaddafi should be of serious concern to all strategists. The Soviets, poised behind the cloak of Gaddafi's eccentricity, are ready to take immediate advantage of any opportunity. The treaty between Libya, Ethiopia and South Yemen is one such opportunity with grave implications for the stability of the Sudan and ultimately for the security of Egypt and Saudi Arabia. Likewise, Gaddafi's meddling in the Iran-Iraq war is a further threat to the security of the area and to the oil routes, while his presence in the Lebanon alongside Syria undermines stability and peace in the region. In West Africa he supported and sustained the Rawlings' coup in Ghana which led, in turn, to the overthrow of the military regime in Upper Volta. Undoubtedly he sees Ghana as a staging post for subversion in West Africa and both Niger and Togo recently experienced attempted coups. Gaddafi, facing French forces in Chad where he now controls half the country through his satrap, Goukouni

Oueddei, is well on course to entrench his authority over the rest of the country.

In Latin America he continues to support the Sandinista regime in Nicaragua and the guerrillas in El Salvador with huge disbursements of aid and arms. He has established a network of subversion throughout the Caribbean – his People's Bureau was the only Embassy in Grenada before the American assault on the island – and in key South American countries. During Britain's war with the Argentine over the Falklands, he gave the Argentine's dictatorial regime moral and practical backing.

The Politics of Trade

Yet – despite all – Gaddafi commands little censure. Trade with oil rich Libya is apparently too valuable to recession-hit industrial economies to put at risk by taking any moral stands. In the last year Gaddafi has squared up to the French army in Chad, successfully blackmailed the West German government, and imprisoned the nationals of other countries, such as the unfortunate Robert Maxwell from Britain – all actions taken with total impunity, secure in the knowledge that these countries will continue to trade with him. Only the U.S.A. has tried trade sanctions, and these have been widely ineffective.

Plots and Purges

What, then, of the unfortunate people of Libya? Gaddafi lives as many dictators have lived. He never sleeps in the same bed on consecutive nights. He directs his policies from the main Libyan army headquarters at Bab Al Azizia where he is protected by the elaborate security systems set up by his East German advisers. Under him power rests with trusted confidantes and relatives. The gap between this ruling clique and the Libyan people widens every day.

Even the power structures created by Gaddafi for the new dawn of his *"Jamahiriya"* are now suspect in their loyalty to him, none less than the army, disillusioned after the Chad adventures. Groups of officers have stood out against him and plots and purges are frequent. Indeed, open opposition to Gaddafi has been evident from the early days of his rule. There have been at least five major take-over attempts – in 1970, 1971, 1975, 1980 and 1982. Students uprisings occurred in 1975, 1976, 1977 and 1982, in addition to several direct attempts on Gaddafi's life.

Last year, as oil revenues fell, the Libyan economy came under further strain, and criticism from the "people's committees" and "congresses" in the provincial areas began to filter through to an extent that the annual "general people's congress" had to be postponed. This trend was more evident this year when the "congresses" blocked a number of key laws that Gaddafi wanted to have passed.

Human Rights

Amnesty International, the human rights organization, has been assiduous in its monitoring of Libya's appalling human rights violations. It reported that, in the first half of 1977, a large number of executions had been carried out and it had drawn attention, following a mission to Libya in October 1976, to the numbers of people held for political reasons, often for lengthy periods before being brought to "trial." It expressed concern at the inadequacy of legal safeguards, at the use of the death penalty, and at reports of torture. Amnesty has continued to make representations on behalf of "prisoners of conscience" and has attended the trials of journalists and writers, 18 of whom were seized and imprisoned in December 1978. The stories that have come out of Libya invariably speak of increased torture and the death, in custody, of political prisoners. These form only the tip of a sizeable iceberg.

Extra Judicial Killings

But perhaps the greatest international revulsion of all was caused by the "extra judicial killings" of the opponents of the regime following Gaddafi's official call early in 1980, to liquidate Libyans living abroad who did not make arrangements to return to Libya. The first intimation that the assassination programme was going to be launched came from the publication in Libyan newspapers in February of that year of a declaration issued by the third meeting of "revolutionary committees" at Gar Younis University, Benghazi, authorizing the "physical liquidation" of "enemies of the revolution abroad." Gaddafi was to repeat this threat on a number of occasions while, in several European capitals—London, Rome, Milan, Athens and Bonn (and Beirut)—trained assassination squads murdered totally innocent civilians. At least a dozen Libyan exiles met their deaths.

Pausing in his grisly task only because of an international outcry, Gaddafi still never repudiated his obscene assassination programme.

Instead he strengthened his security services through his "People's Bureaux" (embassies) and watched his enemies, determined to strike again.

In March 1983 a similar series of statements emanating from Gaddafi intimated that the terror campaign in European cities was about to resume. Intensive foreign diplomatic activity finally persuaded him to hold off. But for how long? The more he feels threatened the more certain it is that he will strike again–at any imaginary foe, and in any direction, as the recent bombings in London and Manchester have shown.

And Gaddafi is threatened as never before. Both inside and outside Libya a growing body of men and women now have the courage to say "enough." Enough to degradation; enough to paranoia; enough to suppression of human rights; enough to terror and murder; enough to the perversion of the sacred religion of Islam. The movement, the motivation and the organization of an end to tyranny have begun.

Planning for Tomorrow

Founding Declaration

The National Front for the Salvation of Libya (NFSL) was formed in October 1981. According to the Founding Declaration made on the seventh of that month, the Front would initially "encourage and unite all Libyan national forces to expose further the destructive reality of Gaddafi's rule, to restore the national will and organize all the resources and efforts of the Libyan people to achieve the liberation of their country and work towards a righteous and better alternative."

It was emphasized in the Founding Declaration that the Front would concentrate all its energies on the struggle to come, which would demand an organized and controlled programme of action. It would not seek to put forward alternative forms or styles of government to the Gaddafi regime; nor would it impose any ideological views on its supporters.

Apart from the overthrow of the Gaddafi regime, the Front has one other binding commitment–to establish a democratic form of government after Gaddafi, to be underwritten by a permanent constitution which itself would be endorsed by a national referendum. It would be the responsibility of a Supreme Council and a transitional government "to run the country's affairs in the inevitable period of upheaval" following Gaddafi, this period to last no longer than one year. The

Supreme Council and transitional government would "make all the necessary preparations to ensure and guarantee the honest and speedy formation of a constitutional national government."

To achieve this end, "all the Libyan people must participate in the making of the future of their country." The Front "belongs to all Libyans, regardless of their age, social status and outlook. We are confident that they will find in the Front's principles, and its work, a true expression of their hopes and aspirations."

All Shades of Opinion

It is indeed the strength of the Front that it embraces all shades of opinion, united in common cause. And consequently its growth and progress have been rapid—not only among the large numbers of Libyans who live, or are exiled, abroad (over 50,000—a huge total for a country with little more than three million people) but within the country itself: significantly, too, in those areas of power which have benefitted most from Gaddafi's patronage.

There have been noteworthy defections to the Front since its formation. The Front was given direction and inspiration by the former Libyan Auditor General and Ambassador to India, Dr. Mohamed Yusef al-Magariaf, who, shortly after leaving his post to join the opposition to Gaddafi in July 1980, prepared the ground for the announcement of the new movement. He has been sentenced to death *in absentia* by a "revolutionary committee" in Libya. He was joined by other senior diplomats sickened, like himself, by Gaddafi's excesses, including Abd-ussalam Ali Aaila, a former diplomat at the Libyan Embassy in India, Ahmed Ibrahim Ehwass, former Libyan Chargé d' Affaires in Guyana, and Ibrahim Abdel-Aziz, formerly Chargé d' Affaires in Argentina. In September 1983, Aziz Omar Shennib, until shortly before, Ambassador in Jordan, declared for the Front. Others have seized the opportunity while travelling abroad to join the Front. In June 1983, ten civilians attached to the Libyan army on a course in West Germany, flew to the Sudan and offered their services.

First Congress

The Front has gained momentum even more rapidly than its founders had dared to hope. Within a year the first National Congress was held which was attended by 130 delegates representing all sections of Libyan society. Decisions taken at the Congress enabled the Front's executive functions to be set up and a programme of action to be democratically adopted. Dr. Magariaf was elected as Secretary General and spokesman, supported by a Permanent Bureau and an executive committee. Six offices were then established in six key areas of the world to act as a focus for support and to coordinate and implement policies. Committees in growing strength were formed within Libya with cells of activists infiltrating the very system initiated by Gaddafi himself to perpetrate his rule. As a result a constant stream of information reaches the Front's organization outside Libya, enabling the Front to monitor the regime's actions – and their effects – in different parts of the country.

Dissemination of information on the Front, its objectives and activities has, of course, been a priority – and results have been rewarding. Immensely damaging to Gaddafi have been the regular broadcasts into Libya on a daily basis. Through these the people of Libya have been given the confidence to hope at last for change. Gaddafi has, on many occasions, indicated his extreme irritation at these broadcasts. He is equally sensitive to interviews with Front officials put out occasionally by foreign broadcasting organizations such as the BBC, which are picked up in Libya. On one occasion this led to a furious protest to the British Ambassador in Tripoli.

Apart from the broadcasts, newsletters in several languages are now being published, as is a bi-monthly magazine in Arabic. Lists of opinion formers in selected countries are being added to growing mailing lists as the campaign against Gaddafi gathers ground internationally. The Front's opinions on issues outside Libya and its immediate sphere of influence are being listened to and acknowledged.

Recognition and Support

A number of countries, in the Middle East, North Africa and elsewhere, are now giving recognition and support in varying degrees to the Front – not least those countries which have been threatened by Gaddafi, openly or otherwise. As the Founding Declaration states:

> "While we in the Front believe that the Libyan people's confrontation with Gaddafi is their own responsibility in the first instance, and that they are capable of achieving victory with their own resources and sacrifices, we do, nevertheless, look forward to seeing other countries, especially our neighbours and sister countries, taking the right moral and political stand towards the Gaddafi regime."

Gaddafi's reaction to a coordinated and organized opposition – the first time he has had to face such a threat – has been as unpredictable as the man himself. Conciliatory [gestures] have been followed by brutal repression of any dissent, imagined or otherwise: bodies as diverse as the People's Bureaux (embassies) and the army, have felt his wrath in recent months. He has strengthened his security network and reactivated the death squads while trying to cultivate the image of being moderate and understanding in all things. These are the signs that he is fully aware of the challenge to his regime. Yet he cannot expose and isolate this challenge. Nor can he stop it.

The Front's influence has now reached all sections of Libyan society, and has penetrated Gaddafi's own government and state apparata, for the Libyan people have found in the Front's programmes, activities and leadership a true expression of their own convictions and aspirations that have far too long been suppressed and frustrated. Over the last year or so resistance has escalated, and the regime has grown more isolated and frightened as well as more brutal and oppressive in dealing with critics and opponents.

For Gadaffi, the future holds further rejection and ultimate defeat. For the Libyan people, confrontation with the regime has now become irreversible. A new chapter will soon be written in the history of Libya.

*Published by the National Front for the Salvation of Libya, Munich, West Germany, April 1984, pp. 5-12.

NOTES

Introduction

1. Frederick Muscat, *My President, My Son*. McLean, Va.; People's Committee for Students of the Socialist People's Libyan Arab Jamahiriya, (n.d.), p. 15.
2. Mirella Bianco, *Al-Kadhafi: Rasoul Al-Sahará (Al-Kadhafi: Messenger of the Desert)*. Beirut, Lebanon: Dar Al-Shawra, 1974, p. 33.
3. *Ibid.*, pp. 33-34.
4. *Ibid.*, p. 38.
5. Muscat, p. 11.
6. *Thus Spoke Colonel Moammar Kazzafi*. Beirut, Lebanon: Dar Al-Awda Publishing Co., 1974, p. 33.
7. *Ibid.*, p. 30.
8. Muscat, p. 12.
9. *Thus Spoke Colonel*, p. 30.
10. Muscat, pp. 10-11.
11. *Thus Spoke Colonel*, p. 30.
12. *Ibid.*, p. 31.
13. *Ibid.*
14. *Ibid.*, p. 35.
15. Muscat, pp. 11-12.
16. Bianco, pp. 38-39.
17. John Wright, *Libya: A Modern History*. Baltimore, Md.: The Johns Hopkins University Press, 1982, p. 126.
18. *Thus Spoke Colonel*, p. 37.
19. *Ibid.*
20. *Ibid.*, p. 39.
21. Muscat, p. 32.
22. *Ibid.*, p. 31.
23. *Ibid.*, p. 12.
24. Omar I. El Fathaly, Monte Palmer and Richard Chackerian, *Political Development and Bureaucracy in Libya*. Lexington, Mass.: D.C. Heath and Company, 1977, pp. 41, 95.
25. "No Democracy Without Popular Congresses," Revolutionary Committees. Publication obtained from People's Bureau, Socialist People's Libyan Arab Jamahiriya, Washington, D.C., (1980).
26. *The Washington Post*, May 10, 1984.
27. Ruth First, *Libya: The Elusive Revolution*. Harmondsworth, England: Penguin Books, 1974, p. 172.
28. Muammar Al Qadhafi, "A Message to the American People." A speech at the First Arab-American People-to-People Dialogue Conference, held in Tripoli, Socialist People's Libyan Arab Jamahiriya, October 9-12, 1978. New York: Aramtek, March 1979, p. 5.

29. *Jamahiriya Review*, no. 16, September 1981, p. 17.
30. *Jamahiriya News*, vol. 1, no. 1, October 15, 1984, p. 7.
31. P. Edward Haley, *Qaddafi and the United States Since 1969*. New York: Praeger Publishers, 1984, pp. 74-83.
32. "Libya's Empire of Terror," *Africa Insight*, vol. 12, no. 1, 1982, pp. 4-10.
33. First, p. 18.
34. Mu'ammar El-Qathafi, *Discourses*. Malta: Adam Publishers, 1975. An Interview by Talal Salman, "The Issue of the Revolution and the Issue of the Unity," *Assafir Newspaper*, April 28, 1974.
35. *Ibid.*, p. 66. An interview by Fuad Mattar, "Inter-Arab Relations," *An-Nahar Newspaper*, April 29, 1974.
36. *Ibid.*, p. 132. An interview by Dara Janikovic, "Comprehensive Talk[s]," *Zagreb Newspaper*, April 29, 1974.

Chapter 1

37. Henri Habib, *Libya: Past and Present*. Malta: Aedam: Publishing House Ltd., 1979, p. 131.
38. *Ibid.*, p. 132.
39. Muammar Al Qadhafi, *The Green Book Part 1: The Solution of the Problem of Democracy, "The Authority of the People."* London: Martin Brian & O'Keeffe, 1976, p. 23.
40. Farouk A. Sankari, "The Validity of Qadhafi's Critique of Representative Democracy: An Appraisal." Paper presented at the International Colloquium on Muammar Al Qadhafi's Thought: "The Green Book" at the Autonomous University of Madrid, Spain, December 1980, p. 10.
41. "Compared with Other Democratic Nations, the U.S. Ranks Poorly in Voter Turnout—Your Vote Can Help Change," *Parade*, October 26, 1980.
42. Qadhafi, *The Green Book, Part 1*, p. 11.
43. "A Unique Revolution," *Africa Report* vol. 22, no. 4, July-August 1977, p. 23.
44. Qadhafi, *The Green Book, Part 1*, p. 14.
45. *Ibid.*, p. 15.
46. *Ibid.*, p. 16.
47. *Ibid.*, p. 19.
48. *Ibid.*, p. 17.
49. *Ibid.*, pp. 19-20.
50. *Ibid.*, p. 9.
51. *Ibid.*, p. 27.
52. *Ibid.*, p. 24.
53. *Qadhafi's Thesis, Book 2*. Qadhafi's answers to questions raised at "The International Colloquium on Muammar Al Qadhafi's Thought" held at Madrid, Spain, December 1-4, 1980.Ottawa, Canada: The Supporters of the "Green March" in North America, April 1981, pp. 22, 29.
54. Qadhafi, *The Green Book, Part 1*, p. 29.
55. *Ibid.*, p. 28.
56. Muammar Al Qathafi, *The Green Book, Part 2: The Solution of the Economic Problem, "Socialism."* Runcom, England: Astmoor Litho Ltd., (n.d.), p. 15.

57. *Africa Report,* July-August 1977, p. 26.
58. *Commentary on the Green Book.* Tripoli, Libya: World Center for Researches and Studies of the Green Book, 1983, p. 74.
59. *The Human March in the Libyan Arab Republic.* Libya: Department of Information and Cultural Affairs, 1976, pp. 41-42.
60. *Ibid.,* pp.42-43.
61. Qathafi, *The Green Book, Part 2,* pp.24-26.
62. *Ibid.,* p.17.
63. *Commentary on the Green Book,* pp.216-217.
64. *Ibid.,* p.88.
65. Qathafi, *The Green Book, Part 2,* p.4.
66. *Ibid.,* pp.3-4.
67. *Ibid.,* p.5.
68. *Ibid.,* pp.8-12.
69. *Commentary on the Green Book,* pp.206-207.
70. Qathafi, *The Green Book, Part 2,* pp.7, 19.
71. *Commentary on the Green Book,* p.208.
72. *Ibid.,* p.207.
73. *Ibid.,* p.208.
74. *Ibid.,* p.209.
75. *Ibid.,* p.83.
76. *Ibid.,* p.212.
77. *Ibid.,* pp.212-213.
78. *Ibid.,* p.213.
79. *The Green Book, International Colloquium in Benghazi,* October 1-3, *1979,* Vol.2. Tripoli, Libya: Foreign Liaison Office, General Secretariat of the General People's Congress, (n.d.), p.117.
80. *Ibid.*
81. *Ibid.*
82. Muammar Al Qathafi, *The Green Book, Part 3: The Social Basis of the Third Universal Theory.* Runcom, England: Astmoor Litho Ltd., (n.d.), p.15.
83. *Ibid.,* p. 12.
84. *Ibid.,* p. 17.
85. *Ibid.,* p. 16.
86. *Ibid.,* p. 18.
87. *Ibid.,* p. 15.
88. *Ibid.,* p. 11.
89. *Ibid.,* pp. 21-23
90. *Ibid.,* pp. 6-7.
91. *Ibid.,* p. 9.
92. *Ibid.*
93. Speech delivered by Col. Mo'ammar El-Gadhafi in the Opening Session of the Euro-Arab Youth Conference, held in Tripoli, Libya on May 14, 1973. Tripoli, Libya: Ministry of Information and Culture, (n.d.), pp. 44-45.
94. *Ibid.,* p. 25.
95. *Ibid.,* p. 39.
96. *Ibid.,* p. 32.
97. *Ibid.,* p. 33.

98. *Ibid.*, p. 60.
99. *Ibid.*, p. 40.
100. *Ibid.*, p. 41.
101. *Ibid.*, p. 39.
102. *Ibid.*, p. 40.
103. First, p. 24.
104. *Ibid.*, p. 135.
105. Habib, pp. 134-137.
106. First, p. 23.
107. Qathafi, *The Green Book, Part 3*, p. 26.
108. *Ibid.*, p. 30.
109. *Ibid.*, p. 32.
110. *Ibid.*, p. 38.
111. *Ibid.*, p. 39.   •
112. *Ibid.*
113. *Ibid.*, p. 41.
114. *Ibid.*
115. *Ibid.*, p. 42.
116. *Ibid.*, p. 43.
117. *Ibid.*, p. 44.
118. *Qadhafi's Thesis.* Ottowa, Ontario: Jerusalem International Publishing House, October 1981, 4th Edition, p. 26.
119. *Ibid.*, p. 27.
120. *Ibid.*
121. *Ibid.*, p. 28.
122. *Ibid.*
123. *Ibid.*
124. *Ibid.*
125. *Ibid.*
126. Qathafi, *The Green Book, Part 3*, p. 45.
127. *Qadhafi's Thesis*, p. 29.
128. Qathafi, *The Green Book, Part 3*, pp. 45-46.
129. *Qadhafi's Thesis*, p. 29.
130. Qathafi, *The Green Book, Part 3*, p. 45.
131. *Qadhafi's Thesis*, p. 29.
132. *Ibid.*, p. 30.
133. *Ibid.*
134. Qathafi, *The Green Book, Part 3*, p. 47.
135. *Ibid.*, p. 48.
136. *Ibid.*
137. *Ibid.*, p. 49.

Chapter 2

138. Muscat, p. 12.
139. First, pp. 124-125.
140. Ḥabib, pp. 153-154.

141. *Ibid.*, p. 156; First, pp. 123-124.
142. El Fathaly, p. 95.
143. *Ibid.*
144. M. El-Shahat, *Libya Begins the Era of the Jamahiriyat.* Rome: International Publication House, 1978, pp. 34-35.
145. El Fathaly, p. 96.
146. Frederick Muscat, *September One: A Story of Revolution.* (n.c.): Link Books 1981, p. 14.
147. Qadhafi, *The Green Book, Part 1,* p. 24.
148. *Ibid.*, pp. 28-29.
149. Muscat, *September One,* p. 28.
150. *Ibid.*, p. 30.
151. Habib, pp. 171-174.
152. *Ibid.*, pp. 176-178.
153. El-Shahat, p. 35.
154. *Ibid.*, pp. 44-45.
155. *Ibid.*, p. 46.
156. *Ibid.*
157. *Ibid.*, p. 44.
158. *Ibid.*, p. 43.
159. *Ibid.*, p. 45.
160. *Ibid.*, p. 46.
161. *The Human March* p. 35.
162. Qadhafi, *The Green Book, Part 1,* p. 35.
163. El-Shahat, p. 103.
164. *Ibid.*, p. 30.
165. *Ibid.*, p. 104.
166. *Ibid.*, p. 105.
167. *Ibid.*, p. 104.
168. *Ibid.*, p. 105.
169. *Ibid.*, p. 106.
170. *Ibid.*, p. 107.
171. *Ibid.*
172. *Ibid.*, p. 104.
173. "Declaration on the Establishment of the Authority of the People in the Socialist People's Libyan Arab Jamahiriya," *Libyan Papers No. 12.* Published by the Libyan Mission at the United Nations, New York, 1979.
174. *Newsweek,* July 20, 1981, p. 42.
175. *Ibid.*
176. *Time,* December 28, 1981, p. 58.
177. Lisa Anderson, "Assessing Libya's Qaddafi," *Current History,* vol. 84, no. 502, May 1985, p. 200.
178. "No Democracy Without Popular Congresses."
179. "Celebrations Mark the Eleventh Anniversary of the Great First of September Revolution." Speech delivered by Muammar Al-Qaddafi. Published by People's Bureau, Socialist People's Libyan Arab Jamahiriya, Washington, D. C., September 1, 1980, p. 3.
180. Speech delivered by Muammar Al-Qaddafi at the Conference of the Revolu-

tionary Committees held at Sebha on November 13, 1979. Published in *From Speeches and Conversations by Muammar Al-Qaddafi* (Arabic). McLean, Va.: People's Committee for Students of the Socialist People's Libyan Arab Jamahiriya in the U.S.A., (1984?), pp. 121-122.

181. *Ibid.*, pp. 120-124.
182. "Celebrations Mark the Eleventh Anniversary," p. 5.
183. *Time*, December 28, 1981, p. 58.
184. *Jamahiriya Review*, July 1980, p. 11.
185. *Newsweek*, July 20, 1981, p. 43.
186. Omar I. El Fathaly and Monte Palmer, *Political Development and Social Change in Libya*. Lexington, Mass.: Lexington Books, 1980, pp. 197-198.
187. *Qadhafi's Thesis, Book 2*, p. 25.
188. *Ibid.*, p. 30.
189. *Al-Inqad* (Arabic), The Magazine of the National Front for the Salvation of Libya, August 1985, nos. 14-15, pp. 5-6.
190. *Al-Sigel Al-Qawmi, 1977-1978* (National Registry). Tripoli, Libya: Department of Information and Cultural Affairs, (n.d.), pp. 593-598.
191. *Al-Sigel Al Qawmi, 1982-1983*. Tripoli, Libya: World Center for Researches and Studies of the Green Book, (n.d.), p. 95.
192. Anderson, p. 226.

Chapter 3

193. *[The] 1st September Revolution Achievements: 5th Anniversary*. Tripoli, L.A.R.: Ministry of Information and Culture, (n.d.), p. 3.
194. First, p. 172.
195. Habib, p. 207.
196. Mohamed S. Abugassa, "Oil in the Political Economy of the Libyan Arab Jamahiriya." Paper presented at the African Studies Center, Howard University, Washington, D.C., April 1980, p. 4.
197. Habib, pp. 211-212.
198. Qathafi, *The Green Book, Part 2*, p. 17.
199. *Ibid.*, pp. 24-26.
200. Speech delivered by Gadhafi, May 14, 1973, pp. 48-49.
201. *Ibid.*, pp. 55-56.
202. *The Human March*, pp. 42-43.
203. *[The] 1st September Revolution Achievements: 5th Anniversary*, p. 3.
204. *Al-Sigel Al-Qawmi, 1977-1978*, p. 732; Text of an address by Col. Muammer Gadaffi delivered to a rally on International Workers Day in Tripoli, Libya on May 1, 1978. Published by Arab Dawn, London, p. 6.
205. Qathafi, *The Green Book, Part 2*, pp. 7-12, 19.
206. *Al-Sigel Al-Qawmi, 1977-1978*, p. 739.
207. *Commentary on the Green Book*, p. 83.
208. *Ibid.*, p. 207.
209. *Ibid.*, p. 212.
210. *Al-Sigel Al-Qawmi, 1977-1978*, pp. 739-741.
211. *Time*, December 28, 1981, p. 56.

212. Ronald Bruce St John, "Libya's Foreign and Domestic Policies," *Current History*, vol. 80, no. 470, December 1981, p. 429.

213. *Ibid.*

214. *Commentary on the Green Book*, p. 80.

215. *Qathafi, The Green Book, Part 2*, p. 18.

216. *Jamahiriya Review*, July 1980, p. 15.

217. *Al-Fateh Revolution in Ten Years* (1979), p. 80.

218. Bob Abdrabboh, *Libya in the 1980's: Challenges & Chances*. Washington, D.C.: International Economics & Research, Inc., 1985, p. 20; Themba Sono, ed., *Libya: The Vilified Revolution*. Langley Park, Md.: Progress Press Publications, 1984, Introduction, p. xii.

219. *Al-Fateh Revolution in Ten Years*, pp. 82-83.

220. *Jamahiriya Review*, July 1980, p. 15.

221. Qathafi, *The Green Book, Part 2*. p. 15.

222. *Al-Sigel Al-Qawmi, 1977-1978*, p. 578.

223. Qathafi, *The Green Book, Part 2*, p. 16.

224. Farouk A. Sankari, "Al-Qadhafi's 'Economic Solution' and Some Achievements Since the 1969 Revolution." Unpublished paper, January 1969, p. 8.

225. St John, pp. 428-429.

226. *Jamahiriya Review*, July 1980, p. 16.

227. *Jamahiriya Review*, September 1981, p. 21.

228. *Jamahiriya Review*, July 1980, p. 16.

229. *Al-Fateh Revolution in Ten Years*, p. 83.

230. *Jamahiriya Review*, September 1981, p. 22.

231. "Celebrations Mark the Eleventh Anniversary," p. 4.

232. *Commentary on the Green Book*, p. 99.

233. First, p. 153.

234. *Al-Fateh Revolution in Ten Years*, p. 170.

235. *Ibid.*, pp. 172, 175.

236. Abugassa, p. 7.

237. *Al-Fateh Revolution in Ten Years*, p. 175.

238. *Jamahiriya Review*, September 1981, pp. 24-25.

239. *Ibid.*, p. 25; Abdrabboh, p. 17; *Al-Fateh* (Arabic), no. 25, November 1984, p. 7.

240. *Al-Fateh Revolution in Ten Years*, pp. 180-185.

241. *Ibid.*, p. 192.

242. *Jamahiriya Review*, September 1981, p. 23.

243. *Jamahiriya Mail*, October 30, 1981, p. 9.

244. *Jamahiriya Review*, September 1981, p. 24.

245. *Al-Fateh Revolution in Ten Years*, pp. 136-137.

246. *Ibid.*, p. 137.

247. *Third World News & Views*, May 18/June 1, 1982, p. 5.

248. *Jamahiriya Review*, September 1981, pp. 19-23.

249. *Ibid.*, p. 25.

250. Abdrabboh, p. 19.

251. *Jamahiriya Review*, July 1980, p. 19.

252. *Jamahiriya Review*, September 1981, p. 24.

253. *Ibid.*, p. 25.

254. *Ibid.*, p. 23.

255. *Ibid.*
256. Anderson, p. 200.
257. *Ibid.*, pp. 199-200.

Chapter 4

258. El Fathaly, *Political Development and Bureaucracy*, p. 11.
259. *Thus Spoke Colonel*, p. 65.
260. El Fathaly, *Political Development and Bureaucracy*, p. 65.
261. *Ibid.*
262. Lisa Anderson, "Qaddafi's Islam." Published in *Voices of Resurgent Islam*, edited by John L. Esposito. New York: Oxford University Press, 1983, p. 137.
263. El Fathaly, *Political Development and Bureaucracy*, p. 12
264. *The Socialist People's Libyan Arab Jamahiriya: The Basic Facts*. Ottawa, Canada: Jerusalem International Publishing House, 1982, p. 64.
265. First, p. 122.
266. Henri Habib, *Politics and Government of Revolutionary Libya*. Montreal: Le Cercle du Livre de France Ltee, 1975, p. 27.
267. *Ibid.*, p. 229; Anderson, "Qaddafi's Islam," p. 140.
268. First, p. 122.
269. *Thus Spoke Colonel*, p. 126.
270. *Ibid.*
271. Habib, *Politics and Government*, pp. 30, 228-229.
272. First, p. 136.
273. Habib, *Politics and Government*, p. 229.
274. Anderson, "Qaddafi's Islam," p. 143.
275. *Thus Spoke Colonel*, p. 61.
276. *Ibid.*, p. 49.
277. *Ibid.*, p. 50.
278. *Ibid.*, p. 49.
279. *Ibid.*, p. 50.
280. *The Basic Facts*, p. 60.
281. *Ibid.*, p. 64.
282. *Ibid.*, p. 62.
283. *Thus Spoke Colonel*, p. 49.
284. Anderson, "Qaddafi's Islam," p. 144.
285. *Thus Spoke Colonel*, p. 124.
286. Habib, *Politics and Government*, p. 28.
287. Speech delivered by Gadhafi, May 14, 1973, pp. 48-49.
288. *Ibid.*, p. 50.
289. *Ibid.*, pp. 50-51.
290. *Ibid.*, p. 55.
291. *Ibid.*, pp. 55-56.
292. Qathafi, *The Green Book, Part 2*, pp. 24-26.
293. Speech delivered by Gadhafi, May 14, 1973, p. 57.
294. *Ibid.*, p. 59.
295. *Ibid.*, p. 62.

296. Habib, *Libya*, pp. 29, 133-137.

297. Qathafi, *The Green Book, Part 3*, p. 10.

298. Speech delivered by Gadhafi, May 14, 1973, p. 64.

299. *Ibid.*, p. 65.

300. Qathafi, *The Green Book, Part 3*, p. 26.

301. Mohamed Al-Jarrah, "Review of the Third Part of the Green Book." Published in the *International Colloquium in Benghazi, 1979*, Vol. 2, p. 181.

302. Qathafi, *The Green Book, Part 3*, p. 41.

303. Dora Henderson, "Libyan Women and their Place in the Revolution." Published in *Libya: The Vilified Revolution*, edited by Themba Sono. Langley Park, Md.: Progress Press Publication, 1984, p. 83.

304. El-Shahat, pp. 44-45.

305. Henderson, p. 82; *Al-Fateh Revolution in Ten Years*, p. 42.

306. Henderson, pp. 84-85.

307. *Ibid.*, p. 83.

308. *Jamahiriya Review*, September 1981, p. 21.

309. Habib, *Libya*, p. 24.

310. Habib, *Politics and Government*, p. 28.

311. *The Basic Facts*, p. 68.

Chapter 5

312. *The Washington Post*, November 8 and 13, 1985.

313. Anderson, "Assessing," p. 199.

314. Address to citizens concerning some items on the agenda of the Basic People's Congresses in its first session, March 19, 1978, *Al-Sigel Al-Qawmi, 1977-1978*, pp. 563-608; Explanations by the Leader of the Revolution on the agenda of the popular congresses in its third session, December 19, 1982, *Al-Sigel Al-Qawmi, 1982-1983*, pp. 305-373.

315. Zdenek Cervenka, "The World of Muammar Qaddafy," *Africa Report*, vol. 27, no. 2, March-April 1982, p. 14.

316. *The Economist*, vol. 291, no. 7341, May 12, 1984, p. 46.

317. "The Islamic System is the Jamahiriya System." Speech by Muammar Qadhafi in Tripoli on June 29, 1984. Published by People's Committee for Libyan Arab Students, (n.d.), p. 6.

318. *Ibid.*, p. 7.

319. *The Economist*, May 12, 1984, p. 46; *The Washington Post*, May 9, 1984.

320. *Ibid.*, May 10, 1984; Libya: *Daring to Hope Again*. Munich, West Germany: National Front for the Salvation of Libya, April 1984, pp. 5-6.

321. *The Economist*, May 12, 1984, p. 46.

322. *Ibid.*

323. *The Observer* (London), October 21, 1984.

324. *Ibid.*

325. *The Basic Facts*, p. 61.

326. *The New York Times*, December 2, 1981.

327. *The Washington Post*, June 13, 1984.

328. *Ibid.*, April 1, 1984.

329. Anderson, "Assessing," p. 226.
330. *USA Today*, May 9, 1984.
331. *The Washington Post*, November 3, 1985.
332. Jack Anderson and Dale Van Atta, "Libya's Qaddafi Is Heading for a Fall," *The Washington Post*, November 6, 1985.
333. *Ibid.*
334. *Ibid.*, November 3, 1985.

Chapter 6

335. Qadhafi, "A Message to the American People," October 1978, p. 11.
336. Habib, *Libya*, p. 279.
337. Haley, pp. 4-5.
338. *Jamahiriya News*, October 15, 1984, p. 5.
339. First, p. 172.
340. Habib, *Libya*, p. 207.
341. Abugassa, p. 4.
342. Haley, p. 24.
343. *Ibid.*
344. Qadhafi, "A Message to the American People," p. 5.
345. *Ibid.*, p. 7.
346. Mohamed El-Khawas and Samir Abed-Rabbo, *American Aid to Israel: Nature and Impact*. Brattleboro, Vt.: Amana Books, 1984, pp. 27-31.
347. Mansur R. Kikhia, "Libyan-American Relations," *Africa Report*, vol. 22, no. 4, July-August 1977, pp. 50-51.
348. Qadhafi, "A Message to the American People," p. 12.
349. *Jamihiriya International Report*, vol. 2, no. 25, April 14, 1984, p. 4.
350. Haley, p. 60.
351. *Ibid.*, p. 39.
352. Qathafi, *Discourses*, p. 28.
353. *Ibid.*
354. Jeff McConnell, "Libya: Propaganda and Covert Operations," *Counterspy*, vol. 6, no. 1, November 1981/January 1982, pp. 28-29.
355. The Libyan Problem, *Special Report No. 111*. U.S. Department of State, Bureau of Public Affairs, Washington, D.C., October 1983, p. 2.
356. Haley, p. 62.
357. *The Washington Post*, March 10, 1981.
358. *The Human March*, p. 81.
359. *Al-Zahf Al-Akhdar*, September 20, 1980, p. 5.
360. *Ibid.*
361. *Ibid.*
362. *The Jamahiriya Review*, July 1980, p. 8.
363. *The Washington Post*, August 20, 1981.
364. *Ibid.*
365. *Jamahiriya News*, October 15, 1984, p. 7.
366. *Ibid.*
367. *Ibid.*, p. 8.

368. Qathafi, *Discourses*, p. 66.
369. *Jamahiriya International Report*, April 14, 1984, p. 5.
370. *Al-Sigel Al-Qawmi, 1974-1975*, vol. 6, p. 13.
371. Haley, p. 36.
372. Qathafi, *Discourses*, p. 15.
373. Haley, p. 36.
374. Mohamed A. El-Khawas, "Qaddafi's Foreign Policy: A Balance Sheet," *The Search*, vol. 2, nos. 3 & 4, 1981, pp. 639-640.
375. *Ibid.*
376. Haley, p. 49.
377. *Jamahiriya News*, October 15, 1984, p. 8.
378. *Ibid.*, p. 7.
379. *Jamahiriya Review*, July 1980, p. 8.
380. *Thus Spoke Colonel*, p. 98.
381. *The Washington Post*, June 10, 1983.
382. *Thus Spoke Colonel*, p. 32.
383. *Ibid.*, p. 21.
384. Qathafi, *Discourses*, pp. 30-32.
385. *Thus Spoke Colonel*, p. 149.
386. *Ibid.*, p. 83.
387. *Ibid.*, p. 98.
388. Qathafi, *Discourses*, p. 43.
389. *Thus Spoke Colonel*, p. 98.
390. *Jamahiriya Review*, September 1981, p. 7.
391. Haley, p. 49.
392. *Africa Insight*, 1982, p. 9.
393. *Ibid.*
394. Haley, p. 40.
395. *Africa Insight*, 1982, p. 9.
396. *Ibid.*
397. Qathafi, *Discourses*, pp. 30-32.
398. *Ibid.*, p. 31.
399. *Ibid.*, p. 45.
400. *Ibid.*
401. *Ibid.*, p. 46.
402. Haley, p. 76.
403. Qadhafi, "A Message to the American People," p. 16.
404. *Al-Zahf Al-Akhdar*, July 5, 1980, p. 5.
405. *Jamahiriya Review*, September 1981, p. 7.
406. Haley, p. 49.
407. *The Washington Post*, May 30, 1981.
408. *Ibid.*
409. *Jamahiriya Review*, September 1981, pp. 6-7.
410. Hermann Fr. Eilts, "President Reagan's Middle East Peace Initiative," *American-Arab Affairs*, no. 2, Fall 1982, p. 1.
411. *The Washington Post*, June 12, 1983.
412. *Ibid.*, June 12 and 22, 1983.
413. *Ibid.*, June 10 and 21, 1983.

414. *Ibid.*, June 22, 1983.
415. *Ibid.*, June 9, 1983.
416. *Ibid.*, July 1 and 14, 1984.
417. Habib, *Politics and Government*, p. 359.
418. *Ibid.*, p. 358.
419. *Jamahiriya Review*, July 1980, p. 9.
420. *Ibid.*, p. 7.
421. Statement by Ahmad Shahati, then Head of the Office of External Relations of Libya's General People's Congresses. Published in *The First Arab American People-to-People Dialogue*, held in Tripoli, Socialist People's Libyan Arab Jamahiriya, October 9-13, 1978. New York: Aramtek, December 1979, pp. 25, 31.
422. *Liberation* (formerly the Movement for Colonial Freedom), vol. 24, no. 4, September/October 1981, p. 9.
423. Kikhia, p. 51.
424. *The Human March*, p. 81.
425. *Jamahiriya Review*, July 1980, p. 6.
426. *Africa Confidential*, December 19, 1975, pp. 1-2.
427. *Jamahiriya Review*, July 1980, pp. 13, 14.
428. *The Washington Post*, August 7, 1979.
429. Mohamed A. El-Khawas, "Arab Involvement in the Horn of Africa: The Ogaden War, 1977-1978," *The Search*, vol. 2, nos. 3 & 4, 1981, pp. 570-572.
430. *Ibid.*, pp. 576-577.
431. *Jamahiriya Review*, September 1981, p. 17.
432. Haley, pp. 105-107.
433. *The Christian Science Monitor*, December 21, 1984.
434. John Howe, "Chad: Strategic Tug O'War," *South* (London), no. 36, October 1983, p. 19.
435. *The Washington Post*, February 10, 1980.
436. *Ibid.*, July 27, 1979.
437. *The Sun*, January 7, 1981.
438. *The Washington Post*, March 26, 1981.
439. *Ibid.*
440. *Ibid.*, July 31, 1982.
441. *The Christian Science Monitor*, December 21, 1984.

Chapter 7

442. El-Khawas, "Qaddafi's Foreign Policy," pp. 637-638.
443. *The Washington Post*, March 6, 1981.
444. *Ibid.*, May 7, 1981.
445. *Ibid.*, May 27, 1981.
446. *Ibid.*, March 10, 1981.
447. Richard Deutsch, "Dealing with Qaddafy," *Africa Report*, vol. 27, no. 2, March-April 1982, p. 47.
448. *The Washington Post*, May 6, 1981.
449. *Ibid.*, August 20, 1981.

450. Deutsch, p. 47.
451. *The Washington Post*, March 21 and August 20, 1981.
452. *Newsweek*, July 20, 1981, p. 46; *Time*, December 21, 1981, p. 22.
453. "The Libyan Problem," p. 2.
454. *Jamahiriya Review*, September 1981, p. 4.
455. *The Washington Post*, March 10, 1981.
456. *Ibid.*
457. "The Libyan Problem," p. 3.
458. *Ibid.*
459. Deutsch, p. 47.
460. *Ibid.*
461. *Ibid.*
462. *The Washington Post*, March 16, 1981.
463. *Ibid.*, March 21, 1981.
464. Haig, News Conference, *Current Policy No. 258*. U.S. Department of State, Bureau of Public Affairs, Washington, D.C., p. 5.
465. *The Sun*, January 7, 1981.
466. *The Washington Post*, January 16, 1981.
467. Howe, p. 19.
468. *The Washington Post*, March 26, 1981.
469. *Ibid.*, March 21, 1981.
470. *Ibid.*
471. Raymond W. Copson, "Libya: U.S. Relations," *Issue Brief No. IB81152*. Congressional Research Service, Washington, D.C., October 19, 1981, p. 10.
472. *The Washington Post*, March 21, 1981.
473. *Ibid.*, August 20, 1981.
474. *Time*, December 21, 1981, p. 17.
475. Deutsch, p. 49.
476. U.S. Department of State, *Bulletin*, July 1981, p. 62.
477. *The Washington Post*, August 20, 1981.
478. *Ibid.*
479. *The DISAM Journal*, vol. 4, no. 4, Summer 1982, p. 55.
480. U.S. Department of State, *Bulletin*, April 1982, p. 36.
481. *Newsweek*, July 20, 1981, p. 46.
482. Statement made by Qaddafi quoted in *The Washington Post*, May 6, 1981.
483. *Time*, December 21, 1981, pp. 21-22; *Newsweek*, July 20, 1981, p. 44.
484. *Parade*, August 9, 1981.
485. *The Washington Star*, May 13, 1981.
486. Copson, p. 7.
487. *The Washington Post*, May 6 and 7, 1981.
488. *Ibid.*, November 8, 1983.
489. *Ibid.*, August 20, 1981.
490. *Ibid.*
491. *Ibid.*
492. *Jamahiriya Review*, September 1981, p. 0.
493. *The Washington Post*, August 20, 1981.
494. *Ibid.*
495. *Ibid.*

496. Gatrasat Al-Quwa Al-Am kiya (The Arrogance of American Power). Prepared by the Administrative Committee for Revolutionary Guidance of the Socialist People's Libyan Arab Jamahiriya, Tripoli, 1981, p. 75.
497. Cervenka, p. 13.
498. *The Washington Post*, August 20, 1981.
499. *Ibid.*
500. Deutsch, p. 50.
501. *Ibid.*
502. *The Washington Post*, July 17, 1982.
503. Marsha Coleman, "A Quantitative Analysis of U.S. Press Coverage of Libyan Leader Muammar Qaddafi," *International Journal of World Studies*, vol. 1, no. 2, Spring 1984, p. 203. For more information, see Themba Sono, *Reaganism Over Libya: Politics of Aggression*. Langley Park, Md.: International Center for Democracy, 1984, pp. 45-78.
504. *Time*, December 21, 1981, p. 18.
505. *Ibid.*, p. 24; *U.S. News & World Report*, December 21, 1981, p. 10.
506. *Time*, December 21, 1981, p. 24.
507. *The Washington Post*, May 8, 1981.
508. *The Wall Street Journal*, July 14, 1981.
509. *The Washington Post*, August 20, 1981.
510. Deutsch, p. 25; Sono, *Reaganism*, p. 189.
511. *Time*, December 21, 1981, p. 25 and December 28, 1981, p. 58.
512. *Newsweek*, July 20, 1981, p. 46.
513. *Time*, December 21, 1981, p. 25.
514. *The Washington Post*, August 20, 1981.
515. *Time*, December 21, 1981, p. 25.
516. *Ibid.*
517. *Ibid.*, p. 24.
518. *Ibid.*, p. 26.
519. *Ibid.*
520. *Ibid.*
521. *Ibid.*
522. *U.S. News & World Report*, December 21, 1981, p. 10.
523. *Newsweek*, July 20, 1981, p. 46; *Time*, December 21, 1981, pp. 25-26.
524. Sono, *Reaganism*, p. 189.
525. *The Christian Science Monitor*, May 16, 1983.
526. Sono, *Reaganism*, pp. 163-169.
527. *The Christian Science Monitor*, May 16, 1983.
528. *The Washington Post*, July 31, 1982.
529. *The Sun*, August 4, 1982.
530. *The Christian Science Monitor*, August 9, 1982.
531. *The Washington Post*, November 26, 1982.
532. *Ibid.*
533. *Ibid.*; Sono, *Reaganism*, p. 169.
534. *The Christian Science Monitor*, May 16, 1983.
535. *The Washington Post*, July 19 and August 5, 1983; *The New York Times*, July 26, 1983; *The Wall Street Journal*, August 5, 1983.
536. *The Washington Post*, August 2, 1983.

537. *Ibid.*
538. *Ibid.*, August 6, 1983.
539. *Ibid.*
540. *Ibid.*
541. *Ibid.*
542. *Ibid.*, August 7, 1983.
543. *Ibid.*, August 8, 1983.
544. *Ibid.*, August 9, 1983.
545. *Ibid.*, August 10, 1983.
546. *Ibid.*, August 11, 1983.
547. *Ibid.*, August 12, 1983.
548. *Ibid.*, August 11, 1983.
549. *Ibid.*, September 6, 1983.
550. *Time*, August 29, 1983, pp. 22-23.
551. *The Washington Post*, March 16, 1984.
552. *The New York Times*, September 26, 1984.
553. *The Washington Post*, November 3, 1985. For Qaddafi's reaction, see *Al-Zahf Al-Akhdar*, November 11, 1985.
554. *Time*, October 21, 1985, p. 24.
555. *The Washington Post*, January 8, 1986.
556. *Time*, January 13, 1986, pp. 26-31.
557. President Reagan: Libyan Sanctions, *Current Policy No. 780*. U.S. Department of State, Bureau of Public Affairs, Washington, D.C., [January 1986].
558. *The Washington Post*, January 9, 1986.
559. *The Christian Science Monitor*, January 10, 1986.
560. *The Washington Post*, January 8, 1986.
561. *Time*, January 20, 1986, p. 16.
562. *The Washington Post*, January 10, 1986.
563. *Time*, January 20, 1986, p. 16.
564. *The Washington Post*, January 10, 1986.
565. *Ibid.*, January 8, 1986.
566. *Time*, January 20, 1986, p. 17.
567. *The Washington Post*, January 9, 1986.
568. *Ibid.*, January 10, 1986.
569. *Ibid.*, January 16, 1986.
570. *Ibid.*, February 11 and 13, 1986; *Time*, February 3, 1986, p. 18.
571. *Ibid.*
572. *Ibid.*
573. *Ibid.*, April 7, 1986, pp. 16-24; *The Washington Post*, March 28, 1986.
574. *Ibid.*
575. *Ibid.*, April 16, 1986.
576. *The Washington Times*, April 17, 1986.
577. *The Washington Post*, April 18, 1986.
578. *Time*, April 28, 1986, p. 18.
579. *Ibid.*
580. *Ibid.*, pp. 17-18, 24, 28-31.
581. *The Washington Post*, April 22, 1986.
582. *Ibid.*, May 6, 1986.

583. *The Los Angeles Times*, February 27, 1983.

584. *The Washington Post*, January 16, 1986.

585. *Al-Jamahiriya* (Weekly News Bulletin), October 24, 1985.

586. *Al-Ahram*, July 27, 1985.

587. "Inside Libya: What Could Bring Down Qaddafi," *Business Week*, February 3, 1986, pp. 43-44.

588. *USA Today*, April 15, 1986; *Time*, April 28, 1986, p. 18.

589. *The Washington Times*, April 17, 1986.